THE HUMAN CON

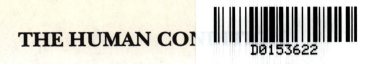

THE HUMAN CONDITION

Anthropology in the Teachings of Jesus, Paul, and John

Udo Schnelle

Translated by
O. C. Dean, Jr.

FORTRESS PRESS   **MINNEAPOLIS**

THE HUMAN CONDITION
Anthropology in the Teachings of Jesus, Paul, and John

First English-language edition published by Fortress Press in 1996.

Translated by O. C. Dean, Jr., from *Neutestamentliche Anthropologie: Jesus, Paulus, Johannes,* Biblisch-Theologische Studien 18, published by Neukirchener Verlag des Erziehungsvereins in 1991.

Library of Congress Cataloging-in-Publication Data

Schnelle, Udo.
    [Neutestamentliche Anthropologie.   English]
    The human condition : anthropology in the teachings of Jesus, Paul, and John / Udo Schnelle ; translated by O. C. Dean, Jr. – 1st English-language ed.
        p.   cm.
    Includes bibliographical references and indexes.
    ISBN 0-8006-2715-6 (alk. paper)
    1. Man (Christian theology)–Biblical teaching.   2. Bible.   N.T.--Theology.   I. Title.
BS2545.M27S3613   1996
233'.09'015–dc20   95-36776
                                                                          CIP

                                                                          AF 1-2715
00   99   98   97   96   1   2   3   4   5   6   7   8   9   10

Page make-up by Trinity Typesetting, Edinburgh
Printed and bound in Great Britain by Page Bros, Norwich

Contents

Abbreviations   vii

Translator's Note   ix

1.   Introduction   1

1.1   Preamble   1
1.2   The Appropriate Starting Point for New Testament
      Anthropology   2
1.3   New Testament Anthropology in Relation to
      Christology, Soteriology, and Ethics   5
1.4   The Binding Force of New Testament Anthropology   6
1.5   The Methodology of a New Testament Anthropology   6

2.   The Image of Humankind in the Proclamation of Jesus   11

2.1   Human Beings as Creatures   11
2.2   The Will of God and Human Beings   19
2.3   Human Beings as Sinners   23
2.4   The Acceptance of Human Beings   25
2.5   God, Jesus, and the New Reality of Humankind   34

3.   Pauline Anthropology   37

3.1   The Presupposition of Pauline Anthropology:
      The World as God's Creation   37
3.2   The Appropriate Starting Point for Pauline
      Anthropology: God's New Reality in Jesus Christ   39
3.3   The Actual Starting Point of Pauline Anthropology:
      Reflection on Humankind *vis-à-vis* Death   40
3.4   Humankind and the Reality of God: πνεῦμα in
      Pauline Anthropology   44
3.5   Being Received into God's Salvific Action: Faith   49
3.6   Corporeality and Human Essence: σῶμα in Paul   55
3.7   Human Beings in Their Corporeality: σάρξ in Paul   59

3.8   Human Beings Are Not Their Own Masters:
       The Power of Sin   63
3.9   God's Power and Human Volition: Free Will   77
3.10 Not License but Responsibility: Freedom in Paul   84
3.11 The Appeal to an Inner Court: Conscience in Paul   92
3.12 Human Dignity: εἰκών in Paul   98
3.13 Centers of the Human Self: καρδία, ψυχή, νοῦς,
       ὁ ἔσω ἄνθρωπος   102
3.14 God's Action and Human Deeds: Justification as a
       Christological and Anthropological Phenomenon   107

4.   Johannine Anthropology   114

4.1   The Human Realization of God and the Self-
       realization of Human Beings: Incarnation in John   114
4.2   The Enabling of the New Life: Faith in John   118
4.3   The Elect of God: Predestination in John   125
4.4   Humankind between Good and Evil: Johannine
       Dualism   128
4.5   Decision Today: Johannine Eschatology   130
4.6   The Powerful Presence of the Divine: Spirit in John   134
4.7   Human Beings: Sinful or Righteous?   137
4.8   Everlasting Communion with God: Life and Eternal
       Life in John   141

5.   God's Reality and Human Life: New Testament
       Anthropology and the People of Today   145

Bibliography   150

Index of Modern Authors   164

Index of Ancient References   167

Abbreviations

Dead Sea Scrolls

CD	Cairo (Genizah) text of the *Damascus Document*
1QH	*Thanksgiving Hymns* from Qumran Cave 1
1QpHab	*Pesher on Habakkuk* from Qumran Cave 1
1QM	*War Scroll*
1QS	*Rule of the Community, Manual of Discipline*

Ancient Authors

Epictetus:
    Diss.   *Dissertationes*
Josephus:
    Bell.   *De bello Judaico*
Philo:
    Agr.   *De Agricultura*
    All.   *Legum Allegoriae*
    Cong.   *De Congressu Eruditionis Gratia*
    Det.   *Quod Deterius Potiori insidiari soleat*
    Fug.   *De Fuga et Inventione*
    Gig.   *De Gigantibus*
    Her.   *Quis Rerum Divinarum Heres sit*
    Imm.   *Quod Deus sit Immutabilis*
    Migr.   *De Migratione Abrahami*
    Plant.   *De Plantatione*
    Prot.   *Protagoras*
    Virt.   *De Virtutibus*
    Vita Mos.   *De Vita Mosis*
Plato:
    Rep.   *Republic*
Seneca:
    Ben.   *De Beneficiis*
    Ep.   *Epistulae Morales*

Other Ancient Texts

2 Apoc. Bar.	Syriac *Apocalypse of Baruch*
As. Mos.	*Assumption of Moses*
Did.	*Didache*
1 Enoch	Ethiopic *Enoch*
Jos. As.	*Joseph and Aseneth*
Jub.	*Jubilees*
LXX	Septuagint
NHC	Nag Hammadi Codices
Pss. Sol.	*Psalms of Solomon*
T. Benj.	*Testament of Benjamin*
T. Jos.	*Testament of Joseph*

Translator's Note

Translating German works that deal with scripture always means a balancing act that involves at least three languages, as well as various translations of the Bible in German and English. Attempting to use only one modern version – in this work the New Revised Standard Version – never proves entirely satisfactory, because of differences between modern German and English translations. Sometimes it is necessary to turn to a more literal version (for example, the RSV) or a literal translation of the Greek word to convey the point the author is trying to make.

In this work translations of the scripture, including the Apocrypha, that are in regular quotation marks (' ') are from the NRSV. Double quotation marks (" ") are used here to gloss Greek words and phrases in a literal way and may or may not correspond to the NRSV translation. The choice of words is often influenced by the author's German gloss.

1

Introduction

1.1 Preamble

New Testament anthropology examines the foundation, enablement, structure, and realization of human existence as they are presented in the New Testament. Although such an anthropology has its basis in the claim of the New Testament to be God's authentic word about humankind, there are also topical reasons for its presentation. In a time of anonymous images of human beings shaped by advertising and by directed behavior trends, the Christian faith is especially challenged to make known the image of humanity in the New Testament. Is human essence realized in achievement, in beauty, in love, in unlimited individual freedom and unrestrained self-realization? Must human existence assimilate to the scientific-technical view of the world and thus be understood in terms of functional aspects? What interests form the basis for defining human essence? Are human beings at all capable of finding themselves on their own? Must they not be told who and what they are? A New Testament anthropology that claims to make insightful and valid statements about human existence cannot avoid these questions.[1]

In addition to the current situation of our time, it is the scientific history of our century that points to a New Testament anthropology as a desideratum. Knowledge about human beings is constantly increasing in all scientific disciplines, and in biology (evolutionary

---

[1] The quest of human beings for themselves is among the most basic aspects of the human essence and is found in every age. A classical and at the same time topical example is the following text, ascribed to the Gnostic Valentine (d. ca. AD 165): 'Not only the bath liberates us but also knowledge: Who were we? What have we become? Where were we? Where have we been cast? Where are we hurrying to? From what are we liberated? What is birth? What is rebirth?' (cited according to W. Foerster, *Die Gnosis* 1:297).

humanism), psychology, education, sociology, and behavioral research, numerous theories have been proposed regarding the nature of human existence,[2] theories that in scientific or popular form continue to determine people's thinking even in the present time. The anthropological turning point in recent philosophical and theological history is connected with the names of Martin Heidegger, Rudolf Bultmann, and Emil Brunner and exerts an ongoing influence in both disciplines, as shown by the numerous anthropological outlines in philosophy (A. Gehlen, H. Plessner) and theology (H. Thielicke, W. Pannenberg, O. H. Pesch).[3] In view of this development,[4] it is surprising that while there are numerous works on anthropologically relevant concepts and themes, there is no anthropology of the New Testament.[5] The normative significance of the New Testament for theology and the church make consideration of the New Testament statements about human beings unavoidable if we are to press on to a theological anthropology and speak what from the Christian viewpoint is the decisive word of God about the nature of humankind.

If a New Testament anthropology seeks to do justice to its appointed task, it must first define its appropriate starting point, its relationship to Christology, soteriology, and ethics, its binding force, and its methodology.

1.2 The Appropriate Starting Point for New Testament Anthropology

One possible starting point for a New Testament anthropology is an inquiry into the theological implications of the social science of anthropology. The openness of humans to the world, their capacity for language, their biological make-up, their ability to hope, their capabilities of abstraction and organization, their capacity for love and hate, their knowledge of the finite nature of

---

[2]   On these scientific fields cf. the seven–volume anthology *Neue Anthropologie*, edited by H. G. Gadamer and P. Vogler.

[3]   An introduction to the main anthropological outlines is offered by Chr. Frey, *Arbeitsbuch Anthropologie*, pp. 37ff.

[4]   W. Pannenberg, *Was ist der Mensch?* (p. 5), aptly characterizes the situation: 'We live in an age of anthropology.'

[5]   Now as before, the studies of W. G. Kümmel, 'Römer 7 und die Bekehrung des Paulus' (Munich, 1974) and 'Das Bild des Menschen im Neuen Testament' (Zurich, 1948), offer the best introduction to this topic.

all life are accessible to a theological determination and at the same time available for inclusion in philosophical and social-scientific knowledge. This possible approach in systematic theology[6] leads to a presentation and interpretation of the results of social scientific anthropology from a theological viewpoint but not to a New Testament anthropology in the strict sense, that is, to a presentation of the essence of humankind based on the revelation of the Word in Jesus Christ, as it is handed down to us in the New Testament. The object of a New Testament anthropology must not be the possibilities of the human essence and their theological understanding but the reality and structure of human existence in view of the Christ event attested in the New Testament. 'Objectivity,' that is, the neutrality and distance of the investigator from the object in the spirit of social scientific anthropology, cannot be the aim of New Testament anthropology, because it must always start with faith as its axiomatic and only appropriate way of understanding the world and humankind.

This basic insight was broadly implemented by Rudolf Bultmann. He emphasized 'that the theological ideas of the New Testament are the development of faith itself, growing out of the new understanding of God, world, and humanity given in faith – or as we can also formulate: out of the new self-understanding.'[7] For Bultmann the fundamental significance of anthropology results from the union of the understanding of God and self-understanding. Because God is 'the all-determining reality,'[8] he also provides the basis of human existence, so that statements about human beings are at the same time statements about God. 'Every sentence about God is simultaneously a sentence about human beings and vice versa.'[9] This does not make God a component part of the world; rather, precisely because he is the totally other, inaccessible One, we can talk of him only by talking of ourselves. Thus anthropology

---

[6] Cf. programmatically W. Pannenberg, *Anthropologie*, p. 21: 'In contrast to traditional dogmatic anthropology, the investigative procedures to be developed here are as a whole to be designated fundamental theological anthropology: the latter does not argue from dogmatic axioms and presuppositions but rather turns to the phenomena of human essence as they are investigated by human biology, psychology, cultural anthropology, or sociology, in order to examine the assertions of these disciplines in regard to their religious and theologically relevant implications.'

[7] R. Bultmann, *Theologie*, p. 587. On Bultmann's anthropology as a whole cf. E. Kamlah, 'Anthropologie als Thema der Theologie bei Rudolf Bultmann.'

[8] R. Bultmann, 'Welchen Sinn hat es, von Gott zu reden?' p. 26.

[9] R. Bultmann, *Theologie*, p. 192; cf. idem, *Die liberale Theologie*, p. 25.

is the necessary and appropriate theological form of expression in that theology is the explication of faith. Faith, in turn, cannot be defined apart from one's own existence, for it is God's creation in human beings and shows itself in the act of obedience to God's word. Thus faith is the giving up of the old and acceptance of the new self-understanding, according to which human existence is determined solely by God's inaccessible future. Therefore, statements about faith are always at the same time statements about existence and vice versa. 'If one wants to talk of God, one apparently must talk of oneself.'[10] Thus theology must be done in the form of theological anthropology.

Bultmann's broad definition of theology as theological anthropology is of fundamental and lasting significance, because he succeeded in making the New Testament statements about humankind transparent for the present time and also in proceeding in a considered and precise manner on the level of both exegesis and hermeneutics. The question remains, however, whether Bultmann can in any case avoid turning the New Testament assertions into a mere factor of human self-understanding. New Testament statements can have an anthropological significance, but their meaning is by no means revealed only and exclusively on the anthropological level. God appears in the New Testament as the freely acting Other, whose existence is different and independent from human beings and whose self-revelation in Jesus Christ occurred as an unfathomable act of love. By linking understanding of God and self-understanding as closely as possible, Bultmann falls into the danger of an anthropological restriction.[11] This is seen on the level of hermeneutical methodology in the adoption of Heidegger's analysis of existence (cf. 1.5 below) and in the determination to interpret – and thereby also to reduce – all mythological and eschatological statements in terms of their understanding of existence, as well as in the guiding assumption that only in this way can New Testament texts be understood. A possible anthropological restriction is also revealed in the concrete execution of this initiative, for Bultmann begins with human beings in order to present their situation *vis-à-vis* the Christ event. His authority for such a procedure is the outline of the Letter to the Romans, in which Paul does not begin with a presentation of the

---

[10] R. Bultmann, 'Welchen Sinn,' p. 28.
[11] For a critique of Bultmann cf., e.g., K. Barth, *KD* 3/2, pp. 534ff.; G. Eichholz, *Paulus*, pp. 44–8.

salvation event. 'Instead he begins by disclosing the human situation, so that the proclamation of the salvific act then becomes a question of decision.'[12] Thus anthropology has both a leading and a basic function, in that it reveals the lost situation of human beings before God and thereby prepares the way for the proclamation of the salvation event and the decision of faith.[13] It is not coincidental that Bultmann begins with anthropology in the presentation of Paul and John in the center of his *Theology of the New Testament.*[14]

For the New Testament authors, however, the starting point of their anthropology is not the lost situation of human beings but solely God's unconditional act of salvation in Jesus Christ for humankind.[15] Therefore, anthropology as the development of the statements about human beings contained in the New Testament can be considered appropriate only if it begins broadly with the foundation of God's revelation in Jesus Christ attested in the New Testament, in order to describe, within the presupposition and context of this revelation of God's word, the essence and situation of humankind.

1.3 New Testament Anthropology in Relation to Christology, Soteriology, and Ethics

Since the New Testament authors never speak in isolation about the nature of human existence, the question arises of the relationship of anthropology to Christology, soteriology, and ethics. The placing of Christology and soteriology before anthropology results from the foregoing considerations, for anthropological statements are not made for their own sake; rather, they appear in consequence of God's salvific act in Jesus Christ for humankind, which is reflected upon in Christology and soteriology. Therefore, in the explication of anthropological statements, we must always take into consideration their basis in Christology and soteriology. If Christology and soteriology speak of the fundamental event of God's *becoming human* in Jesus Christ, then anthropology speaks of the *being human* that this makes possible. This being human or

---

[12] R. Bultmann, *Theologie*, p. 301.
[13] Cf. ibid., pp. 301–2.
[14] Cf. ibid., §§17–20, 42, 43.
[15] Cf. here E. P. Sanders, *Paul and Palestinian Judaism*, pp. 442–3.

human essence is more than a certain way of living; that is, anthropology and ethics are to be clearly distinguished.[16] If anthropology describes the basic composition of human beings, their self-being, then ethics describes their ways of behaving. A New Testament anthropology must resist a mixing of the two areas, because human essence and human action are by no means equated in the New Testament. Action does not constitute human essence but, on the contrary, results from human essence. Human beings are not the product of their achievements. Human essence does not correspond to certain deeds; rather, it was defined long ago in God's salvific act for humankind in Jesus Christ. Only with the preservation of these fundamental distinctions can the close relationship between anthropology and ethics be appropriately grasped.

1.4 The Binding Force of New Testament Anthropology

The New Testament image of humankind stands in the middle of a multiplicity of implicit and explicit interpretations of human existence, and this necessarily raises the question of the truth and thus the binding force of the New Testament statements about humankind. The normative character of New Testament anthropology is not evidenced outside its self-testimony: it results solely from the New Testament itself, from its claim that it is the word of God in written form. Because in the one person Jesus Christ, God revealed himself completely and finally, the shape, sense, and goal of human life are to be read only in this Jesus of Nazareth. One must pursue this self-testimony, self-understanding, and self-claim in order to be able to comprehend God's authentic word about humankind. Thus an understanding of human essence is not accomplished outside of faith; it is rather an element of faith itself.[17] Human beings cannot know themselves on their own; they are dependent on the self-revelation of God in Jesus Christ.

1.5 The Methodology of a New Testament Anthropology

New Testament anthropology is first of all an exegetical discipline and thus a historico-theological discipline. This determination,

---

[16] Cf. G. Sauter, 'Mensch sein – Mensch bleiben,' pp. 108ff.
[17] Cf. R. Bultmann, *Theologie*, pp. 586–7.

however, does not solve the methodological problem of a New Testament anthropology. Does theological anthropology require establishment through a philosophical analysis of existence in order to achieve conceptual clarification and thus understanding? Rudolf Bultmann answered a decisive yes to this question and adopted Martin Heidegger's determination of the relationship between philosophy and theology.

Theology and philosophy have the same object: existence. But they make it their theme in different ways:

> ... philosophy by making the essence of existence its theme, that is, by examining the formal structures of existence ontologically; theology by talking of concrete existence to the extent that it [i.e., existence] believes ... to the extent that its how is characterized by the fact that it has been met by or is supposed to be met by a certain proclamation.[18]

If philosophy talks in an ontological-existentialist way of the possibilities of the human essence, theology speaks in an ontic-existential way of the concrete how. In this way every ontic interpretation moves 'on an initially and generally hidden ground of an ontology.'[19] These basic structures are not set aside by faith; rather, 'the overcome pre-Christian existence is included in an existentialist-ontological way in existence by faith.'[20] Therefore theology can appropriately explicate its concepts of existence only if it has previously considered the phenomena themselves in their existentialist-ontological structure with the help of philosophy. 'All theological concepts contain the understanding of being that human existence as such has of itself, to the extent that it exists at all.'[21] Even if the previous existence is overcome through faith in an existentially ontic way, the existentialist-ontological structures of being itself still remain. Because Christian existence is not relieved of the ontological conditions of being, it must also take them into consideration. In addition to this basic approach, Bultmann also adopted central concepts from Heidegger's analysis of existence (e.g., real and unreal existence), which proved to be especially fruitful in the interpretation of Pauline and Johannine theology.

---

[18] R. Bultmann, 'Die Geschichtlichkeit des Daseins,' p. 343.
[19] M. Heidegger, *Phänomenologie und Theologie*, p. 28.
[20] Ibid., p. 29.
[21] R. Bultmann, 'Die Geschichtlichkeit des Daseins,' p. 347.

Bultmann's theology represents the most significant attempt thus far to do New Testament anthropology on the methodological basis of a general analysis of existence. The strength of this model consists in the precise naming of its methodological pre-suppositions and their application in the completion of the exegesis. On the other hand, there are methodological questions regarding this concept: Does phenomenology as the method of fundamental ontology make possible a formal and at the same time neutral description of the basic structures of the human essence without prejudicing the concrete contents on the existential-ontic level? Both the determination of what is considered existentiality and the formal description of the ontic characteristics of existence necessarily have an influence on the concrete ontic-existential conception of the how of existence. Far more important is a second objection: Can the structures of existence on an ontological-existentialist level be conceived and described for theology without God? Are not they, and not just their ontic-existential expression, already determined by God? This will be made clear with the example of the concept of history.

For Heidegger, in his concrete development of temporality, the problem of the historicity of existence is itself already an existentialist phenomenon.[22] From this it follows 'that genuine historicity, which is an ontological possibility of existence as such, happens ontically only under a certain ontic condition that can no longer be made understandable ontologically.'[23] If historicity, as possible real or unreal historicity, is an ontic characteristic of existence, then factual expression, for example, through faith, is achieved on the ontic level. God, as Creator and Lord of history, cannot be conceptualized in this system, for he touches only the ontic-existential level. Nor does the history of Jesus Christ come into view in its fundamental significance, for it is, of course, by no means only one among many possibilities for the realization of actual historicity; rather, it bestows meaning and purpose on history in general, according to the testimony of the New Testament.

Thus it is no accident that Bultmann reduces the history of Jesus to the fact of his having come and ignores Paul's theology of history as seen in Romans 9–11. In the New Testament, history, as well as historicity itself, is a predicate of God and not vice versa: God as a possibility of history.

---

[22] Cf. M. Heidegger, *Sein und Zeit*, pp. 382ff.
[23] R. Bultmann, 'Die Geschichtlichkeit des Daseins,' p. 359.

The application of the existentialist analysis of existence to the area of theological anthropology by Bultmann reveals the problem involved in the adoption of closed systems of interpretation into New Testament scholarship: the prior decisions inherent in the system prevent the complete reception and interpretation of the New Testament corpus. Thinking in system categories channels and levels perception. Systems incline toward the principle of the pure form; that is, non-integratable statements and comments are either adapted or omitted. Hence, for the adoption of concepts foreign to theology, Luther's principle must apply: 'Lead them to the bath.'[24] At this very point there is a still unsolved hermeneutical problem. The blotting out of the idea of God in other sciences is by no means a state of affairs to be subsequently corrected by theology, but a basic decision that affects even the details of methodology. On the other hand, theology cannot completely forgo using concepts from other areas of scholarship, and thus it has a twofold task. First, like any discipline, theology has, as Luther put it,[25] its own words, namely, the holy scripture. Therefore, it should not only examine the concepts used in the Bible but also use them and not cling to the deceptive hope of being able to express what is meant better through other concepts. Second, the concepts and methods adopted from other sciences must be structured so that they correspond to the form of tradition in the New Testament text and at the same time help as neutrally as possible to lift up the New Testament corpus.

These requirements are still best met by the methods of historical-critical Bible exegesis.[26] Hence the tradition of the New Testament text leads to the unavoidable necessity of reconstructing text-critically the presumed original text of the New Testament. As the linguistic documents of Christian faith, the New Testament texts must be examined according to the various dimensions of their linguistic structure. The literary form of individual New Testament writings requires in various ways literary-critical assumptions in order to explain the present text. The demonstrable similarity of form in the tradition of certain text units is reflected in the form history. Redaction history comes from the basic insight that the authors of New Testament writings worked not only as tradition bearers but as consciously formulating theologians. The links

---

[24] M. Luther, WA 39/1, 229.1819.
[25] Cf. ibid., 229.6ff.
[26] Cf. U. Schnelle, 'Sachgemässe Schriftauslegung,' pp. 116ff.

between the New Testament and a particular historical-cultural situation result in historical and religious-historical questions. The methodological canon of historical-critical exegesis does not represent an apparatus brought to the text from the outside; it results rather from the tradition structure of the text itself. This is the basis of the relative neutrality of the historical-critical method.

The preceding considerations yield the following methodological requirements for a New Testament anthropology:

1. As an exegetical discipline, New Testament anthropology should forgo perception-prejudicing system borrowings from other scientific areas and on the basis of the historical-critical method lift up the meaning and significance of the New Testament statements about humankind and in the process make use of the conceptual system of the New Testament.

2. In terms of content, the starting point for a New Testament anthropology cannot be the lost situation of human beings but only the salvific act of God in Jesus Christ for humankind.

3. Therefore, a New Testament anthropology cannot limit itself purely to the examination of concepts[27] but rather brings to full expression the fact that anthropology is bound to Christology, soteriology, and ethics.

[27] Cf. W. G. Kümmel, 'Das Bild des Menschen,' p. 164.

2

The Image of Humankind in the Proclamation of Jesus

The proclamation of Jesus[1] leads into a variety of encounters between human beings and God. In the Synoptic Gospels we find a wealth of stories, scenes, and programmatic individual statements that deal with God and his attention to humankind. In this way Jesus lets us participate in his special relationship with God. He leads us to reflect on God and humankind; he helps human beings receive insights that they themselves could not reach.[2]

2.1 Human Beings as Creatures

In the proclamation of Jesus, human beings appear first of all as God's creatures. God is the Lord of heaven and earth (Mt 11:25/

---

[1] On the historical and theological difficulty of inquiry into Jesus, cf. K. Kertelge, ed., *Rückfrage nach Jesus* (esp. important in regard to methodology are the contributions by F. Hahn and F. Mussner). The classical basic criteria for developing the proclamation of Jesus (dissimilarity, coherence, multiple attestation) must be expanded in at least two respects: (1) through the criterion of historical continuity: 'A picture of Jesus can be historical only if it makes understandable both the proclamation of Jesus against the background of the Judaism of his time and the development from Jesus to early Christianity' (U. Luz, 'Jesus und die Tora,' p. 116, n. 13); (2) through the 'growth criterion,' according to which original Jesus material, in the course of being handed down, was enriched by secondary text units (cf. G. Strecker, *The Sermon on the Mount*, pp. 13–14). The literary-critical analysis makes it possible here to regain the logia of Jesus as the starting point of tradition.

[2] We cannot speak of an 'anthropology of Jesus' in the sense of a system of teachings. Nevertheless, the authentic Jesus tradition contains many statements about the relationship of humankind to God and thus also about the nature of the human essence, so that it is possible to trace the 'picture of humankind in the proclamation of Jesus.' I am naturally aware that in the construction of this section, as well as in the selection of texts, other emphases are possible.

Lk 10:21), who can do everything (Mk 14:36a).[3] Jesus can exuberantly praise the goodness of God as Creator, who makes the sun rise on the good and the evil (Mt 5:45) and without whose will not a hair falls from one's head (10:29–31).[4] God cares for the birds and the lilies; how much more will he be there for human beings (6:25–33).[5] Worry about food and clothing leads people away from themselves, for ψυχή ("life") and σῶμα ("body") are by no means exhausted in the mere maintenance of life. Naturally the ψυχή, the designation of the life force, requires food and drink, and the σῶμα, the place of actual life, needs clothing,[6] but precisely through worry real life could be missed. Struggle and anxiety about existence are not life! This wisdom idea[7] (cf. Sir. 30:23b–31:2) in its various forms in Mt 6:25–26, 28–32 leads Jesus, however, not to an affirmation of unconcern as a maxim for life; rather, in 6:33 it receives a specific substantiation: 'Strive first for the kingdom of God… and all these things will be given to you as well.'[8] The life of the disciples is fulfilled in orientation toward the kingdom of God. The eschatological shaping of wisdom thinking reveals a characteristic of Jesus' proclamation. The exhortation to unconcern is not given for its own sake; rather, the disciples are to be freed from the worries of the world and for the kingdom of God. This is made possible by the riches of creation and God's concern for his own. Human activity is given a new goal: it is not for its own existence but for the kingdom of God. In turning to God's kingdom and thus to God the Creator, human life experiences its intended destiny in accordance with creation.

Human beings conform to their creatureliness above all through obeying the original will of the Creator. The re-establishment of the original will of the Creator, which is identical with the correctly

---

[3] Cf. here J. Jeremias, *Theologie*, pp. 68ff.

[4] Verse 30 was inserted into the sequence of verses 29 and 31, but there is no convincing reason to deny Jesus this wisdom saying; cf. J. Gnilka, *Matthäus* 1:390.

[5] The basic content of this text, which goes back to Jesus (without redactional additions), comprises verses 25–6, 28–33; for substantiation cf. U. Luz, *Matthäus* 1:364–66 (without verses 25d–e, 32a); J. Gnilka, *Matthäus* 1:252. A penetrating analysis and interpretation is offered by H. Merklein, *Handlungsprinzip*, pp. 174–83.

[6] Cf. G. Dautzenberg, *Sein Leben bewahren*, pp. 94–5.

[7] In terms of form history it is a question here of wisdom admonitions; cf. D. Zeller, *Logienquelle*, p. 79.

[8] In Mt 6:33 καὶ τὴν δικαιοσύνην αὐτοῦ is a Matthean addition; cf. G. Strecker, *Der Weg der Gerechtigkeit*, p. 152.

understood Torah, seems to have been the real center of Jesus' proclamation.[9] Thus in Mk 10:2–9 Jesus bases the indissolubility of marriage on the original creator will of God. It conforms to the will of God – and thus at the same time to the creatureliness of humankind – that husband and wife are joined to each other for life (Mk 10:9: 'What God has joined together, let no one separate'). This form of communion fulfills the intended purpose of human sexuality in accordance with creation. The possibility of divorce, on the other hand, is regarded by Jesus as a concession of Moses to people's σκληροκαρδία ('hardness of heart'), which ultimately directs itself against people. By rejecting divorce, Jesus not only raises the position of the wife in Jewish society; he also places himself above the authority of Moses and claims for himself the task of again making known the original will of God, which is directed toward the welfare of humankind.

In its present literary form, of course, Mk 10:2–9 does not go back to Jesus but may substantially represent his position.[10] This is confirmed by 1 Cor. 7:10–11 (without Paul's parenthetical insertion in v. 11a), where Paul bases the indissolubility of marriage on the word of the *kyrios*. The exceptions in Mt 5:32 (παρεκτὸς λόγου πορνείας, 'except on the ground of unchastity') and 19:9 (μὴ ἐπὶ πορνείᾳ, 'except for unchastity') are Matthean.[11]

The restitution of the original will of the Creator is also served by Jesus' abolishing the fundamental distinction between clean and unclean. This distinction did not exist in the beginning of creation; not until Gen. 7:2 do we find the sudden separation of clean and unclean animals. For Jesus the purity laws as legitimation of religious demarcation and exclusion have lost their meaning, because for him uncleanness comes from another source: 'There is nothing outside a person that by going in can defile, but the things that come out are what defile' (Mk 7:15). Supporting the authenticity[12] of Mk 7:15 are the form of antithetical parallelism,[13] the possibility of a reverse translation,[14] the isolated position in

---

[9] Cf. H. Stegemann, 'Der lehrende Jesus,' pp. 12ff.
[10] Cf. for analysis B. Schaller, 'Die Sprüche über Ehescheidung und Wiederheirat,' pp. 238ff.
[11] Cf. G. Strecker, *The Sermon on the Mount*, p. 74.
[12] Redactional incursions by the evangelist are not probable; on εἰσπορευόμενον εἰς αὐτόν and ἐκπορευόμενα cf. W. G. Kümmel, 'Aussere und innere Reinheit,' p. 121.
[13] Cf. J. Jeremias, *Theologie*, p. 202.
[14] On the problems cf. W. Paschen, *Rein und Unrein*, pp. 173–7.

the immediate context,[15] the variations in Mk 7:18b, 20,[16] the adoption of Mk 7:15 into Rom. 14:14 as a saying of the Lord,[17] and finally the underivable newness.[18] The concrete thrust of this saying can no longer be discerned with certainty, and its meaning and significance are vigorously debated. The original sense of Mk 7:15, in contrast to the Markan understanding, can hardly have been limited to the realm of ritual, for τὰ ἐκ τοῦ ἀνθρώπου ἐκπορευόμενα ('the things that come out of a person') in verse 15b hardly allows such a restriction. Hence not only ritually unclean foods are intended; instead, with these words Jesus is saying that everything that comes out of a person, thoughts as well as deeds, can make him or her unclean before God.[19]

Formally, of course, Jesus does not abolish the idea of impurity before God, but he denies that such impurity can come to a person in any form from the outside. This means not only an abrogation of the purity laws of Lev. 11–15; Jesus also violates a fundamental principle of Jewish thinking and understanding of the world. For both the Pharisees[20] and the Sadducees,[21] as well as for the Essenes

---

[15] Mk 7:15 does not refer to the theme of ritual handwashing treated in verses 1–13, for this saying goes far beyond the problem of 'defiled through touching'; cf. W. G. Kümmel, 'Äussere und innere Reinheit,' p. 120. The immediate context of verse 15 was formed by Mark, for in verse 14 the evangelist produces the public again (cf. Mk 3:23; 8:34), and verses 17–18a contain elements of the Markan mystery theory (separation from the crowd, παραβολή, the disciples' lack of comprehension).

[16] Verses 18b and 20 are either pre-Markan variations or Markan interpretations of the logion in Mk 7:15. Those who argue for the first possibility and draw on verses 18, 20 for reconstruction of the Jesus saying (thus esp. H. Hübner, *Das Gesetz in der synoptischen Tradition*, pp. 166ff.) must explain why a saying of the Lord was so greatly modified. More plausible is the assumption that verses 18b, 20 are doublets of verse 15 formulated by the evangelist, which were necessary in the context of the special instruction of the disciples conceived by Mark himself.

[17] This in my view is the way ἐν κυρίῳ Ἰησοῦ, 'in the Lord Jesus,' is to be understood; cf. also Mk 7:19b with Rom. 14:20b. Versus H. Räisänen, 'Jesus and the Food Laws,' p. 88, who assumes the influence of Rom. 14:14 on Mk 7:15.

[18] R. Bultmann, *Die Geschichte der synoptischen Tradition*, p. 110, correctly emphasizes: 'Thus, what is characteristic of Jesus' proclamation must be found here, if anywhere.' Cf. also H. Braun, *Jesus*, p. 73; E. Haenchen, *Der Weg Jesu*, p. 265.

[19] Cf. W. G. Kümmel, 'Äussere und innere Reinheit,' p. 122.

[20] Cf. J. Neusner, 'Die pharisäischen rechtlichen Überlieferungen,' pp. 43–51.

[21] Cf. on the position of the Sadducees E. Schürer, *Geschichte des jüdischen Volkes* 2:482–3.

of Qumran,[22] the cultic ritual norms – despite contemporary variation in practice – were of essential significance, for they not only functioned as a visible mark of distinction from the Gentiles and the religiously indifferent among the Jews, but were also an expression of their obedience to the Torah and of the ongoing validity of the word of God handed down through Moses. Therefore E. Käsemann correctly stated: 'Whoever questions that impurity penetrates a person from outside strikes at the presuppositions and wording of the Torah and at the authority of Moses himself.'[23] Thus Mk 7:15 is to be understood in an exclusive sense and has a meaning that is critical of the Torah;[24] it is not at all simply a matter of the priority of the love commandment over the purity laws.[25] The argument that such a critical position *vis-à-vis* the Torah is inconceivable in Jesus does not have argumentative value here simply because what is not supposed to be cannot be. Paul already understood this Jesus saying in a Torah-critical sense (Rom. 14:14), and even in Jesus himself there are parallels. In addition to his contact with the cultically unclean, his critique of the Pharisees (cf. Mt 23:25; Lk 11:39–41), and the Sabbath healings, we must mention here above all Lk 10:7, where in his mission speech Jesus commissions his disciples to eat and drink everything that is set before them. If in view of the coming kingdom of God the present is no time to fast (cf. Mk 2:18b–19a; Mt 11:18–19/Lk 7:33–34), then the food laws have also lost their significance for the relationship of people to God and among people themselves. The purity of human beings willed by the Creator cannot be instrumentalized; rather, it concerns people's whole existence. The

---

[22] Cf. the analysis of important texts from Qumran in W. Paschen, *Rein und Unrein*, pp. 85ff.

[23] E. Käsemann, 'Das Problem des historischen Jesus,' p. 207.

[24] In addition to R. Bultmann, E. Haenchen, H. Braun, W. G. Kümmel, and E. Käsemann, Mk 7:15 is also understood in a Torah- critical sense by, e.g., J. Gnilka, *Markus* 1:284; W. Schrage, *Ethik des Neuen Testaments*, p. 68, and H. Hübner, 'Mk VI. 1–23,' p. 345.

[25] Thus, e.g., U. Luz, 'Jesus und die Pharisäer,' pp. 242–3; H. Merklein, *Jesu Botschaft von der Gottesherrschaft*, 96; Chr. Burchard, 'Jesus von Nazareth,' p. 47. H. Räisänen, 'Jesus and the Food Laws,' pp. 89ff., sees behind Mk 7:15 not the earthly Jesus but 'an "emancipated" Jewish Christian group engaged in Gentile mission' (p. 90); similar is the argumentation in E. P. Sanders, *Jesus and Judaism*, pp. 266–7. Both can note some arguments against the authenticity of Mk 7:15 but cannot weaken the main arguments for its originality. Ultimately each exegete's pre-existent image of Jesus determines whether he or she has room for Mk 7:15.

creatureliness of human beings reaches its goal not in religious or
social separation but in the true acceptance of the life given by
the Creator.

The re-establishment of the creative order is also the aim of the
Jesus saying[26] in Mk 2:27 according to which the Sabbath was
created for humankind and not humankind for the Sabbath.[27] In
Mk 2:27 ἐγένετο ("is made") in particular points back to God's
will as Creator. The hallowing of the Sabbath serves people by
tearing them away from everyday busyness, and thus also from
themselves, in order to create time for the all-determining
relationship with God. Already in the priestly creation story the
seventh day appears as time qualified by God to help people orient
themselves in time and history (Gen. 2:2–3). This serving function
of the Sabbath was partially lost in the history of post-exilic
Judaism.[28] It is true that the Sabbath moved to the center of the
understanding of the Torah, but at the same time the qualification
of time turned into a static opposition of Sabbath and humankind.
People now had to subordinate themselves to the Sabbath and its
requirements. That is what it says in CD 11.16–17 within a Sabbath
halakah: 'A living person who falls into a water hole or into some
other place shall no one haul out with a ladder or a rope or any
[other] object' (cf. also *Jub.* 2.25–33; 50.6ff.; CD 10.14–12.22; Philo
Vita Mos. 2.22). Jesus breaks through these reversals and with his
Sabbath healings demonstrates the original significance of the day:
it helps people live (cf. Lk 13:10–17) and enables them to fulfill
their destiny: to meet the Creator.

---

[26] Among those tracing this logion back to Jesus are E. Lohse, 'Jesu Worte,'
p. 68; J. Roloff, *Kerygma*, pp. 52ff.; H.-W. Kuhn, *Sammlungen*, p. 75; J. Gnilka,
Markus 1:123; D. Lührmann, *Markus*, pp. 64–5; H. Hübner, *Gesetz in der
synoptischen Tradition*, p. 121; V. Hampel, *Menschensohn und historischer Jesus*,
pp. 199ff.

[27] The complex and very controversial history of the origin of Mk 2:23–28
transpired, in my opinion, as follows. The starting point of the tradition is the
independent Jesus logion in verse 27. In the second stage the pre–Markan
church, in justification of its liberal Sabbath practice, added verses 23–4. Verse
28 was then added as a christological interpretation of verses 23–4, 27. The
interpretation of the Sabbath commandment is not decided by people; rather,
Jesus Christ has authority even over the Sabbath. Finally, a new level of
interpretation was introduced by verses 25–6. Jesus – here that means the
church – now refers to the scripture; a biblical precedent is constructed. In
this way the church confirms its Sabbath practice.

[28] Cf. here E. Lohse, s.v., 'σάββατον,' *TDNT* 7:1–31.

Also in Mk 3:4 the topic is the original will of God in regard to the Sabbath: 'Is it lawful to do good or to do harm on the sabbath, to save life or to kill?'[29] The Sabbath should serve the good, and this consists in maintaining and saving life. God wants to create salvation in a broad sense for humankind, and the Sabbath is also to be subordinated to this radical turning to humankind. To fail to do good does not represent a neutral position in Jesus' view; it means to do harm, to kill. God's yes to humankind, his caring about and for people, stands above the commandments. An interpretation of God's commandments that does not take this into consideration misses the meaning of the manifestation of the divine will. Therefore, the Sabbath cannot be desecrated by doing good.

Jesus' healings also have a creation-theology dimension (cf. Mk 1:29–31, 32–34; 2:1–12; Mt 8:5–13 par.). Their aim is the reestablishment of a state that accords with creation; they are a sign and protest against the enslavement of people by evil (cf. Lk 13:16: 'And ought not this woman, a daughter of Abraham whom Satan bound for eighteen long years, be set free from this bondage on the sabbath day?'). The driving out of demons and the healings, the petition in the Lord's Prayer for deliverance from evil (Mt 6:13b), Jesus' vision in Luke 10:18 ('I watched Satan fall from heaven like a flash of lightning'), the reproach that Jesus is in league with evil spirits (cf. Mt 9:34; Lk 11:14–19), and the nullification of Satan's power presupposed in Lk 11:21–22 make clear that the struggle against evil or the evil one is the central content of Jesus' teaching and activity.[30] At this point he shares the conviction of ancient Judaism that the neutralization of the power of the devil and his demons is a sign of the inbreaking end time (cf. *As. Mos.* 10.1: 'And then [God's] dominion over his whole creation will appear, and then the devil will be no more, and sadness will be taken away with him'; cf. also 1QS 3.24–25; 4.20–22; 1QM 1.10; etc.). In view of the inbreaking kingdom of God becoming apparent in the miraculous activity of Jesus[31] (cf. Lk 11:20: 'But if it is by the finger of God that I cast out the demons, then the

---

[29] Those who hold Mk 3:4 to be from Jesus include H. Hübner, *Gesetz in der synoptischen Tradition*, p. 129; J. Roloff, *Kerygma*, pp. 63ff.; J. Gnilka, *Markus* 1:126; E. Lohse, 'Jesu Worte,' p. 67.

[30] Cf. H. Stegemann, 'Der lehrende Jesus,' p. 15.

[31] The linking of eschatology and the doing of miracles in Jesus in this form is unique in the history of religion; cf. G. Theissen, *Urchristliche Wundergeschichten*, p. 277.

kingdom of God has come to you'), people are liberated from the enslaving powers of Satan and led again to the destiny accorded them in creation (cf. Mt 11:5–6).

The creatureliness of humankind is likewise expressed in addressing God as πατήρ ("Father"). God is praised as Father, as Creator of all life (Mt 11:25/Lk 10:21). He cares for his own and gives them what they need (Mt 6:32/Lk 12:30). In the Lord's Prayer Jesus instructs the disciples to pray to God as their Father (Mt 6:9b/Lk 11:2b). All petitions are for God the Father, who is called upon for the complete maintenance of life. When Jesus speaks to the disciples of 'your Father' (Mt 6:32/Lk 12:30; Mt 6:45),[32] he takes them into his unique fellowship with God, which is shown in his addressing God as ἀββά ("dear Father"; cf. Mk 14:36; also Rom. 8:15; Gal. 4:6).[33] He lets them participate in the goodness and revelation of God given to him. The creatureliness of human beings and their dependence on God is revealed in the petition for bread in the Lord's Prayer (Mt 6:11/Lk 11:3).[34] Here bread, as the basic means of nourishment, represents human material needs in general. God gives humankind what is necessary for existence; this is the way to translate ἐπιούσιος, a word attested only in the New Testament. God's providence, his generous goodness as Creator, includes what is necessary for life, and it alone makes possible the attitude of unconcern advocated by Jesus in Mt 6:33. The petition for bread articulates trust in the caring Creator.[35] Even in the mere fact that human beings are sustained day by day, we see their indissoluble connection with God. In the all-determining God-relationship humans can comprehend themselves only as creatures. As beings created by God they do not have their existence in themselves; rather, God is in like manner both Giver and Sustainer of life. If human beings do not want to be lacking in their existence, they must always be conscious of their origin in God and at the same time follow the life-sustaining will of God.

---

[32] An analysis of the phrase 'our Father' is found in J. Jeremias, 'Abba,' pp. 41–5. On the connection of the 'Father' form of address with Jesus' message of the lordship of God, cf. H. Merklein, *Handlungsprinzip*, pp. 206–11.
[33] Cf. J. Jeremias, 'Abba,' pp. 56–67.
[34] The phrase τὸ καθ' ἡμέραν ('each day') is Lukan; cf. Lk 19:47; Acts 17:11.
[35] Here Jesus stands in the wisdom tradition; cf. Prov. 30:8: 'Remove far from me falsehood and lying; give me neither poverty nor riches; feed me with the food that I need.'

2.2 The Will of God and Human Beings

As creatures, human beings are obligated to the will of God. This does not mean that they must submit to an arbitrary despot; rather, God's will is comprised in his love, which takes shape in his activity as Creator. The will of God proclaimed by Jesus is to make it possible for people to live together and to overcome disturbances caused by new and unexpected behavior. The antitheses of the Sermon on the Mount articulate loudly and clearly God's absolute will.

In his special material the evangelist Matthew had before him the first, second, and fourth antitheses and on this basis created a series of six antitheses.[36] Through πάλιν ("again") in 5:33a Matthew sets the first series of three off from the second. If the first three antitheses deal with relations with fellow Christians (anger against a brother, adultery, divorce), then the second three deal with relations with non-Christians (swearing, retaliation, love of enemy). In terms of tradition history the oldest component of the first, second, and fourth antitheses includes 5:21–22a (ἠκούσατε ... ἔσται τῇ κρίσει), 5:27–28a–b (ἠκούσατε ... ἐμοίχευσεν αὐτήν), and 5:33–34a (ἠκούσατε ... μὴ ὀμόσαι ὅλως) and can be credited to Jesus' proclamation. In the course of being handed down, this oldest sayings material was augmented with examples and explanations. The antitheses formed by the evangelist also contain old traditions, though only the demand to forgo retaliation (Mt 5:39b–40/Lk 6:29), the absolute ἀγαπᾶτε τοὺς ἐχθροὺς ὑμῶν in Mt 5:44a/Lk 6:27a, and the creation-theological substantiation in Mt 5:45/Lk 6:35 may go back to the historical Jesus.

In the first antithesis Jesus places his own authority against the Old Testament prohibition of murder (Exod. 20:15; Deut. 5:18): 'You have heard that it was said to those of ancient times, "You shall not murder"; and "whoever murders shall be liable to judgment." But I say to you that if you are angry with a brother or sister, you will be liable to judgment' (Mt 5:21–22a). Even anger against another person subjects one to judgment. Jesus does not interpret the Old Testament commandment here: he goes beyond it. What is demanded is the radical devotion of people to each other. Otherwise liability to judgment follows unavoidably. In terms of content, the rejection of anger is not new in Judaism (cf. 1QS 6.25–27).[37] Surprisingly, however, Jesus' rejection of anger goes

---

[36] Cf. G. Strecker, *The Sermon on the Mount*, pp. 62–4.
[37] Cf. H. Merklein, *Handlungsprinzip*, p. 261, n. 306; U. Luz, *Matthäus* 1:254.

beyond the Torah and thus characterizes it as inadequate. God's will is interpreted by Jesus in such a way that it applies to people constantly and even includes their involuntary impulses. Even to ask whether there is also justified anger would be to attempt to limit God's will. Jesus himself accepted no boundaries that could be drawn around God's will. If we let God's unrestricted will apply to us, we will realize that we cannot conform to this will. This means recognition of our own liability to judgment. The only way left open to us in this situation is to repent, to trust in the grace of God, and to act out of this grace.

In the second antithesis Jesus adds to the Old Testament prohibition of adultery (Exod. 20:14; Deut. 5:17) the thesis that even looking with lust amounts to adultery: 'You have heard that it was said, "You shall not commit adultery." But I say to you that everyone who looks at a woman with lust has already committed adultery with her in his heart' (Mt 5:27–28). What is reprehensible is not the looking but the intention that is behind it, the ἐπιθυμία ("lust"). With this term Jesus designates one's longing to appropriate someone else's property,[38] which promises an increase in the feeling of being alive, a gain in pleasure and meaning. Jesus puts an end to this striving because it develops a destructive power. The sanctity of marriage is broken, and people are torn away from their created destiny. Finally, lust destroys the very existence of the one who lusts by promising satisfaction where in reality it cannot be given, because it happens at the expense of other people. According to God's will, human life can succeed only when it is lived in truthfulness and does not destroy others but supports and loves them for their own sake.

Jesus' prohibition of swearing in the fourth antithesis also aims at the whole of human existence (Mt 5:33–34a: 'Again, you have heard that it was said to those of ancient times, "You shall not swear falsely, but carry out the vows you have made to the Lord." But I say to you, Do not swear at all'). Because of the oath that documents the truth of sworn statements, unsworn statements are exempt from the truth. In fact, in this way the oath serves the toleration of lies. An area of life in which the will of God – truthfulness – is valid is separated from another in which it is not. Through Jesus' commandment this separation is to be abolished. God's will is valid for people in all areas of life.

---

[38] Cf. H. Weder, *Die 'Rede der Reden,'* p. 114.

Jesus demands the forgoing of retaliation (Mt 5:39b–40/Lk 6:29).[39] Here it is not at all a question of purely passive behavior that leads to suffering. On the contrary, Jesus' provocative challenge to turn the other cheek also and with the coat to give also the cloak requires of the disciples extreme activity, for they are supposed to practice the basic attitude of love in seemingly hopeless situations. Jesus lived and demanded an unusual, uncalculated, and purpose-free behavior, which for this very reason is productive.

The commandment to love one's enemies in its unrestricted form (Mt 5:44a/Lk 6:27a: ἀγαπᾶτε τοὺς ἐχθροὺς ὑμῶν, 'love your enemies') is without analogy.[40] There are close parallels, to be sure, in both the Jewish and Hellenistic realms, which, however, reveal various motivations. Though Prov. 25:21 reads, 'If your enemies are hungry, give them bread to eat; and if they are thirsty, give them water to drink,' the continuation in verse 22a ('for you will heap coals of fire on their heads, and the Lord will reward you') shows that unrestricted love of enemy can hardly be intended. Epictetus (ca. AD 55–135) can say about the Cynic: 'He must be beaten like a donkey and love those who beat him like a father of all or a brother' (*Diss.* 3.22.54). The driving motive here seems to be self-control rather than unconditional love of enemy. Similar is Seneca (d. AD 65), who argues in a wisdom fashion: 'If you want to emulate the gods, then also do good to the ungrateful, for the sun rises also on the evil ones and the sea also lies open for pirates' (*Ben.* 4.26.1). Marcus Aurelius (AD 121–80) says: 'It is characteristic of human beings also to love those who abuse them' (*Semet.* 7.22).

In 1QS 10.18 we read: 'I will not repay anyone for an evil deed; I will pursue everyone with good.' Here too the continuation reveals the motivation behind the action: 'For judgment over everything living belongs to God, and he will repay the man for his deed.' The principle of retribution remains intact, except that the punishment is left to God. Jesus, by contrast, makes love boundless. A limitation is no longer possible, not even one that includes the neighbor. With the extreme example of the enemy Jesus shows how far love goes. It knows no boundaries; it is for all people. God's

---

[39] On the analysis cf. U. Luz, *Matthäus* 1:292; G. Strecker, *The Sermon on the Mount*, pp. 82–8. Matthew adds τὴν δεξιάν ("the right") in verse 39b.

[40] Only the absolute 'Love your enemies' is definitely from Jesus; on the analysis cf. J. Gnilka, *Matthäus* 1:187ff.

radical, unrestricted love reaches into the everyday lives of people, who are expected with love of enemy to participate in the love of God. A rational basis for the love of enemy cannot be derived from present reality; such unusual behavior can receive its meaning and obligation only from the hands of God. Because the Creator himself, in his goodness *vis-à-vis* good and evil, breaks through the friend-foe schema, people can cross boundaries, and enemies can become friends. The perfect deeds of the heavenly Father are to be practiced also by his children (cf. Sir. 4:10, LXX). The children are in accord with the Father when they practice love of enemy. On their own, people cannot love their enemies; they remain instead dependent on the God who loves them. Only the unrestricted love of God for humankind makes the demand of love of enemy possible for human beings.

A further ethical radicalism of Jesus is represented by the prohibition of judging in Mt 7:1 ('Do not judge, so that you may not be judged').[41] Jesus forbids all judging, because every judgment conceals the seed of a prejudgment. With the *passivum divinum* κριθῆτε ("be judged") in Mt 7:1b Jesus points to the last judgment as substantiation. Because divine judgment is imminent, human beings should anticipate it even now and forgo any judging, for this necessarily has the condemnation of oneself in judgment as a consequence. Here we see a trait that is of great significance for the human image of Jesus. Faced with the will of God, human beings recognize themselves as sinners. In failure their liability to judgment is obvious. Out of failure, however, a person can also turn to God. In this way, ultimately, it is only the mercy of God toward people that makes possible the end of judging among people.

The boundary-crossing ethical radicalisms of Jesus are drastic challenges to overcome divisions between people, which are unwanted by God, and to bring the Creator's will again to reality. Unlimited by nature and understandable only on the level of the imminent kingdom of God, these radicalisms demand a behavior that is determined exclusively by God.[42] In the inauguration of God's kingdom the will of God is proclaimed again in a new, radical, and final way. Jesus formulates that will on his own authority; he does not derive it from the Old Testament, which in the light of

---

[41] The provenance of Mt 7:1 from Jesus is undisputed; cf. G. Strecker, *The Sermon on the Mount*, pp. 143–4; U. Luz, *Matthäus* 1:376.

[42] Cf. H. Weder, *Die 'Rede der Reden,'* p. 154.

the kingdom of God is therefore surpassed, deepened, and expanded. Only in the will of God does humankind reach its destiny in accordance with creation. Human beings can hold to the final word of God, for it is from that word that we are to live and act. When people orient themselves completely toward God and are thereby freed from themselves, they can let love be decisive for themselves in order to seek the well-being of other people. Even in failure *vis-à-vis* God's will and the threat of liability to judgment, human beings are dependent exclusively on God, for only in repentance can they escape their just verdict. Thus the radicality of Jesus' demand corresponds to the totality of human dependence on God.[43] The question of whether the ethical radicalisms are fulfillable is not raised by Jesus, for it would lead to a legalism and functionalization unwanted by him. In view of the imminent kingdom of God, the radicalisms amount to appeals[44] to rely entirely on the will of God and precisely in this way to make being human possible.

2.3 Human Beings as Sinners

In his understanding of sin Jesus begins with the message of John the Baptist. John's proclamation is a preaching of judgment and repentance; he addresses all the people, even the pious, and demands of them radical repentance (cf. Mt 3:2).[45] For him it is not merely a question of moral improvement; the expression βάπτισμα μετανοίας εἰς ἄφεσιν ἁμαρτιῶν ('baptism of repentance for the forgiveness of sins'; Mk 1:4) involves an anthropological premise: all of Israel, in its present state, is a 'collective disaster' and liable to judgment. Trust in kinship with Abraham is deceptive; the ax is already lying at the root of the trees (Mt 3:9–10/Lk 3:8–9). The repentance preached by John demands of Israel the confession that God is justly angry with his people. In the understanding of John the Baptist, this confession represents the last possibility granted Israel by God to escape the coming judgment.

---

[43] Cf. J. Eckert, 'Radikalismen,' p. 319.

[44] Ibid., p. 325.

[45] On the person and message of John the Baptist cf. the recent comprehensive work of J. Ernst, *Johannes der Täufer.*

In adopting baptism Jesus documents that he shares the historical view of John the Baptist in its essential traits. Jesus also calls Israel to repentance. The news of Pontius Pilate's murder of Galilean pilgrims in Jerusalem (Lk 13:1)[46] is not interpreted by Jesus in the sense of the prevalent faith in retribution, according to which suffering was considered punishment for guilt. Rather, Jesus does not except his listeners from the threatening judgment. All are sinners and will be subject to judgment unless they repent (Lk 13:3). Also the unexpected death of many people through the fall of the tower at the pond of Siloam (cf. Jos. *Bell.* 5.145) does not attest to an excess of sins (Lk 13:4–5). Rather, 'Unless you repent, you will all perish as they did' (Lk 13:3b, 5b).

Announcement of judgment and call to repentance as the central content of Jesus' proclamation also appear in the woes to the cities of Chorazin and Bethsaida in Lk 10:13–14:[47] 'Woe to you, Chorazin! Woe to you, Bethsaida! For if the deeds of power done in you had been done in Tyre and Sidon, they would have repented long ago, sitting in sackcloth and ashes. But at the judgment it will be more tolerable for Tyre and Sidon than for you.' Even the pagan cities Sidon and Tyre would have repented if Jesus had done within their walls the deeds that he accomplished in Chorazin and Bethsaida. Now things will be more bearable in the judgment for Sidon and Tyre than for these unrepentant cities. Whereas the Ninevites are led to repentance by the preaching of Jonah, this generation refuses Jesus' message (Lk 11:32: 'The people of Nineveh will rise up at the judgment with this generation and condemn it, because they repented at the proclamation of Jonah'). But here is something greater than Jonah; hence the Ninevites will condemn Jesus' unrepentant listeners.

Human beings are also seen as sinners in other areas of Jesus' proclamation. When in the fifth petition of the Lord's Prayer one prays for the forgiveness of guilt and declares one's own readiness to forgive (Mt 6:12/Lk 11:4), the confession of one's own guilt is presupposed. Human beings fall short of God's demands and recognize their dependence on God's forgiveness. At the same time they know that God's acceptance of sinners initiates a movement that requires their own readiness to forgive. The aorist ἀφήκαμεν ("we have forgiven") even presupposes forgiveness on the part of

---

[46] On Luke 13:1–5 cf. W. Wiefel, *Lukas*, pp. 251ff.
[47] Cf. here G. Schneider, *Lukas* 1:239–40.

human beings, so that it appears as a prerequisite for the proper petition to God for forgiveness.[48] In the parable of the unforgiving servant (Mt 18:23b–30) Jesus expressly illustrates what happens when God's mercy toward people produces no results.[49] In the story of the Pharisee and the tax collector (Lk 18:10–14a)[50] the tax collector knows his unworthiness before God and asks: 'God, be merciful to me, a sinner!' (ὁ θεός, ἱλάσθητί μοι τῷ ἁμαρτωλῷ, 18:13c). Jesus says of him: 'This man went down to his home justified rather than the other' (18:14a). Before God human beings can know themselves only as sinners. If human parents, who are evil, fulfill the requests of their children, how much more will the Father hear those who make requests of him (Mt 7:11).[51] God's benevolence (cf. also Mt 5:45–46; 19:17 par.) helps people to the insight that as sinners they are always dependent on the goodness of God.

2.4 The Acceptance of Human Beings

Like John the Baptist, Jesus proclaims the liability of human beings to judgment. In contrast to the Baptist, however, Jesus also gives full expression to God's salvific activity. Human beings can enter into a new relationship with God through God's goodness and forgiveness. God accepts the sinner ready to repent. Jesus tells about this in his parables. In the parable of the prodigal son (Lk 15:11–32)[52] the exposition of the division of inheritance (v. 12) holds a central position.[53] The father grants the two sons basic life support, which they can use or misuse. The younger son squanders his inheritance and thereby falls into a rapidly deepening crisis

---

[48] Cf. G. Strecker, *The Sermon on the Mount*, p. 121.

[49] Cf. on interpretation pp. 29–31 below.

[50] Cf. F. W. Horn, *Glauben und Handeln*, pp. 205–9.

[51] In 7:11 the words ὑμῶν ὁ ἐν τοῖς οὐρανοῖς ("your . . . in the heavens") go back to Matthew; cf. U. Luz, *Matthäus* 1:385. Luz correctly holds that the whole section Mt 7:7–11 (except for the Matthean redaction in verses 9 and 11) goes back to Jesus.

[52] Only the ὅτι ("for") statements in verses 24a and 32b are redactional; cf. M. Petzoldt, *Gleichnisse*, p. 88; W. Harnisch, *Gleichniserzählungen*, p. 200. There is a broad consensus on the anchoring of this text in the proclamation of Jesus. Only L. Schottroff, 'Gleichnis vom verlorenen Sohn,' p. 42, holds the text to be Lukan; on this discussion cf. W. Harnisch, *Gleichniserzählungen*, pp. 207–8.

[53] Cf. M. Petzoldt, *Gleichnisse*, p. 91.

(vv. 13b–16). This leads him to the reasonable perception that only a return to his father can provide a way out of his economic distress (vv. 17–20a). The son's coming to his senses climaxes in the formation of a speech to his father (vv. 18b–19), in which he confesses his own misdeeds and the loss of his sonship and begs for a subsistence position as a hired hand.[54] In the closing part of the story of the younger son (vv. 20–24) the perspective changes, for now the reporting is from the father's viewpoint. He comes out to meet his son. Even before the latter can confess his misdeeds, the father runs to him, hugs him, and kisses him (v. 20b). Only after the surprising kindness of the father can the son make his confession of guilt. He forgoes the request to be employed as a hired hand, for this would offend his father. Though the younger brother already regarded his sonship as forfeited, the father now again grants him the status of sonship in full ceremony (by giving him a robe and a ring). In the following meal the joy and love of the father are conspicuously expressed.

The unexpected behavior of the father leads to a crisis for the older son (vv. 25–28a). The safe return of his brother unleashes in him not joy but anger and indignation. In the second part of the story (vv. 28–32a) the father behaves just as kindly toward the older son as earlier toward the younger son. Yet the reaction of the older son to the imploring request of the father is diametrically opposed to the behavior of the younger brother. He complains vigorously about his father and brother (vv. 29–30). Nonetheless, at the unresolved close of the story the father also includes in his fellowship and love the older son, who is not supposed to shut himself off from this prevenient love.

In this parable Jesus interprets in like manner humankind and God.[55] At the center stands the father, who in impartial love cares for his sons. Through the inheritance he grants both what they need to live. He responds to the prodigal life of the younger son not with a withdrawal of his love but with the act of unconditional acceptance, *before* the son can make his confession of guilt. He also makes known his enduring love and fellowship to the older son despite the latter's reproaches (v. 31). In the antithetically developed behaviors of the brothers we see two possible human

---

[54] Legally he was entitled to no higher position after the payment of the inheritance; cf. here W. Pöhlmann, 'Abschichtung,' p. 202.

[55] Cf. M. Petzoldt, *Gleichnisse*, p. 90.

reactions to the promise and experience of acceptance. Only through crisis does the younger son come to the insight that life apart from the father is not possible. With the recognition of his own misdeeds (vv. 18, 21: ἥμαρτον, "I have sinned") comes the expectation of just punishment. What is then new and surprising for the younger son is the magnitude and breadth of the father's loving acceptance. The older brother, by contrast, does not understand himself as accepted for no reason at all; rather, he sees his relationship with his father as one of work and pay. Only those who work and follow the law can celebrate. In this way the older son becomes tangled in a web of achievement and compensation that blocks the vision of human dependence. For him there can be no radical forgiveness as an expression of enduring love. In the figure of the older brother it becomes clear the even when human beings reject the love of God, they still live by it.

Along with the parable of the lost son Luke passes on the related double parables of the lost sheep (Mt 18:12–14/Lk 15:1–7) and the lost coin (Lk 15:8–10).[56] The reconstruction of the Q antecedent of Mt 18:12–14/Lk 15:1–7 leads to the conclusion that Matthew is closer to the original version (Mt 18:12–13).[57] The present position in Mt 18, the framework in Lk 15:1–3, the strong emphasis on sharing the joy in Luke 15:6, and the applications in Mt 18:14/Lk 15:7 are to be regarded as secondary. The parable of the lost coin originally comprised Luke 15:8–9.

The parable of the lost sheep is dominated by the idea of joy over finding the lost.[58] Both the juxtaposition of one and ninety-nine and the unusual behavior of the shepherd in leaving the ninety-nine sheep behind alone serve to express the pain over the loss and the joy of the recovery. The parable of the lost sheep seeks agreement; everyone would behave as the shepherd did.[59] In the parable of the lost coin the intensive searching of the woman is surprising. The listener involuntarily joins in the dynamic of the parable and in the joy over the recovery.

Through these parables Jesus establishes an agreement among his listeners as well as between his activity and his message. He interprets his attention to sinners and tax collectors as a recovery

---

[56] On the fundamental analysis cf. E. Linnemann, *Gleichnisse*, pp. 70–9.
[57] For detailed substantiation (also of the following) cf. H. Merklein, *Handlungsprinzip*, pp. 186ff.
[58] Cf. E. Linnemann, *Gleichnisse*, p. 72; J. Jeremias, *Gleichnisse*, p. 135.
[59] Cf. E. Linnemann, *Gleichnisse*, p. 71.

of the lost. Sinners and tax collectors are not forever lost; in Jesus' behavior there is a recovery that is the occasion for joy.[60] The communion with God that is disturbed by sin is not re-established in a cultic, ritualistic way; instead, God himself takes the initiative. The sins of the past have lost their separating and burdening function, without a prior achievement from the human side. Rather, the sinner lives from the forgiveness of God, from God's groundless acceptance.[61] God's surprising attention to human beings takes concrete form in the behavior of Jesus *vis-à-vis* tax collectors and sinners. At the same time Jesus' activity is based on God's final salvific decision for humankind, which finds its proclamatory expression in the nearness of the βασιλεία τοῦ θεοῦ ("kingdom of God") and its concrete expression in Jesus' deeds.[62]

Also in the parable of the laborers in the vineyard (Mt 20:1–16)[63] Jesus gives expression to human existence *coram Deo*. The text shows a clear structure. Following the recruitment and hiring of the laborers (vv. 1b–7) we have the payment of wages (vv. 8–10) and the closing dialogue (vv. 11–15). We note first the hiring of the five groups of workers, which is spread over the whole day and described stereotypically; each group agrees to a clearly defined work agreement.[64] Only the last and first groups then appear in the crisis situation and in the closing dialogue, so that they, together with the landowner, function as a 'dramatic triangle.'[65] Action in the story results from the landowner's unusual instruction to begin payment with the last hired (v. 8b). Initially the first hired overcome the crisis caused by the landowner's atypical behavior with the hope of an appropriate bonus.[66] When this expectation is not fulfilled, they reproach the landowner for unjust treatment (vv. 11–12). The landowner reacts to their – thoroughly understandable (v. 12) – moral indignation by indicating that he has held to the work agreement and that he is free in his behavior with regard to the

---

[60] Cf. ibid., p. 76.

[61] Cf. H. Merklein, *Handlungsprinzip*, p. 191.

[62] Cf. ibid., p. 192.

[63] Verse 16 and possibly the introductory formula in v. 1a are redactional; cf. H. Weder, *Gleichnisse*, pp. 218–19.

[64] On the question of the description's relation to reality cf. W. Harnisch, *Gleichniserzählungen*, p. 179.

[65] Cf. ibid., p. 184. The manager in v. 8 plays only a minor role.

[66] Pertinent here is M. Petzoldt, *Gleichnisse*, p. 53: 'This hope also appears to be underlined and confirmed by the order. The last are not supposed to learn how much more the first are paid.'

last hired. In the antithesis of landowner and first hired, two orders of being are revealed: the order of the wage and the order of goodness. The thinking of the first hired is determined by the just relationship of work and wage. Those who work more than others can also demand more pay. On this principle the first hired attack the wage payment. The landowner, of course, can refer to the kept agreement, so that now suddenly the plaintiffs become the defendants. Their thinking on the causality of work and wage does not give them the right to criticize the landowner and the last hired. The landowner is free in his unexpected, unbounded goodness, which does no one wrong but at the same time is unexpectedly generous with many. This goodness is subject to no time restriction, as shown by the monotonously repeated offer of work during the whole day. Every time appears to be the right time to take up the offer.[67] The first hired cannot understand this, for they understand their hiring not as a benevolent offer but as a self-evident, performance-related arrangement. The landowner, however, grants to everyone and at every time a subsistence wage. His freedom is not limited; his goodness is not calculating. Thus through the parable Jesus describes God as the one who accepts human beings and gives them what is necessary for life. And human beings for their part learn to understand themselves as accepted people whose existence is defined not by their own performance but by the goodness of God.

God's unconditional forgiveness is also expressed by Jesus in the parable of the unforgiving servant (Mt 18:23–30, 31, 32–34, 35). The parable as told by Jesus may have included only verses 23b–30.[68] There are two reasons for this view. (1) The servant's absolution is withdrawn in the second part of the story (vv. 32–34), so that the lord appears to have broken his word. (2) Verse 31 is to be credited to the evangelist, as indicated especially by its numerous Matthean linguistic peculiarities.[69] The growth process of the tradition's history probably went as follows: (1) At the Jesus stage the parable comprised verses 23b–30.[70] (2) Still on the pre-Matthean level it was expanded with verses 32–34.[71] (3) Matthew

---

[67] Cf. ibid., p. 54.
[68] Thus A. Weiser, *Knechtsgleichnisse*, p. 90; H. Weder, *Gleichnisse*, p. 210–11. Versus W. Harnisch, *Gleichniserzählungen*, p. 259.
[69] Cf. A. Weiser, *Knechtsgleichnisse*, pp. 92–3; H. Weder, *Gleichnisse*, p. 211, n. 6.
[70] A. Weiser, *Knechtsgleichnisse*, p. 90.
[71] Cf. ibid., pp. 86–8; H. Weder, *Gleichnisse*, p. 211, n. 7.

interprets the parable through verse 31, a partial reworking of verses 32–34, the addition of verse 35, and the placing of the story in the community ordering of Mt 18; at this point we should especially note the correspondence between verses 21–22 and verse 35.

The story begins with a debtor relationship that clearly exhibits hyperbolic traits.[72] The owed sum of money (100,000,000 denarii)[73] is unimaginable, which places the position and relationship of the lord and the servant in a special light. At first the lord demands the repayment of the money, even if that requires the sale of the debtor and his family into slavery (v. 25). The idea is unrealistic, for neither the possessions of the debtor nor his being led away into slavery would suffice to discharge the gigantic debt. On the other hand, the debtor's behavior is understandable; he begs for mercy and promises to pay everything (v. 26). Then something strange is reported about the lord. He goes far beyond the offer of his servant, has pity on him, and relieves him of all debt.

Against this background, the behavior of the servant described in verses 28–30 must seem unimaginable. Although he himself has experienced boundless mercy, he behaves unmercifully toward a fellow servant over a ridiculously small amount.

This unjust behavior of the servant plainly demands a reaction from the lord in order to restore justice. This understandable desire probably occasioned the addition of verses 32–34.

In and with the parable of the unforgiving servant Jesus interprets the situation of human beings before God. They appear before God as debtors whose debt is so unimaginably great that they cannot discharge it even with the sale of their own existence. In their need humans turn to God and beg him for patience. God not only grants them a postponement but without any precondition forgives them their immeasurable debt. In this unexpected – indeed, incomprehensible – act of the acceptance of humankind God demonstrates his love and mercy. He does not simply give people time to free themselves from their precarious situation, for this would be a totally hopeless attempt. Rather, through forgiveness God gives people new life. God comes to people preveniently by granting them unearned pardon.

Incomprehensibly, God's action for humankind produces no results. Apparently human beings are not at all conscious of the

---

[72] Cf. W. Harnisch, *Gleichniserzählungen*, p. 257.
[73] Cf. J. Jeremias, *Gleichnisse*, p. 208.

magnitude of their debt before God and the hopelessness of their situation. They are unaware of what God has done for them; instead, they give themselves immediately to the world's agenda. They do not know that they live only through God's mercy. In them God's grace has ungracious consequences. Thus both God and humankind in their own way behave incomprehensibly. Without illusion Jesus places God's prevenient love over against the selfishness of humankind.

Jesus' parables point beyond themselves; they attempt to press upon the listeners the insight that the parables are talking about nothing less than the listeners' own lives. They are offered possibilities for identification; they are led to basic decisions to seize and change their lives.

Jesus' message of the unconditional acceptance of humankind by God is made clear in his practice of turning his attention to sinners and tax collectors. This behavior apparently soon gained him the reputation of being a friend of tax collectors and sinners (cf. Mt 11:18–19/Lk 7:33–34: 'For John the Baptist has come eating no bread and drinking no wine, and you say, "He has a demon"; the Son of Man has come eating and drinking, and you say, "Look, a glutton and a drunkard, a friend of tax collectors and sinners!"').[74] The table fellowships practiced by Jesus represented an attack on the Old Testament's basic distinction between clean and unclean[75] (cf. Lev. 10:10: 'You are to distinguish between the holy and the common, and between the unclean and the clean').

Because in ancient Judaism meals always had a religious character and God was thought to be present in worship as the actual host, the table fellowship served both the preservation of Jewish identity and public separation from Gentiles and the religiously indifferent (cf., e.g., *Jub.* 22.16: 'But you, my son Jacob, remember my words and keep the commandments of your father Abraham. Separate yourself from the Gentiles. Do not eat with them. Do not act according to their deeds, and do not be their comrade. For their work is uncleanness, and all their ways are defilement, abomination, and uncleanness'; cf. also 3 Macc. 3:4; 4

---

[74] Cf. on reconstruction of the Q sources S. Schulz, *Q,* pp. 379–80. On the tracing of this text back to Jesus cf. H. Merklein, *Handlungsprinzip,* pp. 198–9; V. Hampel, *Menschensohn und historischer Jesus,* pp. 214–22.

[75] In the New Testament period the Pharisees attempted to make this distinction obligatory in all areas of life; cf. here J. Neusner, 'Die pharisäischen rechtlichen Überlieferungen,' p. 51, who with justification designates the 'legalism' of the Pharisees as 'a matter of the food laws.'

Macc. 1:35; 5:16ff. Jos. *Bell.* 2.137–39: not until after a year of probation and a two-year novitiate did the Essenes admit someone to their common meals; cf. 1QS 6.20–21; Jos. *Bell.* 2.143–44: excluded Essenes starved to death, because they did not accept food from strangers). Hence Jesus' eating habits could not fail to evoke a reaction. According to Mk 2:16[76] the scribes among the Pharisees raised the – in their view discrediting – question of whether Jesus ate with tax collectors and sinners. Jesus responds to this reproach by taking up a pair of terms from the thinking of his opponents: 'I have come to call not the righteous [δίκαιοι] but sinners [ἁμαρτωλοί]' (Mk 2:17c). This pair of terms was not foreign to Jesus' proclamation (cf. Lk 15:7; 18:9–13) and may describe the aim of his mission precisely. Jesus' message of the approaching reign of God was for all of Israel and also for those who were by no means only ironically called the righteous. Above all, however, it was sinners to whom God's mercy and love had to be brought, so that they might return to God. The righteous should and must not hinder them in that.[77]

If Jesus not only proclaimed but also practiced God's radical salvific decision for humankind, the question arises whether he also directly granted God's forgiveness to people. Both the encounter with the sinful woman (Lk 7:36–50) and the healing of the paralytic (Mk 2:1–12) point to a forgiveness of sins by Jesus. In their present literary form, however, neither text goes back to Jesus, but they contain old traditions (Mk 2:5b, 10; Lk 7:37, 38, 47?) that make a pledge of God's forgiveness of sins or an immediate forgiveness of sins by Jesus seem possible.[78] Such a practice by Jesus would correspond to his message of God's unconditional support for humankind. Jesus claims for himself what actually seemed reserved for God. Because God's dominion is present in a liberating way in the person of Jesus (Lk 17:20–21), the deeds of Jesus show that God himself seeks sinners and those who are lost.

Jesus also speaks of the acceptance of humankind in the beatitudes of the Sermon on the Mount.

The beatitudes on the poor (Mt 5:3/Lk 6:20b), the hungry (Mt 5:6/Lk 6:21a), and the mourners (Mt 5:4/Lk 6:21b) go back to

---

[76] Mk 2:15–17 represents an independent text unit, which reproduces the oldest traditions; cf. for reconstruction R. Pesch, *Markus* 1:162–9; H. Merklein, *Handlungsprinzip*, pp. 199–201.

[77] Cf. R. Pesch, *Markus* 1:168.

[78] Cf. H. Merklein, *Handlungsprinzip*, pp. 201–3.

Jesus.[79] This statement is based not only on the agreements between Matthew and Luke but also on the fact that all three beatitudes are marked by alliteration with the Greek letter π and in this way are distinguished from the other beatitudes. Luke may come very close to the original wording of the beatitudes (only the νῦν ["now"] in vv. 21a, 21b is clearly redactional; κλαίοντες ["weeping"] in v. 21b is secondary), whereas interpretations are undertaken by the pre-Matthean community (change to third person plural παρακληθήσονται ["shall be comforted"] in v. 4b) and the evangelist Matthew (τῷ πνεύματι ["in spirit"] in v. 3a, τῶν οὐρανῶν ["of the heavens"] in v. 3b, καὶ διψῶντες τὴν δικαιοσύνην ["and thirsting (after) righteousness"] in v. 6a).

Form-historical parallels to the speech form of the beatitude are found both in the Old Testament (Deut. 33:29; Ps. 127:2; Isa. 32:20; etc.) and in ancient Judaism (Wis. 3:13; *As. Mos.* 10.8; *1 Enoch* 58.2). Especially instructive is *1 Enoch* 99.10, which reads: 'But in those days all those will be blessed who accept and know the words of wisdom, who observe the ways of the Most High, walk in the paths of his righteousness, and do not sin with the godless, for they will be saved.'

In the first beatitude Jesus promises to the bodily poor the kingdom of God. Why to them? The poor, those without rights, the oppressed are in a situation in which they have nothing to offer. They have nothing to give and are dependent on taking. They are prevented from shaping their lives as they please; they can only hope for mercy and help from outside. In this situation of absolute dependence Jesus grants the poor participation in the kingdom of God. Jesus thereby reveals some of the essence of God's kingdom: it is God's abundance, his generous goodness, his acceptance of humankind. Where God's dominion takes place, there God alone is the giver and human beings are the receivers. In view of the kingdom of God they can understand themselves only as the accepted and as recipients of a gift. The poor are dependent on giving, and therefore the abundance of God is for them. It is not the things one has, one's possessions, that enable a person to be open to the kingdom of God, but knowledge of being dependent on God's help.

Like the poor, those who mourn or are hungry find themselves separated from life. Through the death of a loved one, mourners

---

[79] Cf. G. Strecker, *The Sermon on the Mount*, p. 29; H. Weder, *Die 'Rede der Reden*,' pp. 40–1.

have also lost a piece of their own lives. Mourning is the manifest protest against this deprivation of life. The lives of the hungry are threatened by hunger in an immediate way. For them life expresses itself in the elementary longing for food. Jesus blesses both groups and lets them participate in life in the presence of God's dominion. Like the poor, those who mourn and those who are hungry are ready for the kingdom of God, which will bring them comfort and satiety. They do not come before God with demands; they let themselves be given unearned gifts. It is precisely in being cut off from life that they discover acceptance by God.

2.5 God, Jesus, and the New Reality of Humankind

Jesus' proclamation is theocentrically oriented.[80] In the coming of God's kingdom, God himself reaches into the present as a loving father and creates a new reality. It is inseparably bound to Jesus, whose words and deeds appear as the bursting forth of the coming dominion of God. The kingdom of God is the anticipatory presence of what is to come. Jesus qualifies his appearance as the beginning of the eschatological salvation (cf. Lk 17:21; 10:23–24 par.); in his healings God's kingdom is present (Mt 11:5–6 par.; Lk 11:20); faced with the glory of God, Satan must retreat (cf. Mk 3:27; Lk 10:18). In Jesus God himself is acting. When Jesus forgives sinners, he is adopting God's concern. In Jesus' table fellowship with tax collectors and sinners, God himself is seeking the lost. God's original will is heard again in Jesus' ethical radicalisms. The authority of these statements rests not in the Old Testament wording nor in the figure of Moses but solely in the unique authority of the one who says, ἐγὼ δὲ λέγω ὑμῖν ('but I say to you'). The law no longer has the power to determine access to God. In Jesus' appearance the truly new is dawning (Mk 2:21–22: 'No one sews a piece of unshrunk cloth on an old cloak; otherwise, the patch pulls away from it, the new from the old, and a worse tear is made. And no one puts new wine into old wineskins; otherwise, the wine will burst the skins, and the wine is lost, and so are the skins'). In the parables Jesus not only puts God into words; he also brings God so close to people that they let themselves be seized and transformed by his goodness. In so doing, the teller of

---

[80] Cf. here W. Schrage, *Theologie und Christologie bei Paulus und Jesus*, pp. 135ff.

the parables himself vouches for the truth of what is told and demanded. Finally, because Jesus' call to repentance in view of the inbreaking kingdom of God for humankind is realized as acceptance of the call to discipleship, Jesus' sweeping claim and his extraordinary relation to God are also shown through discipleship.[81] In the Old Testament it is God who calls and sends (cf. the prophetic calls in Exod. 3:10–15; Judg. 6:14; Isa. 6:1–8; Jer. 1:4–10; Ezek. 2); now it is Jesus who takes God's place. The immediate and unconditional nature of the call to discipleship (cf., e.g., Mt 8:21–22 par.) clarifies Jesus' claim to represent the presence and nearness of the kingdom of God and to act in God's stead. The category of eschatological prophet of the end time cannot comprise this self-claim, and Jesus rejected it for himself as inadequate (Lk 11:31–32: '… and see, something greater than Jonah is here!'; cf. also Lk 16:16).[82] Although Jesus spoke about his role in the dawning eschatological event only allusively and cryptically, and only the talk of the presently active (cf. Lk 7:33–34; 9:58; 11:30) and coming (cf. Mt 10:23b; 24:30a; Lk 17:24; 17:26; 17:30) 'Son of Man' can be considered Jesus' self-designation,[83] the tradition makes it clear that Jesus appeared with a claim for his person that was not made by any Jew before or after him.[84] He emphasizes that in him the kingdom of God has dawned undetected (cf. Mt 13:31–32/Lk 13:18–19). He demands the highest obligation for his message and ties salvation to his person. The focus here is not on statements about Jesus but on confrontation with his message. Jesus asks people to hear the will of God in a new and final way, to discover the nature of God, and in this way to know themselves.

In terms of content, the image of humankind in the proclamation of Jesus is characterized by a tension-filled intertwining of the message of judgment and the message of grace. In view of

---

[81] The immediacy of the call to discipleship and the unconditionality of obedience are in no way post-Easter interpretations but result appropriately from Jesus' claim; cf. F. Hahn, 'Nachfolge,' pp. 12–13.

[82] M. Hengel, *Nachfolge und Chrisma*, pp. 55–6, correctly emphasizes the uniqueness of Jesus' appearance, which also cannot be understood by analogy with the Jewish rabbi.

[83] A balanced presentation of the Son-of-Man problematic is offered by L. Goppelt, *Theologie* 1:116–253. A comprehensive overview of recent research appears in W. G. Kümmel, *Jesusforschung*, pp. 340–74.

[84] On Jesus' 'self-consciousness' cf. H. Merklein, *Handlungsprinzip*, pp. 212-15, as well as V. Hampel's recent *Menschensohn und historischer Jesus*, pp. 49-372.

the inbreaking kingdom of God and the absolute will of the Creator, human beings can only recognize themselves as sinners who have fallen short of their destiny as creatures. At the same time Jesus – through his behavior and in the his parables – reveals God as the one who seeks the lost and accepts sinners ready to repent. In this way Jesus lets people participate fully in his special relationship with God. He gives insights into the reality of God and the situation of humankind. People are allowed to discover that their lives can succeed only if they understand themselves as creatures, observe the will of the Creator, accept their liability to judgment, and receive God's goodness for themselves. Jesus does not see the aim and meaning of human existence in shaping life on one's own authority, in boundless independence or freedom; rather, one is oneself when one is with God.

Jesus' message and activity articulate an implicit Christology, which at the same time requires an explicit Christology. *After* Jesus one speaks appropriately *of* Jesus, because his person is inseparable from his proclamation and his deeds.

3

Pauline Anthropology

3.1 The Presupposition of Pauline Anthropology: The World as God's Creation

For Paul the whole world is God's creation (1 Cor. 8:6a: 'Yet for us there is one God, the Father, from whom are all things and for whom we exist').[1] Before the world and history stands God, 'who is over all' (Rom. 9:5) and of whom it is said that in the end he will be 'all in all' (1 Cor. 15:28). Not only are creation and humankind of the same origin, but their destinies will also be interwoven in the future. Protology and eschatology go together in Paul (cf. Rom. 8:18ff.[2]). Everything comes from God; everything has its existence in him and moves toward him. God elects and rejects whom he will (Rom. 9:16, 18). His chosen people Israel are defeated and raised up again; the Gentiles share in salvation, but God can also break this new branch of the olive tree off again (Rom. 11:17–24). He is not bound by human standards; he chooses those who from a human standpoint are simple, weak, and unworthy (1 Cor. 1:25ff.). According to his will, it is not human wisdom but the foolishness of the message of cross that saves (1 Cor. 1:18ff.). Reality cannot be understood at all without its reference to God, for 'the earth and its fullness are the Lord's' (1 Cor. 10:26). Everything is and remains God's creation, even if human beings flee from their destiny by worshiping idols.[3] God made himself known in his creation, but though human beings knew about God, 'they did not honor him as God or give thanks to him, but they became futile in their thinking, and their senseless minds were darkened' (Rom. 1:21). Again and again they turn to powers that by nature

---

[1] On creation and cosmos in Paul cf. J. Baumgarten, *Paulus und die Apokalyptik*, pp. 159–79.

[2] On the interpretation of Rom. 8:18ff. cf. S. Vollenweider, *Freiheit*, pp. 375–96.

[3] Cf. J. Becker, *Paul*, pp. 381–2.

are not gods (Gal. 4:8). Despite this compulsion of human beings to create gods for themselves or to take the place of God, humankind and the world remain God's creation. Yet since the fall of Adam sin has set its snare (Rom. 5:12ff.), and Satan has appeared in multiple forms to entice human beings (cf. 1 Cor. 5:5; 2 Cor. 2:11; 11:14; 1 Thess. 2:18); nevertheless, God does not abandon his creation.[4] The apostle is 'convinced that neither death, nor life, nor angels, nor rulers, nor things present, nor things to come, nor powers, nor height, nor depth, nor anything else in all creation, will be able to separate us from the love of God in Christ Jesus our Lord' (Rom. 8:38–39). God calls into being the things that are not; he alone gives life to the dead (Rom. 4:17).[5] Only of him can one say, 'For from him and through him and to him are all things' (Rom. 11:36a).

God does not leave human beings to their own devices in the turmoil of the world and of their own lives; rather, when the fullness of time had come (ὅτε δὲ ἦλθεν τὸ πλήρωμα τοῦ χρόνου; Gal. 4:4a), God sent his Son (cf. Rom. 8:3). As the Lord of history God determines the course of time; he establishes the times, and therefore, 'See, now is the acceptable time; see, now is the day of salvation!' (2 Cor. 6:2b: ἰδοὺ νῦν καιρὸς εὐπρόσδεκτος ἰδοὺ νῦν ἡμέρα σωτηρίας). Jesus Christ was already before Moses (cf. 1 Cor. 10:4); before all time he was with God and was like God (Phil. 2:6). Creation owes its being to the mediator of creation, Jesus Christ, 'through whom are all things and through whom we exist' (1 Cor. 8:6b).[6] In his parousia he will make all things subject to himself (cf. Phil. 3:21). The whole creation is, according to the will of God, indissolubly bound to Jesus. 'Therefore God also highly exalted him and gave him the name that is above every name, so that at the name of Jesus every knee should bend, in heaven and on earth and under the earth, and every tongue should confess that Jesus Christ is Lord, in the glory of God the Father' (Phil. 2:9–11). It is God's salvific will for his creation that powers, authorities, and people know that the mediator of creation, Jesus Christ, is at the same time the mediator of salvation. He frees

---

[4]   Pertinent here is W. Schrage, 'Die Stellung zur Welt,' p. 128: 'God does not leave the world ... to itself forever, because it is his property and he as its Creator has a claim on it.'

[5]   On the concept of the *creatio ex nihilo* in Rom. 4:17, cf. E. Käsemann, *Römer*, pp. 115–16.

[6]   On the traditional character of 1 Cor. 8:6, cf. Chr. Wolff, *1. Korinther*, pp. 7–10.

human beings from bondage to themselves and to the world and makes them what they are by origin: creatures of God.[7]

3.2 The Appropriate Starting Point for Pauline Anthropology: God's New Reality in Jesus Christ

The foundation of Pauline theology is the turn of the times brought about by God in the crucifixion and resurrection of Jesus Christ.[8] Near Damascus the resurrected Jesus Christ appeared to Paul, the Pharisee and persecutor of Christians (cf. 1 Cor. 9:1; 15:8; Gal. 1:16), and led him to faith.[9] Paul rejected his brilliant past (cf. Phil. 3:5–7) because he perceived that God's salvific action for the world in his Son Jesus Christ had achieved its aim once and for all. The Jesus of Nazareth who had died scornfully on the cross was not a Jewish heretic, whose followers had to be persecuted, but the Son of God. To talk of Jesus after Easter meant for Paul to proclaim the significance for salvation of the life, death, and resurrection of Jesus Christ. In the Christ event God was interpreting himself; he is none other than the one who raised Jesus Christ from the dead (cf. 1 Cor. 15:3–5; 1 Thess. 4:14). God's action in Jesus did not occur merely as proof of divine power over life but was in the deepest sense an event for humankind. Jesus died so that we can live with him (2 Cor. 4:14; 1 Thess. 5:10: 'Because we know that the one who raised the Lord Jesus will raise us also with Jesus, and will bring us with you into his presence [= before his face]'). Jesus went obediently to the cross (cf. Rom. 5:19; Gal. 1:4a, 4c; Phil. 2:8), suffered and died ὑπὲρ ἡμῶν ("for us"; Rom. 5:8), ὑπὲρ πάντων ("for all"; 2 Cor. 5:14–15), for the ungodly (cf. Rom. 4:5; 5:6). God made the sinless One to be sin 'for us,' so that we might become the righteousness of God in him (2 Cor. 5:21). 'For us' Christ vicariously took upon himself the curse of the law (Gal. 3:13); God put him forward as a sacrifice of atonement for the forgiveness of 'sins previously committed' (Rom. 3:25). In

---

[7] The creation statements broadly scattered throughout Paul do not form a closed thematic block; they point rather to the turning point in time and in the world achieved in Christ; cf. W. Schrage, 'Die Stellung zur Welt,' p. 126.

[8] Cf. here the basic reflections of W. Schrage, 'Theologie und Christologie bei Paulus und Jesus,' pp. 122–35.

[9] On the interpretation of the Damascus event cf. U. Schnelle, *Wandlungen*, pp. 15–21.

dying Jesus showed his love for us human beings (Rom. 5:8: 'But God proves his love for us in that while we still were sinners Christ died for us'; cf. Rom. 8:39). In Jesus Christ God was reconciling the world to himself, 'not counting their trespasses against them, and entrusting the message of reconciliation to us' (2 Cor. 5:19).[10] Christ died for the brother and the sister (Rom. 14:15; cf. 1 Cor. 8:11); Christ became for us wisdom, righteousness, sanctification, and redemption (1 Cor. 1:30).

In Pauline theology cross and resurrection are the very event of salvation, for 'If Christ has not been raised, your faith is futile and you are still in your sins' (1 Cor. 15:17). But because Christ rose from the dead, death is rendered impotent as God's eschatological adversary (1 Cor. 15:55), and the gracious gift of faith enables people to participate in God's salvific work (cf., Thess. 4:14). Faith in Jesus Christ raises the possibility of eschatological deliverance from the coming wrath of the Judge (cf. Rom. 1:16; 1 Cor. 5:5; 2 Cor. 6:2; Gal. 4:5; Phil. 2:12; 1 Thess. 5:8–9;).[11] It occurs in the acceptance of the gospel's message of grace proclaimed by the apostle.

God's salvific action in Jesus Christ for humankind is the basis and presupposition of all Pauline statements about human beings. With this event God establishes a new reality in which the world and the situation of people in the world appear in a different light. Only in faith in the Son of God, Jesus Christ, can human beings gain access to God and thus to salvation. Outside of this faith rules 'the god of this world' (2 Cor. 4:4) and thus the unfaith that leads to perdition.

3.3 The Actual Starting Point of Pauline Anthropology: Reflection on Humankind *vis-à-vis* Death

The foregoing description of the essential foundations of Paul's image of humankind tells us initially nothing about the concrete theological expression of this anthropology. Also the apostle's background in Hellenistic Judaism[12] can clarify religious-historical

---

[10] On the reconciliation statements in 2 Corinthians 5 cf. C. Breytenbach, *Versöhnung*, pp. 107ff.

[11] On Paul's conception of judgment cf. E. Synofzik, *Gerichts- und Vergeltungsaussagen.*

[12] A good introduction to the theology of the Hellenistic Jewish circle is offered by H. Hegermann, 'Das hellenistische Judentum.'

connections but not the anthropology of the Christian Paul. As the oldest document of Pauline theology, the First Letter to the Thessalonians, shows rather that the continuing passage of time was of great significance in the formation of the apostle's anthropology. This letter lacks all the important anthropological terms of later letters, such as σάρξ ("flesh"), ἁμαρτία ("sin"), θάνατος ("death"), ἐλευθερία ("freedom"), ζωή ("life"). And even the theological concepts of the doctrine of justification, the theology of the cross, the church as the body of Christ, and baptism as burial with Christ are obviously unknown in First Thessalonians.[13]

Of great anthropological relevance, however, are the apostle's reflections on the course of the parousia in 1 Thess. 4:13–18. Paul's description of the eschatological events in this passage was occasioned by unexpected deaths in Thessalonica before the parousia of the Lord.[14] Paul responds by linking here for the first time the idea of the parousia of the Lord with that of a resurrection of deceased Christians. After an introduction to the problem (v. 13) and an initial answer with reference to the kerygma of Jesus' death and resurrection (v. 14), Paul gives a second answer in verses 15–17, which consists of a summary of a traditional word of the Lord (v. 15) and its citing (vv. 16–17). This teaching is closed with the apostle's admonition to console oneself with the answer he has given to the question of the fate of those who have died ahead of time. The description of the end events within the traditional word of the Lord begins with the triumphal coming of the Lord (v. 16a–c), which is followed first by the resurrection of the 'dead in Christ' (v. 16d) and then the combined rapture with the living into the clouds to meet the Lord (v. 17a). Within this process the resurrection of deceased community members has only a subordinate function ('... the dead in Christ will rise first. Then we who are alive, who are left, will be caught up in the clouds together with them ...'). The aim of the whole event is to be with the Lord; its immediate presupposition is the rapture of all, and its intermediate precondition is the resurrection of the dead in Christ. In his founding proclamation in Thessalonica Paul had – in expectation of the imminent parousia of the Lord – apparently dispensed with the idea of a resurrection of the believing dead.[15]

---

[13] Cf. U. Schnelle, 'Der erste Thessalonicherbrief,' pp. 207–14.

[14] On 1 Thess. 4:13–18 cf. the interpretation of H. H. Schade, *Apokalyptische Christologie*, pp. 157–72.

[15] Cf. W. Marxsen, *1. Thessalonicher*, pp. 64–5.

Not until the death of some Christians before the parousia and the accompanying problems of the delay of the parousia and the historicity of the Christian faith was Paul forced to introduce the concept of a resurrection of deceased believers. Even in 1 Thess. 4:13–18, however, he remained true to his original eschatological conception of a rapture of all at the parousia of the Lord. The resurrection of deceased community members functions solely to make possible the following rapture. In 1 Thessalonians the death of Christians before the parousia is clearly still the exception; Paul counts himself and also the community among the living at the return of the Lord (vv. 15, 17: 'we who are alive'), probably in the conviction that the arrival of the Lord is imminent.

A changed situation is reflected in 1 Corinthians.[16] Here deaths before the parousia are no longer unusual (cf. 7:39; 11:30; 15:6, 18, 29, 51). Paul treats this new situation in 1 Cor. 15:35–56 in a broadly developed anthropological argumentation whose objective basis is the reality of the resurrection of Jesus Christ from the dead (cf. 15:20: 'But in fact Christ has been raised from the dead, the first fruits of those who have died'). The actual occasion was an adversarial question about the 'how' of the resurrection of the dead: 'But someone will ask, "How are the dead raised? With what kind of body do they come?"' (15:35). Paul begins his first train of thought in 15:36–38 with the idea – widespread in antiquity – of the necessity of dying as a condition for new life. The element of discontinuity already contained in this view is applied by Paul in verse 38 to the free creative activity of God, who gives all people their own σῶμα ("body, corporeality") as he chooses. Here the basic position of the apostle already becomes clear: for him there is no existence without corporeality, and thus the question about the 'how' of the resurrection can only be the question about the kind of resurrection body (cf. v. 35). Paul presupposes here that the resurrection is a new creative act of God. As in the first creation God's power of life brings forth from itself a new corporeality that is not surrendered to death and perishability.[17] In verses 39–41 Paul emphasizes God's ability to create various earthly as well as heavenly bodies, in order to illustrate again the creator-power of God, which is the guarantee of creation and the maintenance of the individual

---

[16] On the following section cf. U. Schnelle, 'Der erste Thessalonicherbrief,' pp. 214–18.

[17] Pertinent is Chr. Wolff, *1. Korinther*, p. 197: God's 'creative will realizes itself ever anew.'

doxa-body. In verses 42–44 Paul makes full use of what he has said thus far, as he summarizes. As the perishable is sown and the imperishable is raised, so the σῶμα ψυχικόν ("perishable body") is sown and the σῶμα πνευματικόν ("spiritual body") is raised. With this antithesis, the question of the 'how' of the resurrection is answered, in that on the one hand corporeality appears as the basic condition of the resurrection, but on the other hand it is defined as spiritual reality and thus to be clearly separated from the present perishable world. Paul substantiates this basic position christologically in verses 45–49, for as πνεῦμα ζῳοποιοῦν ("life-giving spirit")[18] Christ produces the spiritual resurrection body, and as prototype of the new being he is also its ideal (1 Cor. 15:45: 'Thus it is written, "The first man, Adam, became a living being"; the last Adam became a life-giving spirit'). In verse 50a Paul summarizes his foregoing anthropological argumentation: σάρξ ("flesh") and αἷμα ("blood") as anthropological designations for the perishability of the creaturely cannot inherit the kingdom of God, because perishability cannot acquire imperishability.[19] In verses 51–52 Paul develops his solution to the problem by first informing the community that not all will fall asleep, but all (living and dead) will be changed. The relationship of the dead and the living is clarified more precisely in verse 52: the dead will be raised imperishable, and 'we will be changed.' In verses 53ff. a further antithetical explanation is given in which the metaphor of 'putting on' imperishability or immortality clearly contains the element of identity between the old and the new being.

If at the time of the writing of 1 Thessalonians deaths before the parousia of the Lord were the unexpected exception, then in 1 Corinthians they are part of the reality of the Christian community. This changed the historical position of the first generation of Christians, for the now realistic possibility of dying before the expected imminent arrival of the Lord made it clear that even Christians were included in the perishability and thus in the historicity of all that is, and that their special position consists in a reasonable hope, but not in a visible change. Death as a now acute theological problem not only produced the consciousness of historicity in the young churches; it also required from the

---

[18] On the religious-historical background cf. G. Sellin, *Auferstehung der Toten*, pp. 79–90.

[19] On the analysis of 1 Cor. 15:51–52, cf. G. Lüdemann, *Paulus* 1:264ff.

apostle a new argumentation appropriate to the changed situation. Because the death of Christians before the parousia of the Lord is no longer the exception, Paul feels compelled to solve this problem on the basis of an anthropology that defines individual earthly as well as heavenly existence. In 1 Thessalonians, by contrast, all the important anthropological terms are lacking,[20] because here the problem of death and the historicity of Christian existence is only suggested and has not yet become fully conscious. In the oldest Pauline letter human beings are totally determined by the Spirit of God working in the present, and their whole existence is oriented toward the imminent coming of the Lord. Only the delay of the immediately expected parousia and the thereby necessitated theological overcoming of death by Christians before the arrival of the Lord make it necessary to work out an antithetical anthropology that describes the different individual modes of existence. When Paul wrote 1 Corinthians, he felt compelled to reflect extensively on pre- and post-mortal human existence and to present its christological enablement and concrete antithetical formulation. Pauline anthropology can no doubt be explained in its entirety mono-causally based on the consciousness of the delay of the parousia; on the other hand, however, the significance of this process for the working out of Paul's image of humankind is not to be underestimated, as 1 Thessalonians in particular shows.

3.4 Humankind and the Reality of God: πνεῦμα in Pauline Anthropology

The reality of God in the world is spiritual reality. In the πνεῦμα ("spirit"), which at first always emanates from God (cf. Rom. 5:5; 1 Cor. 1:12, 14; 2 Cor. 1:21; 5:5; Gal. 4:6; 1 Thess. 4:8), we see the life-giving power of the Creator. Even in the pre-Pauline tradition of Rom. 1:3b–4a Christ is regarded in his fleshly existence as the son of David but in his spiritual existence as the Son of God.[21] He is Son of God by virtue of his resurrection, which, however, according to Rom. 1:4a, produces the πνεῦμα ἁγιωσύνης ("spirit of holiness"). It is the Spirit of God that in the resurrection acts creatively in Jesus Christ. This working of the Spirit does not remain

---

[20] On 1 Thess. 5:23 cf. pp. 104–5 below.
[21] Cf. here E. Käsemann, *Römer*, pp. 8ff.

limited to the act of resurrection, but πνεῦμα also describes the new mode of being and acting of the resurrected One, his dynamic, efficacious presence. The exalted Jesus Christ works as πνεῦμα ζῳοποιοῦν and gives his people the σῶμα πνευματικόν ("spiritual body"; 1 Cor. 15:44).[22] What happened to Christ as the first to fall asleep will now also happen to the believers. Human existence, in its perishability (cf. χοϊκός, "made from earth," in 1 Cor. 15:47; φθαρτός, "perishable," in 15:53), corresponds completely to the first Adam; only the resurrected One can open up life in the Spirit for believers. Thus the Spirit acting in Jesus Christ is always the Spirit of God; the power at work in human beings is mostly the Spirit of Christ.

As the life-creating and animating power of God, the Lord is the Spirit (2 Cor. 3:17: ὁ δὲ κύριος τὸ πνεῦμά ἐστιν, 'now the Lord is the Spirit'). Here κύριος and πνεῦμα are identified with each other in the sense of a clarifying definition. It is supposed to assert not the identity of two persons but the mode of existence and activity of the exalted Lord.[23] This is illustrated in verse 17b ('where the Spirit of the Lord is, there is freedom'), in which the soteriological dimension of the Spirit's presence comes into view. In the Spirit, God's salvific act in Jesus Christ is realized as liberation from the powers of sin and death. Communion with the exalted Lord is communion in the Spirit (1 Cor. 6:17: 'But anyone united to the Lord becomes one spirit with him'). The Spirit is thus ultimately a christological designation; Christ and the Spirit correspond to each other (cf. Gal. 4:6: 'And because you are children, God has sent the Spirit of his Son into our hearts, crying, "Abba! Father!"'). Nevertheless, the relationship between Christ and the Spirit cannot be regarded as one of static identity; as the one coming from Christ the Spirit also has his own personal reality, as 1 Cor. 12:11 shows in the context of the charismata: 'All these are activated by one and the same Spirit, who allots to each one individually just as the Spirit chooses' (cf. also 1 Cor. 12:4). The Spirit does not appear in Paul as an independent person, but he is probably regarded in personal terms.

In the religious-historical background here are concepts from the Jewish wisdom literature. 'There is in her [= in wisdom] a spirit that is intelligent, holy, unique, manifold, subtle, mobile, clear ...'

---

[22] Cf. H. Conzelmann, *1. Korinther*, pp. 341–2.
[23] Cf. the analysis of I. Hermann, *Kyrios und Pneuma*, pp. 17–66.

(Wis. 7:22). 'For wisdom is more mobile than any motion; because of her pureness she pervades and penetrates all things' (Wis. 7:24). Like Christ, σοφία ("wisdom") in the wisdom literature can be identified with πνεῦμα (cf. also Wis. 1:6a; 7:7).[24]

The *pneuma* unique to each person individually (cf. Rom. 1:9: 'my spirit'; 1 Cor. 5:4; 14:14; 16:18; 2 Cor. 2:13; 7:1; Gal. 6:18; Phil. 4:23; Philemon 25: 'your spirit') is not removed by the Spirit of God or of Christ but is taken up and transformed. Believers no longer live out of themselves; they now find themselves under the influence of God.

But where does the reception of the Spirit take place for believers? When do they enter the reality of God? For Paul as for the whole of early Christianity, the λαμβάνειν τὸ πνεῦμα ("reception of the Spirit") occurs in baptism (cf. Rom. 8:15; 1 Cor. 2:12; 2 Cor. 11:4; Gal. 3:2, 14).[25] In Paul the solid connection between baptism and bestowal of the Spirit is emphatically attested in 1 Cor. 6:11; 12:13; 2 Cor. 1:21–22. In 1 Cor. 6:11 the calling out of the name of the Jesus Christ (ἐν τῷ ὀνόματι τοῦ κυρίου Ἰησοῦ Χριστοῦ, 'in the name of the Lord Jesus Christ') and the presence of the Spirit (ἐν τῷ πνεύματι τοῦ θεοῦ ἡμῶν, 'in the Spirit of our God') effect the baptismal event: washing, sanctification, and justification. It is an efficacious event: through baptism the baptized are free from sins, belong to the chosen community of God, and are justified. According to 1 Cor. 12:13, through the Spirit (instrumental ἐν) Christians are baptized into the body of Christ: 'For in the one Spirit we were all baptized into one body – Jews or Greeks, slaves or free – and we were all made to drink of one Spirit.' Through the Spirit, Christ himself, present in the Spirit, creates the unity of the church. In 2 Cor. 1:21–22 it is God who in baptism binds the church to Christ ('But it is God who establishes us with you in Christ and has anointed us, by putting his seal on us and giving us his Spirit in our hearts as a first installment'). God gives as down payment (ἀρραβών; cf. 2 Cor. 5:5) the Spirit, who effects the anointing and sealing of Christians in the baptismal event. Significant here is the juxtaposition of the present participle βεβαιῶν ("establishing") with the aorist participles χρίσας ("having anointed"), σφραγισάμενος ("having sealed"), and δούς ("having given"), for in this way the effect of baptism is in no way limited to

---

[24] On the analysis of Wis. 7, cf. E. Brandenburger, *Fleisch und Geist*, pp. 106–13.
[25] Cf. U. Schnelle, *Gerechtigkeit und Christusgegenwart*, pp. 123–35.

the past baptismal act, but rather with the help of the concept of the Spirit, the ongoing effect of the baptismal event is emphasized for the present and the future. God gives (cf. 1 Thess. 4:8: present participle διδόντα) his Spirit to believers in the present. Finally, the internal objective relationship of the bestowal of the Spirit and the baptismal event becomes clear on the macro level of Paul's letters especially in the conscious association of Gal. 2:19–20 with 3:2–5; Gal. 3:26–28 with 4:6–7; and Romans 6 with Romans 8.

Spiritual existence appears as the consequence and effect of the baptismal event, which as the salvation event is in turn an event in the power of the Spirit. In baptism the Christian enters the realm of the spiritual Christ (εἶναι ἐν Χριστῷ, "being in Christ"; cf. Gal. 3:26–28); at the same time the exalted One (cf. Rom. 8:10; 2 Cor. 11:10; 13:5; Gal. 2:20; 4:19) and the Spirit (cf. Rom. 8:9, 11; 1 Cor. 3:16; 6:19) are at work in the believer. The corresponding statements make clear that as the believer is incorporated into the Spirit of Christ, so Christ now works in the believer as πνεῦμα. In this way Paul characterizes a fundamental anthropological state of affairs; the life the Christian has taken a fundamental turn: it is now a ζῆν κατὰ πνεῦμα ("living according to the Spirit"). Those who are defined by the Spirit live in the realm of the Spirit and orient themselves toward the work of the Spirit (Rom. 8:5). Because the Spirit of God lives in them, they are released from the power of the flesh and of death (Rom. 8:6, 9). As children of God and true heirs of the promise they have immediate access to God (cf. Rom. 8:17; Gal. 4:6). The salvific gift of υἱοθεσία ("adoption as sons"; Rom. 8:15; Gal. 4:5) designates the new reality that encompasses the baptized. Rom. 8:14: 'For all who are led by the Spirit of God are children [Gk. "sons"] of God' (ὅσοι γὰρ πνεύματι θεοῦ ἄγονται, οὗτοι υἱοὶ θεοῦ εἰσιν).

The change in Christians' existence, brought about through the Spirit and thus by God himself, reveals the true situation of human beings: they live not from themselves but are always found in a defining realm.[26] There is only life according to the flesh (κατὰ σάρκα) or according to the Spirit (κατά πνεῦμα). Paul's classical formulation of the ethical dimension of the new reality of the baptized is found in Gal. 5:25: εἰ ζῶμεν πνεύματι, πνεύματι καὶ στοιχῶμεν ('If we live by the Spirit, let us also be guided by the Spirit'; cf. also Rom. 6:2, 12; 1 Cor. 5:7; Phil. 2:12–13). The Spirit

---

[26] Cf. R. Bultmann, *Theologie*, pp. 227ff.

is thus the basis and norm of Christian essence and action. The Spirit creates the new being of Christians and also effects their maintenance. The Spirit effectively lays claim on the essence and the will of Christians. They have entered the life determined by the Spirit, so they are now also to let themselves be guided by the Spirit. At the same time it becomes clear that there is no new walk without new action. The self-giving Spirit wants to be grasped. Precisely because the Spirit incorporates baptized believers into the sphere of God and the realm of the church, they no longer find themselves in the vacuum of a dominion-free space but are under the obligation of a new obedience made possible by the Spirit. Consequently, Paul can call the distinguishing marks of the new life fruits of the Spirit (Gal. 5:22): love, joy, peace, patience, kindness, goodness, faith. The περιπατεῖν κατὰ πνεῦμα ("walk according to the Spirit") separates one from the desires of the flesh (Gal. 5:16) and finds its goal in love (cf. 1 Cor. 13), in which the law is also fulfilled (cf. Rom. 13:8–10; Gal. 5:14), for εἰ δὲ πνεύματι ἄγεσθε, οὐκ ἐστὲ ὑπὸ νόμον ('But if you are led by the Spirit, you are not subject to the law'; Gal. 5:18; cf. Rom. 6:14). For those who live in the Spirit's sphere of influence, God no longer approaches from the outside with demands.[27] The 'newness of life' (Rom. 6:4) is fulfilled in the 'new life in the Spirit' (Rom. 7:6).

The visible and actual expression of the presence of the Spirit are the charismata.[28] The Spirit is the power of grace; the χάρισμα ("gift") grows out of the χάρις ("grace"; Rom. 12:6). The charismata attest to the ecclesiological dimension of the Spirit's work, which leads to the unity of the church. The Spirit does what benefits the church (1 Cor. 12:7) and serves its upbuilding (cf. 1 Cor. 14:3, 5, 12). The charismata (cf. Rom. 12:3–8; 1 Cor. 12:4–11) of the utterance of wisdom (λόγος σοφίας), the utterance of knowledge (λόγος γνώσεως), the gift of healing (χάρισμα ἰαμάτων), the working of miracles (ἐνεργήματα δυνάμεων), prophecy (προφητεία), the discernment of spirits (διακρίσεις πνευμάτων), and speaking in tongues (γλῶσσα) do not serve individualistic self-representation but are the visible expression of the multiplicity granted and effected by the Spirit within the unity (cf. 1 Cor. 14). All charismata must be measured against the principle: πάντα πρὸς οἰκοδομὴν γινέσθω ('Let all things be done for building up'; 1 Cor. 14:26).

---

[27] Cf. H. Leitzmann, *Römer*, p. 71.
[28] On the analysis of the texts cf. U. Brockhaus, *Charisma und Amt*, pp. 128ff.

Paul prizes the gifts of the Spirit (1 Cor. 14:1: ζηλοῦτε δὲ τὰ πνευματικά, 'strive for the spiritual gifts'). At the same time he emphasizes that the Spirit wants to work through the elements of order, of discreet self-limitation, and of fitting into the whole, through consideration and complement. The gifts of grace are present only when they are shared and passed on.

For humankind God's new reality is revealed as spiritual reality. Baptism is the turning point between the death-bringing yoke of the σάρξ and the life-giving service of the *pneuma*. A fundamental transformation takes place; acceptance into Christ's realm of life has the dimension of a new creation: εἴ τις ἐν χριστῷ, καινὴ κτίσις. τὰ ἀρχαῖα παρῆλθεν, ἰδοὺ γέγονεν καινά ('So if anyone is in Christ, there is a new creation: everything old has passed away; see, everything has become new!'; 2 Cor. 5:17).[29] God's creative activity for humankind is not limited to a one-time bringing into existence; rather, in the gift of the Spirit God grants human beings a share in his creator-power. The baptized live according to the Spirit, who for them is the assurance of present salvation and the pledge of future redemption. The Spirit is the power (ἐν πνεύματι) and norm (κατὰ πνεῦμα) of the new life. The Spirit enables Christians to remain what they have already become.

Christians are in a new situation and in a new age: the age of the Spirit. Therefore, as spiritual reality, the changed reality of Christians not only determines past and present but likewise encompasses the future. Rom. 8:11: 'If the Spirit of him who raised Jesus from the dead dwells in you, he who raised Christ from the dead will give life to your mortal bodies also through his Spirit that dwells in you.' Here the resurrection of believers appears as an act of creation in which God links up with himself, as it were: the Spirit bestowed in baptism and dwelling in Christians appears as the continuation of the divine power of life. What God achieved in Christ he will also grant to believers through the Spirit.

3.5 Being Received into God's Salvific Action: Faith

Human beings receive God's attention to the world through faith.

---

[29] On the religious-historical background of καινὴ κτίσις in Paul, cf. U. Mell's extensive treatment in *Neue Schöpfung*, pp. 47–257. Yet when he designates καινὴ κτίσις as the 'leading concept of Paul's theological anthropology' (p. 387), this is no doubt exaggerated with only two occurrences (2 Cor. 5:17; Gal. 6:15).

The foundation and enablement of faith is God's salvific initiative in Jesus Christ. Faith does not rest on a human decision; it is a gracious gift of God.[30] This was already true for Abraham: 'For this reason it depends on faith, in order that the promise may rest on grace [διὰ τοῦτο ἐκ πίστεως, ἵνα κατὰ χάριν] and be guaranteed to all his descendants, not only to the adherents of the law but also to those who share the faith of Abraham (for he is the father of all of us)' (Rom. 4:16). The basic structure of Paul's concept of faith is shown clearly in Phil. 1:29: 'For he has graciously granted you [ὅτι ὑμῖν ἐχαρίσθη] the privilege not only of believing in Christ [οὐ μόνον τὸ εἰς αὐτὸν πιστεύειν], but of suffering for him as well.' Faith is a work of the Spirit, for 'no one can say "Jesus is Lord" except by the Holy Spirit' (1 Cor. 12:3b).[31] Faith is one of the fruits of the Spirit (cf. 1 Cor. 12:9; Gal. 5:22). The gift character of πίστις/πιστεύειν ("faith/believe") also determines the close connection between faith and proclamation in Paul. Faith is ignited by the gospel, which is a power of God (Rom. 1:16). It pleased God, 'through the foolishness of our proclamation, to save those who believe' (1 Cor. 1:21). The news about the apostle spread quickly: 'The one who formerly was persecuting us is now proclaiming the faith' (Gal. 1:23). According to Rom. 10:8 Paul proclaims the word of faith (τὸ ῥῆμα τῆς πίστεως). Faith grows out of the proclamation, which in turn goes back to the word of Christ (Rom. 10:17: 'So faith comes from what is heard, and what is heard comes through the word of Christ'). Thus Christ himself acts in the word of proclamation. The hearing of faith (ἡ ἀκοὴ πίστεως, Gal. 3:2, 5; NRSV: 'believing what you heard') is accomplished in the preaching of the gospel. In 1 Cor. 15:11b Paul closes his basic instruction with the words: 'So we proclaim and so you have come to believe' (οὕτως κηρύσσομεν καὶ οὕτως ἐπιστεύσατε). Not the rhetorical art of the preacher or the enthusiastic 'Yes!' of the people leads to faith, but the Spirit and power of God (1 Cor. 2:4–5: 'My speech and my proclamation were not with plausible words of wisdom, but with a demonstration of the Spirit and of power, so that your faith might rest not on human wisdom but on the power of God'). Thus the proclamation of faith

---

[30] On this cf. the general reflections of G. Friedrich, 'Glaube und Verkündigung bei Paulus,' pp. 100ff.

[31] Versus R. Bultmann, *Theologie*, p. 331, who asserts that 'Paul does not designate πίστις ["faith"] as inspired and does not trace it back to the πνεῦμα.'

must bring with it Spirit and power in order to be able to effect faith in people. In 2 Cor. 4:13 Paul speaks of the same Spirit of faith, which unites apostle and church. The Spirit conveys the gift of faith and at the same time shapes its content by providing the unity of the church. Spirit and faith are causally interdependent in Paul in that the Spirit initiates faith and the believer leads a life in the power of the Spirit.[32] 'For through the Spirit, by faith, we eagerly wait for the hope of righteousness' (Gal. 5:5). Finally, Gal. 3:23, 25 shows that in Paul faith receives dimensions that go far beyond individual coming-to-faith: the 'coming' of faith plays a role in the history of salvation, for faith replaces the law and enables human beings to have a new access to God.

The basic structure of the Pauline concept of faith as a saving and thus life-giving power and gift of God makes it seem inappropriate to conceive of faith as a 'condition,'[33] 'free act of decision,'[34] 'acceptance and preservation of the message of salvation,'[35] 'communications process,'[36] 'desired human response to the Christian missionary message'[37] or even to speak of 'faith's character of achievement.'[38] The aspects of the Pauline concept of faith named here are important in part, but at the same time cause and effect are reversed, for only God's action makes faith possible.[39] It is God who enables the will and the work (Phil. 2:13). Faith arises from the salvific initiative of God, who calls people to serve the proclamation of the gospel (cf. Rom. 10:13–14: 'For, "Everyone who calls on the name of the Lord shall be saved." But how are they to call on one in whom they have not believed? And how are they to believe in one of whom they have never heard? And how are they to hear without someone to proclaim him?'). God alone is the giver, human beings the recipients, and thus Paul can logically set life by faith over against life by the law (cf. Rom.

---

[32] Pertinent here is H. D. Wendland, 'Wirken,' p. 464: '... without Spirit, no faith; without faith, no possibility of entering the dimension of the Spirit.'

[33] A. Jülicher, *Römer*, p. 232.

[34] R. Bultmann, *Theologie*, p. 317.

[35] E. Käsemann, *Römer*, p. 101.

[36] A. von Dobbeler, *Glaube*, p. 20. Naturally, also in von Dobbeler 'the authority of God [stands] behind this communications process' (p. 95). But here God not only stands 'behind' a process; he is the acting subject of this event

[37] J. Becker, *Paul*, p. 412.

[38] H. J. Schoeps, *Paulus*, p. 216.

[39] Cf. G. Friedrich, 'Glaube und Verkündigung bei Paulus,' p. 109: '... faith is a decision of God.'

3:21–22, 28; 9:32; Gal. 2:16; 3:12). Justification διὰ πίστεως Ἰησοῦ Χριστοῦ ("through faith in Jesus Christ") occurs as a gift through God's grace (δωρεὰν τῇ αὐτοῦ χάριτι; Rom. 3:24). Precisely as God's gracious gift, faith is the absolutely new thing that opens up to human beings the possibility of letting God's activity come to bear and thereby entering into the realm of this activity.

Faith takes shape in confession, as Paul formulates programmatically in Rom. 10:9–10, 'because if you confess with your lips that Jesus is Lord and believe in your heart that God raised him from the dead, you will be saved. For one believes with the heart and so is justified, and one confesses with the mouth and so is saved.' Faith is faith only if it is confessed. We cannot remain neutral *vis-à-vis* the content of faith; we can only confess it or reject it. Precisely in confession believers point away from themselves and toward God's act of salvation, and in this way they receive a share in the future deliverance. Faith does not remain apart; it communicates itself and crosses boundaries. Therefore it is not silent; rather, '"I believed, and so I spoke" (Ps. 115:1 LXX) – we also believe, and so we speak' (2 Cor. 4:13b: καὶ ἡμεῖς πιστεύομεν, διὸ καὶ λαλοῦμεν).

For Paul the content of faith and the relationship of faith are not to be separated. If the content of faith is the resurrection of Jesus Christ from the dead (cf. 1 Cor. 15:14; 1 Thess. 4:14), then the acceptance of this saving message does not occur in a dispassionate manner, withdrawn from one's own existence; faith in Jesus Christ means recognizing him as Lord and entering into a personal relationship with him. Closely connected with the content of faith is the knowledge of faith, as Paul often reminds the churches with οἴδατε or ἀγνοεῖτε ("you do not know"; ἀγνοεῖν: Rom. 1:13; 11:25; 1 Cor. 10:1; 12:1; 1 Thess. 4:13; etc.; οἶδα: 1 Cor. 3:16; 6:1–11, 15–16, 19; 2 Cor. 5:1; Gal. 2:16; etc.). Abraham is presented as the prototype of the new faith (cf. Gen. 16:6 LXX in Rom. 4:3);[40] his attitude is understood by Paul, in contrast to the interpretive tradition of ancient Judaism, not as a virtue (cf. Sir. 44:20; 1 Macc. 2:52; Philo *Her.* 90ff.) but as reliance on God's promise while rejecting one's own possibilities. Even the Old Testament knows: 'The one who is righteous will live by faith' (Hab. 2:4 in Rom. 1:17; Gal. 3:11).[41] In Rom. 6:8–9a the hope of faith

---

[40] Cf. here A. von Dobbeler, *Glaube*, pp. 116–25.
[41] Cf. here ibid., pp. 146–56. On the religious-historical background of Paul's concept of faith, cf., in addition to D. Lührmann and G. Barth (see Bibliography), esp. A. von Dobbeler, *Glaube*.

rests on the knowledge of faith: 'But if we have died with Christ, we believe that we will also live with him. We know that Christ, being raised from the dead, will never die again.' Faith knows about itself; it is sure of its origin, and it hopes for an activity of God in the future that will match his past activity in Jesus Christ.

As a gift of God faith always contains the individual element of believing and at the same time liberates a person's activity.[42] Paul speaks frequently of 'your faith' (Rom. 1:8, 12; 1 Cor. 2:5; 2 Cor. 1:24; 10:15; Phil. 2:17; 1 Thess. 1:8; 3:2, 5–7, 10; etc.) and especially emphasizes the missionary dimension of the faith of the churches in Thessalonica and Rome. For the apostle there is an increase in faith (2 Cor. 10:15); new insights and perceptions augment, refine, and transform faith. It is subject to changes, but in its basic convictions it does not invalidate itself. In Rom. 12:3 Paul admonishes the charismatics not to go beyond (ὑπερφρονεῖν) the boundaries set even for them but to be sober-minded (σωφρονεῖν) according to the measure of faith (μέτρον πίστεως) given to them.[43] With this Paul introduces the idea of a faith that is accomplished in a particular place and in a particular manner, a faith that must be conscious of its finitude if it does not want to slip into a fanatical overestimation of self. Believers must evaluate the gifts given to them and find their place in the church.

In 1 Thess. 1:3 Paul speaks of a 'work of faith' (ἔργον πίστεως), a 'labor of love,' and the 'steadfastness of hope.' This triad of faith-love-hope is also found in 1 Cor. 13:13 and 1 Thess. 5:8 (cf. Rom. 5:1–5; Gal. 5:5–6) and comprehensively describes Christian existence: it lives from faith, proves itself in love, and is borne by hope. The singular ἔργον makes clear that Paul is not addressing the demonstrable faith accomplishments of the individual but the faith condition of the church as a whole, a faith that is effected by God, is active in love, and is determined by hope.[44] This connection is made precise in Gal. 5:6 (RSV): 'For in Christ Jesus neither circumcision nor uncircumcision is of any avail, but faith working through love' (ἀλλὰ πίστις δι' ἀγάπης ἐνεργουμένη). Faith is grounded in God's loving activity in Jesus Christ (cf. Rom. 5:8), and thus love appears as the active and only visible side of faith. Because love is the essential attribute of faith, everything that does

---

[42] To the point is A. Schlatter, *Glaube*, p. 371: 'Volition grounded in faith is love.'

[43] Cf. on this term E. Käsemann, *Römer*, p. 323.

[44] Cf. W. Marxsen, *1. Thessalonicher*, p. 35.

not come from faith is sin (Rom. 14:23). Paul demands from believers a harmony of thought and deed, of conviction and action.[45] At the same time, however, he knows of transgressions of believers (Gal. 6:1), speaks of those who are weak in faith (Rom. 14:1), promises the Philippians progress in faith (Phil. 1:25), and exhorts readers to stand firm in the faith (Rom. 11:20; 1 Cor. 16:13; 2 Cor. 1:24). Thus faith does not give people a visible new quality; it puts them into a historical movement and testing process, which takes place in obedience (Rom. 1:5: Through Jesus Christ 'we have received grace and apostleship to bring about the obedience of faith among all the Gentiles for the sake of his name'). Faithful obedience in turn is revealed in the acceptance and testing of the gospel.

For Paul faith is always faith in the God who raised Jesus Christ from the dead (cf. Rom. 4:17, 24; 8:11). Jesus Christ is equally the Redeemer and the content of faith.[46] Thus the center of faith is not the one believing but the One believed. Because faith grows out of the proclamation of the gospel, it is ultimately always an act of God, based solely on the Christ event. Therefore faith cannot be the means by which a person creates the presupposition for God's saving activity. Rather, in faith God puts a person on a new path, the ground and goal of which is Jesus Christ. For human beings faith cannot be made, but it can be lived, experienced, and carried out. Faith appears as a creative activity of God in human beings, which in turn enables and requires their activity. Faith no doubt also contains biographical and psychological aspects and the element of human decision, which, however, is preceded by God's fundamental decision. Only God's prevenient act of grace leads to acceptance of the gospel, which again is to be seen as a gift of God.

Thus believers understand their own decision as an act of God's grace. Otherwise faith would also be only a human work, and the Pauline understanding of faith only a variation of the understanding of the law fought by the apostle. Faith does not abolish human decisions; rather, it embraces them and redirects them. In faith we experience and understand ourselves and the world in a new way. We find a new self-understanding and a new relationship

---

45 Pertinent is P. Stuhlmacher, *Römer*, p. 72: 'Faith for the apostle is, for all that, a whole act of life borne by the Holy Spirit.'
46 Cf. G. Friedrich, 'Glaube und Verkündigung bei Paulus,' pp. 102–6.

to the world,[47] because God's reality in Jesus Christ is now the standard of knowledge and action. This is confirmed by the phenomenon of the doubting of faith, which arises from the contrast between the hidden reality of faith (2 Cor. 5:7: 'For we walk by faith, not by sight') and the standards of the generally perceivable world. Faith can orient itself only toward the gospel message, from which it receives the strength to accept the hiddenness of its truth. Faith is always carried out as a tension-filled intertwining of experience of God and experience of the world, in which God's salvific action in Jesus Christ is regarded as the supporting ground of reality and is decisively put into relationship with the present world.

3.6 Corporeality and Human Essence: σῶμα in Paul

For Paul corporeality constitutes the human essence in its creatureliness.[48] Thus he can use σῶμα ("body") in the first place completely neutrally to designate the human condition.[49] Abraham had a body that had already withered away (Rom. 4:19). In his condemnation of the undisciplined in Corinth, Paul is of course absent in body (ἀπὼν τῷ σώματι; 1 Cor. 5:3; cf. also 2 Cor. 10:10) but present in spirit. Paul carries the marks of Jesus on his body (Gal. 6:17), wounds that he received during his missionary activity through beatings, for example (cf. 2 Cor. 11:24–25). In a marriage each partner has a claim on the other's body (1 Cor. 7:4: 'For the wife does not have authority over her own body but the husband does; likewise the husband does not have authority over his own body, but the wife does'). Virgins are supposed to be concerned about the holiness of their bodies (1 Cor. 7:34). As the place of human desires and weaknesses the body must be tamed (1 Cor. 9:27). Even the burning of the body in a fiery martyrdom is of no avail if one does not have love (1 Cor. 13:3). In 1 Cor. 15:38, 40

---

[47] A false alternative is set up by A. von Dobbeler, *Glaube*, p. 276: 'Hence with πίστις it is not a matter of a new self-understanding but of a new group or community understanding of those made equal before God.'

[48] On the history of research cf. K.-A. Bauer, *Leiblichkeit*, pp. 13–64; R. Jewett, *Terms*, pp. 201–50.

[49] Cf. here K.-A. Bauer, *Leiblichkeit*, on each passage.

Paul lifts up being a σῶμα as the basic condition of all existence; God gives every creature a body according to its nature.

In Paul σῶμα also appears in a negative sense. In Rom. 6:6 the apostle speaks of the destruction of the body of sin in baptism. Here σῶμα τῆς ἁμαρτίας ("body of sin") means the same as σῶμα τοῦ θανάτου ("body of death") in Rom. 7:24: human beings in their totality are subject to sin and death. Even after liberation from the powers of sin and death through the Christ event, Paul can exhort his readers not to let sin reign in the σῶμα θνητόν ("mortal body"; cf. 6:12). In Rom. 8:10 (σῶμα νεκρόν) and 8:11 (σῶμα θνητόν) σῶμα is likewise clearly close to σάρξ ("flesh"); it designates the human body confronted with sin. Can Paul equate σῶμα and σάρξ? This seems to be indicated by the parallel use of σάρξ and σῶμα in 2 Cor. 4:11 and Rom. 8:13, where, analogous to σῶμα θνητόν, Paul speaks of 'our mortal flesh' (θνητή σάρξ ἡμῶν; cf. 2 Cor. 5:4). In Paul desires (ἐπιθυμίαι) can also spring from both the σάρξ (Gal. 5:16–17, 24) and the σῶμα (Rom. 6:12). Nevertheless, a simple equation does not capture the Pauline understanding. In Rom. 8:9 the apostle expressly emphasizes the change in existence taking place in baptism from the sphere of the σάρξ into the realm of the Spirit, so that verses 10–11, 13 can no longer talk about being determined by the σάρξ but only of being subject to the σάρξ. The σῶμα has not succumbed completely to the foreign powers of the σάρξ and of ἁμαρτία[50] and thus been robbed of its true will, yet it finds itself constantly in danger of being ruled by them. Paul understands the change in existence historically and not ontologically, and thus it is the baptized that he repeatedly exhorts not to fall back from their attained state of salvation. The baptized have really died to sin (cf. Rom. 6:1ff.), but sin is not dead. It lives on in the world as temptation to the body. Therefore Paul can speak of σῶμα θνητόν or σῶμα τῆς ἁμαρτίας without stressing the fundamental distinction between σάρξ and σῶμα. Σῶμα is the person him- or herself, while σάρξ is a foreign power laying claim on a person.

---

[50] Versus R. Bultmann, *Theologie*, pp. 197–8, who comments on Rom. 8:13 that here the σῶμα has succumbed to a foreign power, and πράξεις τοῦ σώματος ("practices of the body") corresponds to ζῆν κατὰ σάρκα ("living according to the flesh"). On the critique of Bultmann cf. also E. Käsemann, *Römer*, p. 218; K.-A. Bauer, *Leiblichkeit*, pp. 168–9.

Paul uses σῶμα as the comprehensive expression of the human self.[51] According to its essence, the body is much more than food or drink (1 Cor. 6:13a); it is not defined by its biological functions but rather belongs to the Lord (1 Cor. 6:13b: 'The body is meant not for fornication but for the Lord, and the Lord for the body'). The body as the seat of sexuality (cf. Rom. 1:24; 1 Cor. 6:18; 7:4) may not be defiled through fornication. On earth Christians place their bodies at the disposal of the Lord 'as a living sacrifice, holy and acceptable to God, which is your spiritual worship' (τὴν λογικὴν λατρείαν ὑμῶν; Rom. 12:1b). Corporeality is the very place where faith acquires visible form. As temple of the Holy Spirit the body is not subject to one's own arbitrary disposition (1 Cor. 6:19). The autonomous self no longer takes possession of the body of the believer, because God himself established the body as the place of his glorification: δοξάσατε δὴ τὸν θεὸν ἐν τῷ σώματι ὑμῶν (1 Cor. 6:20b: 'Glorify God in your body'; cf. also Phil. 1:20). Human corporeality is the very place where indicative and imperative merge into a unity,[52] because that is where the new essence is tested in faithful obedience (cf. Romans 6). Those who withhold the body from the Lord withhold themselves from him entirely.

For Paul there is no human identity without corporeality, and thus he also thinks of resurrection reality, including post-mortal existence, in bodily terms. As the faithful are connected bodily to Christ on earth, so the resurrected One effects the transition of human beings from pre- to post-mortal existence. God's power of life, present in the Spirit, overcomes even death and creates a spiritual corporeality (σῶμα πνευματικόν) in which the pre-mortal human self and thus personal identity are absorbed and led into a new quality. In his characteristic way Paul develops this idea in 2 Cor. 5:1–10,[53] where he gives emphatic expression to the wish to leave the earthly body and to be clothed with a heavenly dwelling (vv. 1–4). Existence in the body appears as a separation from the Lord (vv. 6–8) that the apostle strives to overcome. Again, it is the gift of the Spirit that as first installment of the new life guarantees being clothed with the σῶμα πνευματικόν (v. 5). The apparently negative valuation of corporeality and the dualistic categories are

[51] R. Bultmann, *Theologie*, p. 195, formulates tersely: 'A human being does not have a σῶμα; he [or she] is a σῶμα.'
[52] Cf. E. Schweizer, s.v. 'σῶμα,' *EWNT* 2:774.
[53] Cf. on the analysis W. Wiefel, 'Hauptrichtung des Wandels,' pp. 74–9.

explained by the apostle's longing to move from believing to seeing
(v. 7). Even here he does not abandon his basic conception,
according to which God places people, precisely in their
corporeality, in the tension between the salvific present in the Spirit
and the anticipated consummation through the Spirit. When Paul
speaks of the redemption of our present bodies (Rom. 8:23), he is
not articulating hostility to the body but longing for unbroken and
everlasting communion with the resurrected One. The present
futile body (Phil. 3:21: τὸ σῶμα τῆς ταπεινώσεως, "body of
humiliation") will be changed and be conformed to the body of
his glory (τὸ σῶμα τῆς δόξης αὐτοῦ). What was accomplished in
Christ as the first fruit of those who have died (1 Cor. 15:20) will
also happen to the believer.

For Paul the σῶμα is the point of intersection between the
presence of humankind in the world and God's activity in regard
to humankind. Precisely because a person has a body and is a
body,[54] God's salvific act in Jesus Christ encompasses and defines
the body and therefore the concrete existence and history of the
person. As the comprehensive definition of the human self, the
σῶμα marks the spot where the powers of the transitory world and
God's salvific will for humankind come together. The believer is
removed by the Spirit from his previous disastrous history and
placed into God's new reality, which is based on the resurrection
of Jesus Christ from the dead and which began for the individual
in baptism in terms of real history and will culminate in the
eschatological gift of the σῶμα πνευματικόν. In Paul, therefore,
σῶμα comprises both one's self-understanding and one's inclusion
in God's creative act of salvation.[55]

The σῶμα concept serves Paul not only for anthropological but
also for ecclesiological statements.[56] The close connection between
the two conceptual areas is documented in 1 Cor. 6:15: 'Do you
not know that your bodies are members of Christ?' (οὐκ οἴδατε

---

[54] Thus K.-A. Bauer, *Leiblichkeit*, p. 185, in a critical extension of R. Bultmann's
definition cited in n. 51; in Paul σῶμα encompasses both essence as a person
and human corporeality.

[55] Relationship to the world and self-understanding are extremely closely
connected in Paul; eschatology and anthropology condition and complement
each other. E. Käsemann, *Zur paulinischen Anthropologie*, p. 53, in his
disagreement with R. Bultmann, pointedly asserts: 'People do not exist without
their worlds.'

[56] Cf. here E. Schweizer, s.v. 'σῶμα,' *TDNT* 7:1064ff.; U. Schnelle, *Gerechtigkeit
und Christusgegenwart*, pp. 139–44.

ὅτι τὰ σώματα ὑμῶν μέλη Χριστοῦ ἐστιν). Because believers belong to the Lord with their entire bodies, they are at the same time members of the body of Christ. For Paul there is no crucified One (Rom. 7:4) or exalted One (Phil. 3:21) without his body, just as conversely participation in the body of Christ is not imaginable without the glorification of God in the σῶμα of the believer.

The starting point for the ecclesiological use of σῶμα in Paul is the talk of the σῶμα τοῦ Χριστοῦ ("body of Christ") in Rom. 7:4 and in the tradition of the Lord's Supper (1 Cor. 10:16; 11:27). Here we find the origin of the term *body of Christ* and observe the transition to ecclesiological statements. If σῶμα τοῦ Χριστοῦ in Rom. 7:4; 1 Cor. 10:16; 11:27 means the body of Christ given at the cross for the church, then in 1 Cor. 10:17 the ecclesiological conclusion is drawn: ἓν σῶμα οἱ πολλοί ἐσμεν ('we who are many are one body'). The identification of the church with the body of Christ, which is fundamental to all ecclesiological statements, is found explicitly only in 1 Cor. 12:27: ὑμεῖς δέ ἐστε σῶμα Χριστοῦ ('now you are the body of Christ'). Paul also employs this concept in Rom. 12:5; 1 Cor. 1:13; 6:15–16; 10:17 and 12:12–27. In 1 Cor. 12:13 ('For in the one Spirit we were all baptized into one body') Paul develops the σῶμα Χριστοῦ idea in a characteristic way. (1) The body of Christ is pre-existent in regard to its members. It is not formed through human decisions and associations but is already present and makes such decisions and associations possible. (2) Through baptism individual Christians are integrated into the already existing body of Christ. Baptism does not constitute the body of Christ, but it is the historical place of acceptance into this body and the real expression of the unity of the church based on Christ. The baptized are placed in the body of Christ, whose reality and unity are based on Christ and attested by the baptized. There is no exalted Christ without his body, the church. Likewise, participation in the σῶμα Χριστοῦ is manifested precisely in the corporeality of the believer.

3.7 Human Beings in Their Corporeality: σάρξ in Paul

Paul can also use σάρξ, like σῶμα, first in a neutral sense as the designation of the external human condition. Paul calls illness a 'weakness of the flesh' (ἀσθένεια τῆς σαρκός, Gal. 4:13) or 'thorn in the flesh' (σκόλοψ τῇ σαρκί, 2 Cor. 12:7). Circumcision occurs 'in the flesh,' there is a 'distress in the flesh' (1 Cor. 7:28), and there are different kinds of flesh (1 Cor. 15:39: human, fish, animal, bird). In 1 Cor. 9:11 the goods actually expected by the apostle are called σαρκικός ("fleshly"; cf. also Rom. 15:27). In the genealogical sense σάρξ stands for belonging to the people Israel in Rom. 4:1; 9:3; 11:14; Gal. 4:23, 29. An already qualified meaning is given to σάρξ when Paul calls the perishable things excluded from the kingdom of God σάρξ καὶ αἷμα (1 Cor. 15:50; Gal. 1:16; cf. also Rom. 6:19; 1 Cor. 5:5; 2 Cor. 4:11).[57] He gathers up all of humankind in the phrase πᾶσα σάρξ (cf. Rom. 3:20; Gal. 2:16 in reference to Ps. 142:2 LXX). Several times the apostle speaks of living 'in the flesh' (cf. 2 Cor. 10:3; Gal. 2:20; Phil. 1:22, 24; Philemon 16), by which he means the ways of human existence. Paul no longer knows Christ κατὰ σάρκα ("according to the flesh"; 2 Cor. 5:16); essential knowledge of Christ cannot be gained from his earthly appearance but only from the cross and resurrection.[58]

Here Paul stands in the tradition of Old Testament anthropology.[59] Thus בָּשָׂר designates the whole person under the aspect of one's corporeality. The form of a person is visible corporeality. God created humankind, and thus בָּשָׂר/σάρξ is the expression of human creatureliness (Gen. 2:23). It is in their very corporeality that human beings stand in relationship to God, who sustains the flesh (2 Kgs 4:34), limits the flesh in its life span (Gen. 6:3), and finally lets it perish (Gen. 6:13). But God also sets boundaries on his wrath, for 'He remembered that they were but flesh [MT: בָּשָׂר, LXX: σάρξ]' (Ps. 78:39a). The first person singular pronoun and בָּשָׂר can be used synonymously: 'My flesh [MT: בָּשָׂר, LXX: σάρξ] trembles for fear of you, and I am afraid of your judgments' (Ps. 119:120). Human beings in their totality are flesh.

Those who live by their own devices and rely on themselves are assigned by Paul to the realm of the flesh.[60] He calls the Corinthians 'people of the flesh' (σαρκινός), infants in Christ (1 Cor. 3:1) who live in human ways and thus according to the flesh (1 Cor. 3:3). They are oriented toward what is in the foreground and external, they let themselves be blinded by the visible, and they cannot press forward to the hidden but all-determining reality of God. Their

---

[57] Cf. Chr. Wolff, *1. Korinther*, p. 205.
[58] Cf. on 2 Cor. 5:16 esp. R. Bultmann, *2. Korinther*, pp. 155ff.; H.-J. Klauck, *2. Korinther*, pp. 54–5.
[59] Cf. here H. W. Wolff, *Anthropologie*, pp. 49–56; M. Krieg, *Leiblichkeit*, pp. 7ff.
[60] Still basic here is R. Bultmann, *Theologie*, pp. 232–9.

judgment takes place on the earthly level (2 Cor. 1:12). Paul, by contrast, lives ἐν σαρκί, of course, but not κατὰ σάρκα (2 Cor. 10:3: ἐν σαρκὶ γὰρ περιπατοῦντες, οὐ κατὰ σάρκα στρατευόμεθα, "for we walk in the flesh but do not fight according to the flesh"). The 'people of the flesh' are characterized by self-involvement and self-sufficiency; they build on their own abilities and make their knowledge the measure of what is rational and real. In so doing, however, they are not aware that they are the ones who are delivered up helplessly to the dominating power of sin. A life κατὰ σάρκα means a life without access to God, a life that is captive to what is earthly and perishable. Of the person outside of faith Paul says: ἐγὼ δὲ σάρκινός εἰμι πεπραμένος ὑπὸ τὴν ἁμαρτίαν ('But I am of the flesh, sold into slavery under sin'; Rom. 7:14b). Here σάρξ not only designates a certain fleshliness but becomes the epitome of a life separated from God and rebelling against God.[61] The real subject of life is sin; the consequence is death. 'While we were living in the flesh [ἐν τῇ σαρκί], our sinful passions, aroused by the law, were at work in our members to bear fruit for death' (Rom. 7:5).

On their own, human beings cannot escape this fateful interplay of sin and death. God alone can liberate them from themselves and the powers of sin and death and place them in the new reality determined by the Spirit. This liberation was carried out fundamentally in the sending of the Son ἐν ὁμοιώματι σαρκὸς ἁμαρτίας ('in the likeness of sinful flesh'; Rom. 8:3). Jesus assumed the mode of existence in which the rule of sin is exercised over humankind. The death and resurrection of Jesus Christ neutralizes the power of sin in the one place where it is effective: in the flesh. God defeats sin in its own territory by breaking its power in the human being Jesus Christ. As one without sin (2 Cor. 5:21) Jesus subjected himself to sin and overcame it. Consequently, believers find themselves removed from the realm of the flesh and subject to the workings of the Spirit. Paul develops this connection fundamentally in Rom. 8:5–8.[62] Here σάρξ and πνεῦμα, flesh and Spirit, appear as two mutually exclusive powers that surround people and take them into service – be it death-bringing or life-giving service (Rom. 8:5: οἱ γὰρ κατὰ σάρκα ὄντες τὰ τῆς σαρκὸς φρονοῦσιν, οἱ δὲ κατὰ πνεῦμα τὰ τοῦ πνεύματος, 'For those who live according to the flesh set their minds on the things of the

---

[61] Cf. A. Sand, s.v. 'σάρξ,' *EWNT* 3:552.
[62] On the interpretation of Rom. 8:5–8 cf., in addition to the commentaries, H. Paulsen, *Überlieferung*, pp. 33ff.; W. Schmithals, *Anthropologie*, pp. 104ff.

flesh, but those who live according to the Spirit set their minds on the things of the Spirit'). Neither mediation nor a natural transition between the two spheres is possible; two ontologically understood realms of power stand starkly over against each other. The antithesis of σάρξ and πνεῦμα results from their different goals: death and life (Rom. 8:13). Because the Spirit of God or Christ is alive and at work in believers (Rom. 8:9), they still live ἐν σαρκί, of course, but no longer κατὰ σάρκα. Their existence in hostility to God is abolished; they do the works of the Spirit (Gal. 5:22). By contrast, natural human beings outside of faith are delivered up to the workings of sin in the flesh; they do the works of the flesh: fornication, idolatry, enmities, factions, etc. (Gal. 5:19b–21).

The σάρξ-πνεῦμα dualism was available to Paul from Hellenistic-Jewish Christianity, as shown by the pre-Pauline tradition in Rom. 1:3b–4a and also Gal. 5:16ff.; 1 Tim. 3:16; and 1 Peter 3:18.[63] In religious-historical terms, the Jewish wisdom literature may be the starting point of this antithesis.[64] In Wis. 7:1–6 the writer describes himself as a mortal being molded into flesh in the womb of a mother (7:1c: καὶ ἐν κοιλίᾳ μετρὸς ἐγλύφην σάρξ). He is exposed to futility without salvation, and therefore he prays for understanding and pleads for the coming of the spirit of wisdom (7:7b). Wisdom leads people out of their finitude, and they attain friendship with God (7:14). The natural person appears as ἄνθρωπος ἀσθενής (9:5: 'a man who is weak'); the perishable body (σῶμα φθαρτόν, 9:15) weighs down the soul. Human beings receive insight into God's plans only if God gives them his wisdom or sends his Holy Spirit (πνεῦμα ἄγιον) from on high (9:17).

A developed σάρξ-πνεῦμα dualism is found in the Jewish philosopher of religion Philo of Alexandria (ca. 20 BC to AD 45).[65] The flesh appears as the shackle of human beings (*Virt.* 78); it burdens them (*Gig.* 31); it is the coffin of the soul (*Migr.* 16). By contrast, God is one of the incorporeal and thus fleshless beings, so that orientation toward God brings both the turning away from the flesh and entry into the realm of the divine spirit. Therefore there are two classes of people and a way to salvation and a way to disaster (cf. *Imm.* 140–83). While the perfected ones take the way of the knowledge of God, this way is avoided by the 'comrades of

---

[63] Cf. H. Paulsen, *Überlieferung*, p. 46.
[64] Basic here is E. Brandenburger, *Fleisch und Geist*.
[65] Cf. ibid., pp. 114ff.

the flesh' (*Imm.* 143). Because they are imprisoned by the flesh, they cannot attain heavenly knowledge; 'because they are flesh, the divine spirit cannot remain' (*Gig.* 29: διὰ τὸ εἶναι αὐτοὺς σάρκας μὴ δύνασθαι τὸ θεῖον πνεῦμα καταμεῖναι).

The Qumran texts exhibit a general agreement with Paul.[66] Here too, creaturely human beings are flesh (בָּשָׂר) and thus separated from God and delivered up to sin without salvation. They belong to the 'communion of the flesh of evil' (1QS 11.9) and have in their flesh the spirit of wickedness (1QS 4.20–21); the flesh is sin (1QH 4.29: עָווֹן), and thus there can be no human righteousness. Everything is up to God, who forms the spirit (רוּחַ; 1QH 15.22) and through the Holy Spirit (1QS 4.21: בְּרוּחַ קוֹרֶשׁ) wipes out the spirit of wickedness from inside the flesh. Only the grace of God enables the pious to obey God's will and practice righteousness (1QS 11.12: 'But when I waver, God's way of grace is my help forever. And when I stumble through the evil of the flesh, my righteousness is sustained by the righteousness of God forever').

The antithesis σάρξ-πνεῦμα seems in Paul to be not a metaphysical but a historical dualism. Because there is no human existence outside the flesh and God's activity with humankind is carried out in the flesh, the flesh appears to be the place where human beings either persist in their self-centeredness or through the power of the Spirit let themselves be placed into the service of God. For Paul, believers are not exactly removed from the flesh in their earthly existence, but the Spirit removes the natural self-assertion of the flesh. If people think they can live by their own devices, they succumb to the flesh, which is then ruled not by the Spirit but by sin.

3.8 Human Beings Are Not Their Own Masters: The Power of Sin

The peculiarities of Paul's understanding of sin are revealed first in the apostle's use of language.[67] Characteristic of Paul is the use of ἁμαρτία ("sin") in the singular (cf., e.g., Rom. 5:21; 6:12; 7:11; 1 Cor. 15:56; 2 Cor. 5:21; Gal. 3:22); plural forms are found mostly in traditional formulations outside the Letter to the Romans (cf.

---

[66] Cf. here K. G. Kuhn, 'Πειρασμός – ἁμαρτία – σάρξ,' *ZTK* 49:209ff.
[67] Cf. on the use of language G. Röhser, *Metaphorik*, pp. 7ff.

1 Cor. 15:3, 17; Gal. 1:4; 1 Thess. 2:16). Romans, as the document of the apostle's intensive reflection on the nature of ἁμαρτία, is clearly dominated by the singular; only in three places does the plural appear (4:7; 11:27, an LXX quotation; and 7:5, conditioned by τὰ παθήματα, "passions"). The concentration on the absolute use of ἁμαρτία and the forgoing of distinctions, differentiations, or refinements within the concept of sin must be considered the hallmarks of Paul's use of ἁμαρτία. The apostle's linguistic usage expresses the fundamental insight that natural human beings are unavoidably under the domination of sin. Paul sees the cause of this hopeless human situation in the trespass of Adam and the guilt of humankind (Rom. 5:12: 'Therefore, just as sin came into the world through one man, and death came through sin, and so death spread to all because all have sinned …').

Thus for Paul sin is at once both fate and an act. In Rom. 5:12 the two stand side by side rather unexpectedly, revealing the aporias of a one-line explanation of the origin and nature of sin.[68] A completely mythological interpretation leaves the personal responsibility of individuals out of consideration, so that they are no longer ethically addressable because they no longer bear the ultimate responsibility for their deeds. Yet if people bear the exclusive responsibility for their situation, then they must also be in a position to turn this situation to the good, that is, to escape from slavery to sin.[69] Then, however, the *meritum Christi* would be diminished, grace would no longer be radically understood as unearned grace, and the specifically Pauline doctrine of justification would be cut to the quick. Thus the juxtaposition of fate and personal responsibility in Rom. 5:12 is essential,[70] for it expresses equally the helplessness and the inexcusability of the human situation under sin. Moreover, there is an inner connection between the universality and the active character of sin, in that the human state of being under sin is realized in sinning.

---

[68] Cf. E. Käsemann, *Römer*, p. 139: 'The real problem of interpretation lies in 12d, where the dominant motif of fate in 12a–c is abruptly replaced by that of the personal guilt of all people.'

[69] Exactly this conclusion is drawn in *2 Apoc. Bar.* 54.15, the closest parallel to Rom. 5:12: 'For if Adam first sinned and brought early death to all, every single one of those who are descended from him has still drawn to him- or herself future torment, and on the other hand every single one has chosen future glory'; cf. also 4 Ezra 7:118–19.

[70] Versus H. Lietzmann, *Römer*, p. 62, who regards Rom. 5:12d as a disturbing secondary idea.

Sin's priority is evidence of its universality and fateful character.[71] Since the sin of Adam the world has been marked by the pregiven and all-determining connection of sin and death (cf. Rom. 5:12; also 4 Ezra 3:7; 3:21; 7:118; *2 Apoc. Bar.* 23.4). Sin was in the world before the law (Rom. 5:13; cf. 7:8b); the law entered only in the meantime (Rom. 5:20: νόμος δὲ παρεισῆλθεν). Also the factual judgment that Jews and Greek are equally under sin (Rom. 3:9; cf. Gal. 3:22: ὑπὸ ἁμαρτίαν) presupposes the priority of sin. For Paul, finally, the reality of sin and sinning forms the starting point of his argumentation. People always find themselves in the realm of sin and death; sin is no longer only an active phenomenon, but rather people are involved in a disastrous situation not caused by themselves.[72] Because they are members of the human race, they are affected by the power of sin.

Nevertheless, Paul does not release human beings from their responsibility. The active character of sin is seen especially in Rom. 3:23 where Paul summarizes the previous broad argumentation: 'All have sinned [πάντες γὰρ ἥμαρτον] and fall short of the glory of God.' Both the vices of the Gentiles (cf. Rom. 1:24–32) and the fundamental antithesis of orthodoxy and orthopraxy among the Jews (cf. Rom. 2:17–29) result respectively from their deeds and non-deeds. 'All who have sinned apart from the law will also perish apart from the law, and all who have sinned under the law will be judged by the law' (Rom. 2:12). The factual judgment in Rom. 3:9 that all are under sin is substantiated by Paul in verses 10–18 with a comprehensive scriptural proof, whose quotations clearly point to the active character of sin.[73] Here being guilty before God (cf. Rom. 3:19b) is not the consequence of fate but the result of a deed. Sin as responsible action appears plainly programmatic in Rom. 14:23: 'Whatever does not proceed from faith is sin' (πᾶν δὲ ὃ οὐκ ἐκ πίστεως ἁμαρτία ἐστίν). Thus the universal dominion of sin results from its character of fate and deed.[74]

---

[71] This aspect alone speaks against the judgment of G. Röhser, *Metaphorik*, pp. 142–3: '*Sin* in Paul means the sum of human trespasses, which develop their own dynamic and become a reality that people themselves have brought forth and that stands over against them and annihilates them (ultimately by virtue of the law).' According to Paul human beings always find themselves in the dominion of sin, without thereby being relieved of their own responsibility.

[72] Cf. H. Weder, 'Gesetz und Sünde,' p. 362.

[73] Cf. on the quotations D.-A. Koch, *Die Schrift als Zeuge*, pp. 179–84.

[74] Cf. G. Röhser, *Metaphorik*, p. 118.

The power of sin is considered by Paul in detail in Rom. 6:6, 12ff., in which Paul's adopted terms δουλεύειν ("to serve"), βασιλεύειν ("to reign"), ὑπακούειν ("to obey"), κυριεύειν ("to have dominion over, command"), ὑπακοή ("obedience"), δοῦλοι ("slaves"), παρίστημι ("submit"), and ἐλευθερωθῆναι ("be made free") clearly reflect the power situation evident in a master-slave relationship.[75] Sin is no longer to reign in the life of Christians (Rom. 6:12, 14); its passions are not to be obeyed (6:12). Believers are exhorted no longer to place their members at the disposal of sin (6:13, 19). The baptized were formerly slaves to sin (6:17, 20), but now they are free from the dominion of sin (6:18, 20, 22).

In Qumran likewise one could say that among human beings one finds 'service to sin and deeds of deception' (1QH 1.27; cf. 1QS 4.10; 1QM 13.5: 'service to uncleanness'). Here too the 'flesh' is the dominion of sin (cf. 1QS 4.20–21).[76] Also in 4 Ezra 4:38; 7:46, 68; 8:17, 35 we find the idea of the general sinfulness of humankind. In the broad circle of Hellenistic Judaism, on the other hand, we find human beings – through their own decision and with the support of the divine wisdom – in a position to lead a life of righteousness in order thus to escape the rule of sin and death (cf., e.g., Wis. 1:12–16; 2:23–3:3; 6:18–19; 9:10, 17–18).

The juxtaposition of Rom. 3:21 and 3:23 shows by itself that the universal rule of sin is not a generally demonstrable and self-evident phenomenon but can only be perceived from the perspective of faith. Because natural human beings live apart from the righteousness of God made evident in Christ, we can say of those persons that they are delivered up helplessly to the power of sin and do sin. Paul considers these connections thoroughly in Romans 7, where the teaching of the law and the central themes of Pauline anthropology meet. The starting point of these reflections is the relationship of νόμος and ἁμαρτία, law and sin, which was already latently present in the previous chapters of Romans as the central problem of Paul's doctrine of justification and had to be considered after the determination of the relationship of ἁμαρτία and χάρις ("grace") in Romans 6.

As his starting point in Rom. 7:1–4 Paul chooses an example from the Jewish marriage law in order to make clear how death

---

[75] Cf. on this conceptual field esp. ibid., pp. 103ff.
[76] On the understanding of sin in the Qumran texts cf. H. Lichtenberger, *Studien zum Menschenbild*, pp. 73–98, pp. 209–12.

affects and limits the law.[77] In verse 4 he interprets the death of Christ and the death of the Christian with him in baptism as liberation from the law. Baptism is not only death *vis-à-vis* sin but also death *vis-à-vis* the law, which has now lost its claim on the baptized person. The situation that from the perspective of faith is already past is now presented by Paul in verse 5 in order then to describe with verse 6 the believer's new form of existence, which is founded on the Christ event. In verse 5 he defines the old existence of people apart from faith as being in the flesh. The flesh appears as the point of attack of 'sinful passions' (τὰ παθήματα τῶν ἁμαρτιῶν), that were aroused by the law. Sin does not simply come to people only from the outside; it takes up residence in them (7:16, 20: ἡ οἰκοῦσα ἐν ἐμοὶ ἁμαρτία) and thus completely rules them. Death appears as the consequence of this vulnerability to sin. In 7:6 Paul uses νυνὶ δέ (cf. 3:21) to mark the eschatological turning point. Through the gift of the Spirit Christians are freed from the realm of the law and thus of sin and death. They now know that they are led by the living Spirit, not by the perishable letter.

The 'once-now' schema that underlies Rom. 7:5–6 is developed by Paul in 7:7–25a and 8:1ff. First, in 7:7[78] he must emphatically guard against the possible identification of νόμος and ἁμαρτία, law and sin. More than once he himself had established a close connection between the two (cf. 3:20; 4:15; 5:13b; 7:5), and thus the equating of νόμος and ἁμαρτία, which would be unfortunate for his doctrine of justification, was but a short step – especially for the apostle's Jewish-Christian opponents. For Paul the law and sin are not identical, but the law has an important function in the process of getting to know sin. Paul conceives of sin as ἐπιθυμία ("desire") in order to describe its nature more exactly.[79] The relationship of sin, law, and desire according to Rom. 7:7 is the following: the knowledge of sin comes through the law, because the law becomes concrete in the commandment, and sin in desire. The law is not sin, but humankind would probably never have known sin as desire if there had been no commandment. In this process sin plays a highly active role, for it uses the law, or the commandment, in order to turn what God willed into its opposite

---

[77] Cf. on this text U. Wilckens, *Römer* 2:62–7.
[78] Cf. on Rom. 7:7 esp. H. Hübner, *Gesetz bei Paulus*, pp. 63–5.
[79] Cf. on the tradition-historical background of ἐπιθυμία in this passage R. Weber, 'Die Geschichte des Gesetzes,' pp. 154–5.

(v. 8). Through the commandment itself sin arouses what is forbidden by the commandment: desire. Already at this point it becomes clear that law and sin are working at cross-purposes and that sin is temporally and practically prior to the law.

In Rom. 7:7ff. Paul relies on the paradise story in order to define comprehensively the situation of pre-Christian humankind. The 'I' in this passage encompasses both Adam and the whole of humankind, including the Jews.[80] The objective determination of the essence of sin is neither temporally nor spatially limitable but is transferable to all people and all times outside of faith. Sin and law appear as trans-individual powers that effect individual circumstances. Paul consciously chooses mythological language to present a general anthropological state of affairs. Sin already existed before the law and without the law, but only through the law does sin become a power that condemns before God. Sin does not originate through the law and is thus not to be equated with it, but the power of sin first becomes apparent through the law when the law awakens desire, which sin uses to dominate the individual. On the anthropological level the encounter with sin-dominated law occurs in the individual commandment.

Paul presents the universality of this process in Rom. 7:8–11 through the corresponding usage of ἐντολή ("commandment") and νόμος ("law").[81] If ἐντολή refers to the paradise commandment given to Adam, νόμος means the Sinai Torah. Thus for Paul there was no period in which sin had not taken the commandment or the law as the occasion to arouse desire. The human self is always found to be ruled by sin. The active role of sin in this process is emphatically stressed in 7:11, where through the power of sin the story of the self becomes a story of disaster. Through this argumentation Paul succeeds in preventing an identification of νόμος or ἐντολή with sin (7:12: 'So the law is holy, and the commandment is holy and just and good'), for sin is the real reason why what is good ultimately brings death (7:13). Sin can even turn good into its opposite, clearly showing its great power. Thus, according to Paul, the law does not have the power to conquer sin.

---

[80] Cf. ibid., p. 157.
[81] On the details cf. H. Hübner, *Gesetz bei Paulus*, pp. 67–9; R. Weber, 'Die Geschichte des Gesetzes,' pp. 155–7.

From this basic insight comes the apostle's anthropological argumentation in Rom. 7:14–25a, in which he develops the unavoidable entanglement of the self under the power of sin. In verse 14 Paul points to a general and currently valid state of affairs: human beings as creatures of the flesh are vassals to sin. The life that is designated as σαρκινός ("fleshly") is separated from God and rebels against God; it stands over against the law, which is spiritual and thus belongs to God.

Νόμος here refers to the Sinai Torah; at the same time, however, the actual qualifying opposition πνευματικός-σαρκινός makes clear that anthropology is the real content level of Paul's argumentation.[82] For Paul this antithesis defines the two sides of the human essence, and here he is unmistakably already pointing to Rom. 8:1ff. The universality of the fundamental assertion in 7:14 is underlined by ἐγώ ("I"). The use of the first person singular is a literary style device that has parallels in the psalms of lament (cf. Ps. 22:7–8) and the Qumran literature (cf. 1QH 1.21; 3.23–24; 1QS 11.9ff.).[83] Both this first person literary style and general character of 7:14 and its reference to 8:1ff. suggest regarding ἐγώ as an exemplary, general 'I' that from the perspective of faith represents the situation of people outside of faith.[84] The human condition of being sold to sin is explained by Paul in 7:15–16: the 'I' finds itself in a fundamental conflict in which it does not do what it wants but what it hates.

The difference thus expressed between the real will and the actual deed is also considered by Epictetus (*Diss.* 2.26.1):[85] 'Every transgression [πᾶν ἁμάρτημα] contains a contradiction. If the one

---

[82] Recently, K. Kertelge in particular (*Anthropologie nach Röm 7*, pp. 105ff.) follows R. Bultmann and pleads for anthropology as the real content level of Rom. 7:7–25. By contrast U. Wilckens, *Römer* 2:75, ascertains that even in Rom. 7:7–25 the topic remains the law. This is an inappropriate alternative, for in Paul the hermeneutic of existence and the hermeneutic of history belong together; cf. R. Weber, 'Die Geschichte des Gesetzes,' pp. 149, 163.

[83] Cf. here W. G. Kümmel, 'Römer 7,' pp. 127–31; G. Theissen, *Psychologische Aspekte*, pp. 194–204.

[84] This insight was thoroughly discussed by W. G. Kümmel, 'Römer 7,' pp. 74ff. Also pertinent is P. Althaus, *Paulus und Luther*, p. 39: 'Romans 7 is thus the picture of human beings under the law, before and without the law, but their picture as it is seen only through faith in Christ. Only from the viewpoint of Romans 8 can one write and fully affirm Romans 7.'

[85] On Rom. 7:15, 19 and the parallels in Epictetus cf. esp. G. Theissen, *Psychologische Aspekte*, pp. 213–23.

who transgresses [ὁ ἁμαρτάνων] wants not to transgress, he apparently does not do what he wants [ὃ μὲν θέλει οὐ ποιεῖ].' A little later (2.26.4–5) Epictetus says:

> It is the one who is convincing in his argumentation who can show the contradiction on the basis of which he transgresses, and who can show why he does not do what he wants and does what he does not want [pw''' o} qevlei ouj poiei' kai; o} mh; qevlei poiei']. If someone points this out to him, he will dissociate himself from it. But as long as you do not point it out to him, do not be surprised if he persists. He does it, you see, because he has the idea that it is right.

For Paul and Epictetus there is a contradiction in human beings between the intention of an action and the practical execution of the action. Yet in giving the cause of this contradiction, Paul and Epictetus are fundamentally different. In Epictetus wrong behavior can be overcome through right knowledge. Here we see an optimistic view of humankind in which knowledge as the standard of action can overcome possible wrong behavior. Paul does not share this confidence, for sin is the real subject of an event, not the knowing person. Natural human beings are not at all in a position to see through their situation. From the contradiction described in 7:15 Paul now concludes in verse 16 that the law in itself is good; it is sin that brings about the contradiction between will and deed. Paul underlines the power of sin in verse 17 with the metaphor of the indwelling of sin in people. Here too the reference to Romans 8 is unmistakable, for in 8:9–10 Paul says that the Spirit of God/Christ, or Christ, dwells in believers. Thus sin and Christ clearly are in competition with each other; human beings function merely passively as the dwellings of powers that bring them death or life.[86] If sin reigns in people, it destroys them, whereas Christ or the Spirit gives them life (cf. 8:11).

The total helplessness of the human situation outside of faith is emphasized in Rom. 7:18–20, where Paul again develops the contradiction between wanting and doing. Human beings can want the good, but the doing is prevented by the sin dwelling within them. In 7:21 the 'I' draws an initial conclusion and ascertains a regularity: wanting good takes concrete form as doing evil.

---

[86] Cf. G. Röhser, *Metaphorik*, pp. 119ff. Romans 7 does not describe a conflict in people but a transpersonal event; versus P. Althaus, *Paulus und Luther*, pp. 41–9, who in dispute with R. Bultmann understands Romans 7 as conflict within a person.

Here νόμος does not mean the Old Testament Torah but must be understood in the figurative sense of a regularity.[87] In 7:22–23 Paul now clarifies the regularity ascertained in 7:21. Clearly νόμος τοῦ θεοῦ ("law of God," v. 22) and νόμος τῆς ἁμαρτίας ("law of sin," v. 23), νόμος τοῦ νοός μου ("law of my mind") and ἕτερος νόμος ἐν τοῖς μέλεσίν μου ("another law in my members") in verse 23, as well as ἔσω ἄνθρωπος ("inner self," v. 22) and ἔξω ἄνθρωπος ("outward self") are contrasted.[88] The law of God and the law of sin each have points of attack in people; there is a battle (v. 23: ἀντιστρατευόμενον, "warring against"; αἰχμαλωτίζοντα, "taking captive") for dominion in human beings. Here νόμος appears in no way to be a thoroughly constant entity (e.g., in the sense of the Sinai Torah); instead, the qualifiers alone in each case decide the understanding of νόμος. The term νόμος τοῦ θεοῦ in verse 22 includes the Sinai Torah but may also mean the law of creation[89] that was given to the Gentiles (cf. Rom. 1:19ff.; 2:14–15). Such an interpretation is already derivable from 7:7–13, where Paul also expresses a fundamental state of affairs for Jews and Gentiles. In terms of content νόμος τοῦ θεοῦ means the original will of God, with which the inmost human self is in agreement. The ἔσω ἄνθρωπος strives to fulfill the will of God. In verse 23 νόμος τοῦ νοός stands on the one hand in continuity with νόμος τοῦ θεοῦ in verse 22 and at the same time in sharp contrast to ἕτερον νόμον ἐν τοῖς μέλεσίν μου and νόμος τῆς ἁμαρτίας. Here Paul is playing with the concept, for he is not referring to the Old Testament Torah but naming structural qualities. This meaning is apparent in νόμος τῆς ἁμαρτίας. As a power antagonistic to the original will of God, the expression must be understood in the sense of a regularity: sin stands over against the law of the Spirit (8:2) and enslaves those outside of faith.[90]

On their own human beings cannot choose good and reject evil; contentious sin dwelling within them rules over them totally (cf. as parallel 1QS 4.20–21). Likewise νόμος τοῦ νοός and νόμος ἐν τοῖς μέλεσίν μου name the conflict between reason and the subjugating powers that shape human existence. Thus Rom. 7:23

---

[87] Cf. D. Zeller, *Römer*, p. 142; R. Weber, 'Die Geschichte des Gesetzes,' p. 159.
[88] Cf. ibid., pp. 160–1.
[89] Cf. W. Schmithals, *Anthropologie*, p. 66.
[90] Versus U. Wilckens, *Römer* 2:90, who believes that in verses 22–3 'νόμος in its various semantic contents always refers to the Torah.'

describes a fundamental anthropological state of affairs: human beings are divided within themselves and are not in a position to re-establish their integrity on their own.[91] For this reason natural human beings find themselves in a hopeless situation; hence the apostle's cry in 7:24: 'Who will rescue me from this body of death?' According to the inner logic of Romans 7 the answer must be: 'No one.' For Paul this does not remain the last word, as verse 25a shows.[92] The deliverance of humankind from this hopeless situation came in Jesus Christ. Therefore Paul thanks God for the salvation from the dominion of sin effected in Jesus Christ and brought by the Spirit. Thus Romans 8 seems to be the correct continuation of Paul's argumentation in 7:7ff.; it is even the essential presupposition, for the perspective of faith developed by Paul in Romans 8 was already the foundation of his argumentation in Romans 7.

The apostle continues his basic argumentation in Rom. 8:2–3 by describing the present reality of believers. Here too νόμος does not designate the Sinai Torah,[93] for in the two phrases νόμος τοῦ πνεύματος τῆς ζωῆς ('law of the Spirit of life') and νόμος τῆς ἁμαρτίας καὶ τοῦ θανάτου ('law of sin and of death') the genitive qualifies the understanding of the two *nomoi*. In no way can νόμος here be a constant entity, because the verb ἠλευθέρωσεν ("freed") clearly expresses the liberation of the one *nomos* through the other. Rather, πνεῦμα and ἁμαρτία stand antithetically opposed, and the *nomoi* belonging to them likewise behave antithetically. Thus νόμος has to be translated as the *rule, norm,* or *principle* that is obligated to the Spirit or to sin.

The first reference to the Sinai Torah comes in Rom. 8:3a, where Paul emphasizes the inability of the Torah to liberate from the power of the σάρξ ("flesh"). Here it becomes completely clear that

---

91 Cf. R. Weber, 'Die Geschichte des Gesetzes,' p. 159.

92 Rom. 7:25b is a gloss, for it speaks again of the unredeemed person, whereas 25a has already made the transition to the situation of redemption in Romans 8. Moreover this summary does not correspond with the foregoing Pauline argumentation. The agreement with the law in verses 16, 22 is not identical with the δουλεύειν νόμῳ θεοῦ, "serve the law of God," in 25b, which is precisely what we do not have in Rom. 7:14ff., because this is prevented by sin; versus P. Stuhlmacher, *Römer*, pp. 104–5, who regards 25b as original.

93 Cf. in this regard, e.g., E. Käsemann, *Römer*, 207; H. Räisänen, *Das 'Gesetz des Glaubens*,' pp. 113ff.; U. Luz (and R. Smend), *Gesetz*, p. 104; R. Weber, 'Die Geschichte des Gesetzes,' p. 116. Versus U. Wilckens, *Römer* 2:122–23; H. Hübner, *Gesetz bei Paulus*, pp. 125–6, and E. Lohse, ὁ νόμος τοῦ πνεύματος τῆς ζωῆς, pp. 285–6, who even here relate νόμος to the Torah.

the νόμος in 8:2 cannot mean the Old Testament Torah, because verse 3a would then reject what verse 2 asserts, liberation from the power of sin and of death. Because Christ placed himself in the realm of ἁμαρτία, through his resurrection he rendered sin and death impotent. This liberation occurs in the lives of Christians through the Spirit,[94] and it is present in the Spirit, as verse 4 shows. Through the transition with ἵνα ("so that") the soteriological element already dominant in verse 3 is taken further. With the sending of the Son the legal claim of the law was fulfilled. But what does δικαίωμα τοῦ νόμου ('just requirement of the law') mean? The answer is given in 13:8, where it is expressly emphasized that the law is fulfilled in the commandment of love.[95] According to the programmatic statements in 7:1–6 this can mean neither the fulfillment of a legitimate claim of the Old Testament Torah nor its restitution;[96] rather, νόμος is to be understood here as in Gal. 6:2 in a paradoxical sense: only through God's act of love in Jesus Christ was the power of sin broken, the law fulfilled and thus redeemed. The new being, however, in no way leads to license; rather, precisely because for Christians the περιπατεῖν κατὰ πνεῦμα ("walking according to the Spirit") is what now counts, they fulfill the commandment of love.

In Rom. 7:7–8:4 Paul comprehensively develops the basic structures of human existence, which are first revealed in faith. Outside of faith human beings find themselves always under the power of sin. Compared to the commandment or wanting what is good, sin has a temporal and practical advantage: it was in the world before the commandment, and with the help of the law it deceives human beings by turning their striving for the good into the opposite. As beings of flesh they are helplessly subject to the power of sin. Out of itself sin releases a regularity that no one can escape. Only the resurrection of Jesus Christ from the dead and with it the neutralization of the power of sin and death can free humankind from this hopeless situation through the present working of the Spirit. And this is perceivable and knowable only

---

94 Versus P. Stuhlmacher, *Römer*, p. 114, who asserts: 'The law no longer stands foreign and threatening over against them but moves them from within, so that they stand in the knowledge of the will of God and fulfill the law's requirement of justice out of the strength of Christ (Rom. 8:4).' It is the Spirit alone who brings about this change.

95 Cf. H. Paulsen, *Überlieferung*, p. 65.

96 Cf. E. Käsemann, *Römer*, p. 209.

for those who in faith let this salvific event have validity for them. Thus it is only in faith that one knows one's true situation of being dependent on the unmerited grace of God. At the same time, however, Paul describes in 7:7–25a the reality of human beings in general, which outside of faith they neither are conscious of nor can escape. Not the existence of this reality but only its knowledge and overcoming is bound to faith for Paul.

Thus, as the fundamental neutralization of sin's power through the cross and resurrection of Jesus Christ occurred in a unique historical event, so concrete incorporation into this event of salvation also occurs in a unique historical event: baptism. The starting point of Paul's argumentation in Romans 6[97] is the relationship of sin and grace (6:1). The two are related to each other antithetically, for the Christian lives in the realm of χάρις ("grace") and has therefore died to sin. But how? The concept of Rom. 6:3 is apparently that by being baptized into Jesus' death the Christian dies to sin.[98] Baptism is in reality a death to sin, precisely because it is a baptism into Jesus' death. The starting point here is the death of Jesus (cf. αὐτοῦ, "his"), who is present in baptism. The act of baptism is understood as the sacramental reliving of the present death of Jesus by the individual Christian. The sacramental paralleling of Jesus' death with the death of the one being baptized establishes the reference to the unique death of Jesus on Golgotha. Even if only one death, the death of Jesus Christ, overcame sin in a final way, this death is nevertheless present in baptism and enables the Christian also really to die to sin. The sacramental reliving of Jesus' death with the consequence of one's own death in baptism is not identical with Jesus' death on Golgotha, but baptism is the place where the salvific meaning of Jesus' death becomes reality for the Christian. Here the life of sin is annihilated, and the new existence is constituted and carried out as a life κατὰ πνεῦμα, according to the Spirit.

Rom. 6:4 strengthens the idea of the common destiny of Christ and his people already contained in verse 3, for both the preposition σύν ("with") and the explanatory ὥσπερ-οὕτως statement

---

[97] On the interpretation of Romans 6, cf. U. Schnelle, *Gerechtigkeit und Christusgegenwart*, pp. 74–88, pp. 203–15 (including discussion of the literature).

[98] The background of Rom. 6:3–5 may include views from the mystery religions; cf. on this complex R. Bultmann, *Theologie*, pp. 142ff.; rather skeptical regarding this attempted derivation is A. J. M. Wedderburn, *Baptism*, pp. 90–163.

("just as … so also") are aimed at the far-reaching correspondence between Christ and the baptized. The salvific character of baptism is stressed by συνετάφημεν ("we have been buried"), for here baptism is effective participation in the whole salvation event, including the resurrection of Jesus Christ. This is clearly shown by the final statement in 6:4b–c, introduced by ἵνα and divided by ὥσπερ-οὕτως. The idea of the material as well as temporal correspondence between Christ and his people in the resurrection, already present in συνετάφημεν, is so strongly emphasized here through ὥσπερ-οὕτως, that a logical completion of the idea would have had to lead to the formulation ὥσπερ … οὕτως καὶ ἡμεῖς ἐκ νεκρῶν ἐγερθῶμεν ("just as … so we too have risen from the dead").[99] Yet Paul does not draw this conclusion but defines the present and future being of Christians in a future, ethical way with the phrase ἐν καινότητι ζωῆς περιπατήσωμεν ("walk in newness of life").[100] Death to sin does not result in a substantial change in a person; baptism effects no ontological transformation. Rather, the new reality of freedom from sin stands under an eschatological proviso and must prove itself historically.

Thus, at a crucial point Paul breaks through the established traditional idea of the temporal and practical correspondence between Jesus and his people. In Rom. 6:6 the apostle takes the subject further by speaking now of the παλαιὸς ἄνθρωπος ('old self'), whose body of sin was destroyed in baptism. Positively, liberation from sin results in a life in righteousness. In verse 7 Paul varies this idea by interpreting death in baptism again as liberation from the power of sin. Summarizing, Paul describes the new situation of the baptized in 6:8–11: because Jesus Christ died and has risen from the dead, and the baptized receive in baptism full participation in this salvation event, they too are removed from the dominion of death and sin. As people who have died to sin, they now live for God. The new life of Christians was enabled by the cross and resurrection of Jesus Christ, appropriated in baptism and carried out by the Holy Spirit.

Are the baptized and Spirit-led Christians now forever separated from sin? Can they again fall under the rule of sin? Paul believes

---

[99] Cf. R. Bultmann, *Theologie*, p. 143.
[100] Here lies the crucial difference from Eph. 2:6; Col. 2:12; 3:1–4, which speak of a resurrection (in faith) already completed in baptism; on the analysis of the texts cf. E. Grässer, 'Kolosser 3,1–4,' pp. 129ff.

this possible, as the juxtaposition of Rom. 6:1–11 and 6:12–23 shows. If in 6:1–11 he emphatically stresses the reality of the salvation event and thus the indicative, then 6:12–23 is filled with the imperative. Christians are not to obey desires. They are exhorted rather to present their members to God as instruments of righteousness but not to sin as instruments of wickedness. Then are the baptized not dead to sin, as verse 2 so emphatically asserts? Yes, they have died to sin, but sin is not dead. It remains in the world as temptation of the body and the spirit. Sin no longer rules over the baptized, but it continues to be a power they face. This explains the clear predominance of the imperative in Rom. 6:12–23. Christians are not immune to the temptation of sin; the righteousness attained in baptism is not a possession but as God's gift must prove itself ever anew in human obedience. People are not removed from their former circumstances; they continue to live under the conditions of a transitory cosmos. It is true that the crucial passage of Christians from the world of death and sin into the world of the Spirit has already occurred in baptism, but the new being stands under an eschatological proviso (cf. also 1 Cor. 13:12; 2 Cor. 4:7; 5:7); that is, it is not demonstrable in the inner world and will not become apparent until the parousia of Christ. In the present the power of the Spirit bears witness as down payment and first fruits of the new salvific reality created by God.

The whole Pauline ethic shows that for the apostle there is a falling away of Christians from the already attained state of salvation. In 1 Cor. 5:1–13 Paul reports an expulsion from the church; because of a serious moral trespass, a Christian is handed over to Satan (cf. 1 Cor. 5:5).[101] Paul's admonitions and imperatives (cf., e.g., 1 Cor. 6:18: φεύγετε τὴν πορνείαν, 'Shun fornication!'; 7:23; 8:12; etc.) as a whole testify to the possibility that Christians can again come under the dominion of sin. Paul knows about the temptations to which Christians are subject (cf. 1 Cor. 7:5; 10:9, 13, Gal. 6:1). Satan appears in the form of an angel of light and attempts to confuse the churches (cf. 2 Cor. 11:13–15). The church in Galatia falls from grace when it places itself under the dominion of the law, which again is only a tool of sin. Freedom from sin for Paul is a divine gift that in historical practice becomes a human task. The indicative sets forth the imperative and at the same time

---

[101] On the problem of church discipline in the Pauline congregations cf. I. Goldhahn-Müller, *Grenze der Gemeinde*, pp. 115–56.

requires it. Nevertheless, the imperative cannot be understood simply as human achievement, for it is the Spirit, of course, that enables Christians to withstand the assaults of sin (cf. Phil. 2:13: 'For it is God who is at work in you, enabling you both to will and to work for his good pleasure'). Finally, even for Paul God is and remains the righteous Judge[102] who judges according to human works (cf. Rom. 2:5ff; 1 Cor. 3:12–15; 2 Cor. 5:10: 'For all of us must appear before the judgment seat of Christ, so that each may receive recompense for what has been done in the body, whether good or evil'.) Only the Judge can forgive sinners for Christ's sake, free them from sin, and justify them through faith.

3.9 God's Power and Human Volition: Free Will

The question of human free will represents a central problem of Pauline theology and anthropology, although the apostle deals explicitly with this problem only in Rom. 9:6–29. The assertions about the dominion of sin in 7:7–25a already allow only the conclusion that human beings have no free will with respect to salvation. Yet Paul chooses another starting point for discussing free will: the question of the righteousness of God and the destiny of Israel. For Paul central biographical and theological lines intersect here.[103] Paul feels deep pain over the persistence of large parts of Israel in unbelief in regard to the ultimate revelation of God in Jesus Christ (9:1–2). He himself would even like to be excluded from salvation if he could thereby save his brothers and sisters (9:3). Israel is the people chosen by God; to them belong the adoption (ἡ υἱοθεσία), the glory (ἡ δόξα), the covenants (αἱ διαθῆκαι), the giving of the law (ἡ νομοθεσία), the worship (ἡ λατρεία), and the promises (αἱ ἐπαγγελίαι). If large parts of Israel refuse the revelation in Christ, then the conclusion could be drawn that the promises of God have failed.

In several chains of thought in Rom. 9:6ff. Paul refutes this possible conclusion. In this he starts with the basic conviction that God's word cannot fail (9:6a). Rather, empirical Israel is not identical with the recipients of the promises of God (9:6b: οὐ γὰρ πάντες οἱ ἐξ Ἰσραὴλ, οὗτοι Ἰσραήλ, 'for not all Israelites truly

---

[102] Cf. here E. Synofzik, *Gerichts- und Vergeltungsaussagen.*
[103] On the position of Romans 9–11 in the structure of the Letter to the Romans cf. U. Luz, 'Zum Aufbau von Röm 1–8,' p. 169.

belong to Israel').[104] For Paul the true Israel is identical with those
who accept God's promises and recognize that God's salvific will
reached its goal in Jesus Christ. For every part of Israel that refuses
the revelation in Christ the Old Testament promises are no longer
valid, because in a theological sense it is not Israel at all.

The idea that the empirical Israel is not identical with the chosen
Israel is found in explicit form in the Qumran literature. Thus in
CD 3.3–4: 'And the sons of Zadok are the chosen ones of Israel,
those called by name, who will appear at the end of days. See the
exact directory of their names according to their tribes and the
time of their appearance.'

In Rom. 9:7–9 Paul supports his thesis in verse 6b. Only the
descendants of Isaac count as true seed in the salvation-historical
sense. Bodily descent alone in no way assures a special salvation-
historical position; but only the τέκνα τῆς ἐπαγγελίας ('children
of the promise') are recognized by God as descendants. Because
for Paul the promises of the old covenant became reality in Jesus
Christ, only those who grasp them in faith are their heirs. If the
sovereignty of God over Israel already stood at the center of the
relationship of Isaac to Ishmael, then Paul illustrates the freedom
of the Creator-God once again in 9:10–13. Although Jacob and
Esau came from the same mother and the same father, God loved
the one and rejected the other. Even before Jacob and Esau were
born and could do anything good or evil, God's judgment was fixed.
Paul provides the reason for this behavior of God in 9:11b ('… so
that God's purpose of election might continue'). The call grows
out of God's purpose alone and not on the basis of works. Thus in
Paul all assertions about divine predestination must be seen as a
consequence of the doctrine of justification.

Both the doctrine of justification and the predestination
statements aim at one single assertion: everything depends on
God's gracious activity.[105] This activity of God occurs in freedom;
no one can, on the basis of his or her origin or adduced
accomplishments, influence or determine God's activity. The
freedom and sovereignty of God are valid with regard to every
person and thus also with regard to his chosen people Israel. The
scripture itself confirms the election of Jacob and the rejection of

---

[104] Cf. on this H. Hübner, *Gottes Ich und Israel,* p. 17.
[105] Pertinent is O. Michel, *Römer,* p. 307: 'In God's activity and in his self-testimony,
according to Paul, lies his justification.'

Esau (cf. Gen. 25:23; Mal. 1:2 LXX in Rom. 9:12–13).[106] In Rom. 9:14 Paul takes up the obvious human objection that God is unjust. He dismisses this reproach by quoting Exod. 33:19 LXX in verse 15: 'I will have mercy on whom I have mercy, and I will have compassion on whom I have compassion.' Here we see a central trait of Paul's argumentation. For Paul the scripture attests and proclaims divine predestination. In the scripture God himself has made his will known, which human beings can indeed perceive but cannot call into question.[107] Paul stresses God's independence again in 9:16 in a downright dogmatic form: 'So it depends not on human will or exertion, but on God who shows mercy.' In verse 17 Paul substantiates the foregoing dogmatic assertion with a further scriptural quotation (Exod. 9:16) in order then to show yet another facet: 'So then he [God] has mercy on whomever he chooses, and he hardens the heart of whomever he chooses.' Again God's being God appears to be the sole reason for his behavior.

In Rom. 9:19–21 Paul deals with a further possible objection, for from his foregoing argumentation the conclusion could be drawn that through the unquestionable arbitrary dominion of God, any responsibility of human beings for their deeds and their destiny is canceled. Why does God blame and reject sinners if everything is still up to his will and human beings can change nothing at all with regard to their destiny? Paul meets this objection in verses 19–21 by holding the questioners' creatureliness before their eyes and thereby making clear the inappropriateness of their question. Whether consciously or unconsciously, the questioners are placing themselves on the same level with God, but they are God's creatures and therefore not at all justified in accusing God. Here the apostle anchors anthropology in creation theology. For him the qualitative difference between Creator and creature is indissoluble and provides the positive basis for the sovereign activity of the Creator, who can choose and reject according to his will.[108] Every self-glory of the creature is for Paul always a falling short of the nature of humankind as determined by creation and an illegitimate rejection

---

[106] On the use of scriptural quotations in Romans 9(–11) cf. esp. H. Hübner, *Gottes Ich und Israel*, pp. 149ff.; D.-A. Koch, *Die Schrift als Zeuge*, under the relevant text.

[107] Cf. G. Maier, *Mensch und freier Wille*, pp. 367–8.

[108] Cf. ibid., pp. 337–8.

of the Creator's will. God's creative power is revealed in two ways
for Paul as wrath and mercy (9:22–23). Here Paul wants to make
clear to the Jews boasting of their privileges that God is not bound
in his activity but completely free to call and reject. God can call
Gentiles and Jews equally, as the scripture has already foretold (cf.
9:25–29).

The quest for human free will had already been considered
intensively and controversially before Paul in ancient Judaism.[109]
Thus in Sirach (Ecclesiasticus) we find statements about both the
free will of humans and the unfree will of humans. In Sir. 15:11–
15, 20 we read:[110]

> Do not say, 'It was the Lord's doing that I fell away';
>   for he does not do what he hates.
> Do not say, 'It was he who led me astray';
>   for he has no need of the sinful.
> The Lord hates all abominations;
>   such things are not loved by those who fear him.
> It was he who created humankind in the beginning,
>   and he left them in the power of their own free choice.
> If you choose, you can keep the commandments,
>   and to act faithfully is a matter of your own choice....
> He has not commanded anyone to be wicked,
>   and he has not given anyone permission to sin.

By contrast Sir. 33:11–15 says about humankind:

> In the fullness of his knowledge the Lord distinguished them
>   and appointed their different ways.
> Some he blessed and exalted,
>   and some he made holy and brought near to himself;
> but some he cursed and brought low,
>   and turned them out of their place.
> Like clay in the hand of the potter,
>   to be molded as he pleases,
> so all are in the hand of their Maker,
>   to be given whatever he decides.

---

[109] For a comprehensive treatment cf. ibid., pp. 1–350. For the Greek-Hellenistic
area cf. A. Dihle, *Die Vorstellung vom Willen*, pp. 31–109.

[110] In each case the quotations from Sirach are from the NRSV.

Good is the opposite of evil,
  and life the opposite of death;
    so the sinner is the opposite of the godly.
Look at all the works of the Most High;
  they come in pairs, one the opposite of the other.

The *Psalms of Solomon* stemming from the Pharisaic tradition
attest that even in this grouping of ancient Judaism the question
of human free will was controversial. Thus *Pss. Sol.* 5.4 reads:[111]
'For human beings and their lot lie in the balance with you; beyond
your decision, O God, they shall add nothing further.' On the other
hand, *Pss. Sol.* 9.4–7 can say:

> Our works happen according to the choice and decision of
> our soul to do right or wrong with the works of our hands,
> but in your righteousness you haunt the children of
> humankind. Those who practice righteousness gather
> themselves life with the Lord, but those who practice wrong
> commit their souls to destruction, for the Lord judges a
> person and that person's house in righteousness. With whom
> are you benevolent, O God, if not with those who call on the
> Lord? He will cleanse the sins of those who praise through
> confession, for on us and our faces lies shame on account of
> everything. And whose sins will he forgive if not those who
> have sinned? The righteous you will bless, and you do not
> punish them for the sins they have committed.

Thus, as a former Pharisee, Paul was already familiar with the
discussion about human free will. His position is very close to Sir.
33:11–15 and also has parallels in the Qumran literature:

> And I have perceived through your insight that there is no
> way in the hand of the flesh and not with humankind, and a
> person cannot determine his or her step. And I perceived
> that in your hand lies the form of every spirit [which] you
> have determined before you created it. How should anyone
> be able to change your words? Only you have created the
> righteous and determined them from the womb on for the
> time of goodwill, so that they may be preserved in your

---

[111] Quotations from the *Psalms of Solomon* follow the German translation of
S. Holm-Nielsen.

covenant and walk in everything in order to do great things
in them in your rich compassion and open every oppression
of their souls to eternal salvation and lasting peace and no
imperfection of any kind. And you establish their glory out
of the flesh, but the ungodly you have created for the time
of your wrath, and from the womb on you have consecrated
them for the day of slaughter.

(1QH 15.12–17)

Within the Qumran catechesis the double predestination of
humankind is extensively substantiated in 1QS 8.13–4.26. Here it
states that God has set over humankind the spirits of truth and of
wickedness, and these two spirits completely determine the life of
humankind. 'In these two spirits is the origin of all people, and
these are shared by all groups in their races. They walk in their
ways, and all deeds of their work happen in their classes
corresponding to the share of each one – be it much, be it little –
for all eternity. For God has set them side by side until the last
time and has ordained eternal strife between their classes' (1QS
4.15–17). In massive form the Qumran texts assert a prior
determination by God of human beings to salvation or destruction.
Positively, God is coupled with the idea of election, which the
community in Qumran relates to itself.

Paul presents a double predestination:[112] God calls and rejects
whom he will (cf. Rom. 9:18; cf. also 2 Cor. 2:15). This brings 'to
expression the idea that the decision of faith does not, like other
decisions, go back to some sort of internal motives, but rather that
these lose all motivational power when confronted with the
kerygma; this means at the same time that faith cannot be based
on itself.'[113] But the Pauline statements on predestination are by
no means wholly based on this interpretation that is centered on
the faithful existence of the individual. They are first of all
theological statements that communicate a state of affairs revealed
by God himself in the scripture. In his unquestionable freedom
God the Creator can choose and reject according to his will. Hence
free will is for Paul exclusively a predicate of God. The infinite
difference between Creator and creature underlies the specific
perspective from which Paul understands humankind. God
confronts human beings as the one who calls; 'Being human means

---

[112] Thus, emphatically, G. Maier, *Mensch und freier Wille*, pp. 356–7.
[113] R. Bultmann, *Theologie*, p. 331.

being called and addressed by God.'[114] As with the apostle (cf. Gal. 1:15), the call of God is the foundation of Christian existence. Thus it is not at the disposal of human beings but can only be accepted when heard. The ὁ καλέσας ἡμᾶς ("the one who calls us") becomes in Paul a central predicate of God (cf. Gal. 1:6; 5:8; 1 Thess. 5:24). Therefore, 'those whom he predestined he also called; and those whom he called he also justified; and those whom he justified he also glorified' (Rom. 8:30). God confronts human beings as the calling 'I' whose will is announced in the scripture.[115] In regard to salvation human beings can never know themselves as more than recipients of a gift. As creatures they are fundamentally incapable of planning and realizing salvation and meaning. They would thereby put themselves in God's place – a dangerous and hopeless illusion.

If human beings want to understand and appreciate themselves and their situation appropriately and realistically, they must recognize and take seriously their creatureliness and thus their finitude. The creature's destiny reaches its goal in hearing and doing the Creator's will. For Paul, God is always the God who acts.[116] The creature does not decide about salvation and disaster; the Creator has already made that decision.

Paul's statements on predestination must therefore be seen in close, substantial connection with the doctrine of justification. They are the consequence of that doctrine, for in the two theological concepts one basic perception is articulated: God's activity is independent of human deeds or presuppositions; his will always precedes our volition. God's election grace is his justification grace. Thus the doctrine of justification and the statements of predestination in like manner preserve the freedom of God and the unavailability of salvation. Paul wants to show in Rom. 9:6–29 that God is free in his salvific activity and can make a people other than the empirical Israel his people. This argumentation goal and the observation that Paul's predestination statements appear as a function of the doctrine of justification should warn us not to force them into a solidly constructed, static doctrine of predestination. At the same time, against relativizing and leveling tendencies we must maintain that Paul presented a double predestination, that in regard to salvation free will is a predicate of God and not of

---

[114] H. Hübner, *Gottes Ich und Israel*, pp. 31–2.
[115] Cf. ibid., pp. 31–5.
[116] Cf. E. Grässer, "'Ein einziger ist Gott,'" pp. 233ff.

human beings, and that this whole complex is organically integrated into Pauline theology and necessarily results from it. Salvation and damnation are both grounded in the unquestionable decision of God alone (versus Jas. 1:13–15.). Yet the two do not stand together on an equal footing; rather, God's universal will to salvation was revealed in Jesus Christ, while God's no is his mystery and as such is not accessible to human knowledge.

3.10 Not License but Responsibility: Freedom in Paul

The ethical dimensions of Paul's concept of freedom are revealed in the conflict in Corinth about the meat offered to idols (cf. esp. 1 Cor. 8:1–13; 10:14–33). The majority of the church members in Corinth were former pagans (cf. 1 Cor. 12:2), but Jews (cf. Acts 18:8) and proselytes or God-fearers (cf. Acts 18:7) also joined the church. Certainly at the time the 'strong' in Corinth belonged to the higher social level; it was possible for them to free themselves from traditional religious ideas through religious knowledge (cf. 1 Cor. 8:1, 4; 10:23).[117] Nonetheless, the 'strong' are not simply to be equated with the social upper class in the church, for the knowledge of the existence of only one God and the futility of idols and demons is an expression of a monotheism that belonged to Jews and pagans (cf. 1 Thess. 1:9–10). The traditions of the Cynics could also have been significant, for out of their monotheistic confession, they, as part of the Corinthian church, claimed the freedom to eat everything.[118] Both Gentile Christians and liberal Jewish Christians were in the group of the 'strong.' Moreover, they were invited by pagans (cf. 1 Cor. 10:27), and their social position alone made it impossible for them to forgo fully the consumption of meat consecrated to idols. The 'weak' in the Corinthian church were apparently a Gentile-Christian minority (cf. 1 Cor. 8:7). Some of this group generally rejected the consumption of meat sacrificed to idols out of fear of the gods. Others were forced just from material need to participate in public

---

[117] This aspect is stressed by G. Theissen, 'Die Starken und Schwachen,' pp. 282–3.

[118] Thus Epictetus, *Diss.* 3.22.50, can say that it is characteristic of the Cynic 'to swallow everything you give [him]'; there are further texts with interpretation in S. Jones, *'Freiheit,'* pp. 59–61.

religious feasts and to eat meat there in the cultic context, thereby burdening their consciences. Still others were led by the behavior of the 'strong' to go against their consciences and eat the meat offered to idols, for the 'strong' took part in the cultic sacrificial meals without thinking and without need (1 Cor. 10:14–22).

In this discussion Paul takes up the slogan of the 'strong,' πάντα μοι ἔξεστιν ('all things are lawful for me'), in order immediately to relativize it and refine it (1 Cor. 6:12: '"All things are lawful for me," but I will not be dominated by anything'; 1 Cor. 10:23: '"All things are lawful," but not all things are beneficial. "All things are lawful," but not all things build up'). Christian freedom is certainly not achieved in unbounded self-presentation and self-realization but rather is by its nature a relational concept: it gains its true shape only in relationship to fellow Christians and to the Christian community. Hence, freedom cannot be understood as an attribute of an autonomous subject; rather, it finds its limitation in the conscience of another person: 'But take care that this liberty of yours does not somehow become a stumbling block to the weak' (1 Cor. 8:9). The freedom of the 'strong' to eat – without desperate need – meat offered to idols must not lead to the 'weak' thereby becoming unfree. Unlimited freedom leads necessarily to unfreedom, because it does not observe the boundaries that are imposed on it by the neighbor. At this point Paul is not formulating maxims of a philosophical concept of freedom; rather, ἐλευθερία is also understood here christologically: 'But when you thus sin against members of your family, and wound their conscience when it is weak, you sin against Christ' (1 Cor. 8:12). In this admonition to the 'strong' the foundation of the Pauline concept of freedom becomes clear. Christian freedom for Paul is freedom gained for us through Jesus Christ; hence a misuse of this freedom as sin against a fellow Christian is also sin against Christ.

This character of service of the Pauline concept of freedom becomes visible in 1 Corinthians 9. Here Paul discusses the relationship of freedom and justice. As an apostle of Jesus Christ he is free and has the right to be supported by his churches (cf. 9:4–6). Paul consciously renounces this right in order not to hinder thereby the proclamation of the gospel (9:12, 15–16).[119] If in antiquity freedom and slavery were mutually exclusive, in Paul they are mutually dependent: the freedom of the apostle is realized

---

[119] On the religious-historical background cf. ibid., p. 52.

precisely in slavery to the gospel (9:19). The renunciation of support serves only the unhindered propagation of the gospel; Paul can be a Jew for the Jews and a Gentile for the Gentiles, in order to win them for the gospel.[120] Here too freedom is a relational concept; it can be realized paradoxically in slavery because it receives its nature and its content from Christ, who himself entered slavery (Phil. 2:6–7). Freedom does not of itself presuppose slavery as such; rather, the freedom that appeared in Jesus Christ is achieved in the mode of service to the gospel. For the missionary Paul it is true that 'I do all for the sake of the gospel, so that I may share in its blessings' (1 Cor. 9:23).

The social-ethical dimension of the Pauline concept of freedom is open to discussion on the slavery issue. In 1 Cor. 7:21b[121] does Paul advise slaves to accept liberation, or are they to remain in their status? Philologically one cannot clearly decide whether the aorist χρῆσαι ("use") is to be completed with τῇ δουλείᾳ ("slavery") or τῇ ἐλευθερίᾳ ("freedom"). The initial ἀλλά of verse 21b can be understood on the one hand as the introduction of something contrary to what has preceded; then it would be translated as 'nevertheless' or 'however' and would support the option of freedom. On the other hand, ἀλλά can also introduce a further reinforcing statement in the sense of "and not only this but also" or "indeed even," which would suggest remaining in the status of slaves. The latter interpretation is clearly supported by the context of 1 Cor. 7:17–24, where the stress of the paraenesis is on *remain* (μένειν in 7:20, 24, also 7:8, 11, 40) in the various callings (7:20: κλῆσις; 7:15, 17, 20–22, 24: καλέω in passive form). Even the clarifying verse 22 points in this direction: 'For whoever was called in the Lord as a slave is a freed person belonging to the Lord, just as whoever was free when called is a slave of Christ.' Paul defines freedom here as inner freedom, which has its possibility and its goal in Jesus Christ alone. In this concept of freedom social structures are unimportant because they can neither guarantee freedom nor abolish unfreedom.[122]

---

[120] In 1 Cor. 9:20–21 Paul illustrates the paradoxical form of his missionary existence using the example of the law, without discussing 'freedom from the law' in the sense of the Galatian and Roman letters; thus with S. Jones, ibid., 52, versus S. Vollenweider, *Freiheit*, pp. 213–14.

[121] A detailed exegesis is offered by S. Vollenweider, ibid., pp. 233–46.

[122] Cf. here the balanced argumentation of E. Fascher, *1. Korinther*, pp. 92–3.

Paul is clearly close to Stoic concepts.[123] For example, Seneca can say about the slave: 'He is a slave. But perhaps free in the soul! He is a slave: that will hurt him? Show me who is not! One is a slave to his sensuality, another to his greed, another to his ambition, all to hope, all to fear. I will show you a former consul, slave to an old woman; I will show you a rich man, slave to a young slave girl; I will show you highly eminent men as slaves of actors: no slavery is more ignominious than that of one's own volition' (*Ep.* 47). For Epictetus (*Diss.* 4.4.33) freedom is identical with inner independence: 'You must let everything go, body, possessions, good reputation, and your books, society, office, and your private life. For where your inclination draws you, there you have become a slave to what is inferior; you are enchained, compelled; in short, you are totally dependent on other things.' So, as no one can really give the Stoic anything, so nothing can be taken from him. It is his goal to live in agreement with himself and in this very way put himself into harmony with the cosmos.

In the world that is passing away (cf. 1 Cor. 7:29–31) Paul advises remaining in one's vocation. Such a course is demanded not by an unchangeable cosmic order given by God but by God's present and future salvific activity. In the Christian community baptism has removed the fundamental oppositions of society: man-woman, slave-free, Jew-Greek (cf. 1 Cor. 12:13; Gal. 3:26–28). The opposition δοῦλος-ἐλεύθερος ("slave-free") was applied among the Jews as well as among the Greeks. Also the third pair of opposites that appears only in Gal. 3:28, ἄρσεν-θῆλυ ('male-female' – Gen. 1:27 LXX), held great significance for Jews and Greeks, for according to the Jewish conception a woman was not and is not qualified for the cult, and Greek thinking is dominated by a line that emphasizes the superiority of men over women. The pre-Pauline traditions obviously aim at a change or removal of fundamental distinctions within the church, because for those baptized ἐν χριστῷ those oppositions have already been lifted. Paul's intention can be seen clearly in Gal. 3:26–28, for through the means of interpretation διὰ τῆς πίστεως ("through faith") in verse 26 a fanatical or libertine misunderstanding of the statements of this piece of tradition is prevented. Paul connects the removal of the named oppositions and thus the new being of Christians to faith and thus to reality, which evades outward demonstration.

---

[123] A comprehensive presentation of the question regarding the history of religion and law is found in S. Jones, *'Freiheit,'* pp. 27–37.

Nevertheless, Paul by no means rules out the attainment of freedom for the Christian slave, as the Letter to Philemon, for example, shows. It is a textbook example of Pauline argumentation.[124] First Paul attempts to win Philemon for himself. He burdens him with his being a Christian by suggesting that he do the good that he can do (Philemon 6–7). If the apostle up to this point appealed only to Philemon's responsibility, in verses 8–9 he subtly brings his own authority into play. He expressly emphasizes that he does not want to use it, but in this very way he applies it all the more effectively. Not until verse 10 does it become clear what Paul really wants: he asks for the slave Onesimus, whose master Philemon was and is.[125] The central theological motif of the letter appears in verse 11: the conversion of Onesimus not only has consequences for the slave himself but also for the judgment of the slave by his master Philemon. Onesimus is now Philemon's brother just as much as Paul is. Philemon is supposed to recognize and accept the new status of the slave Onesimus as his beloved brother 'in Christ.' In this way Paul is encouraging Philemon to break through the ancient social structure and grant Onesimus a new social status to go with his unchanged legal status. The apostle, by emphatically identifying himself with Onesimus (vv. 12, 17–20), pointedly makes the new situation clear to Philemon. If Paul now sends Onesimus back in accordance with the legal situation (vv. 12, 14), then a part of himself will be coming to Philemon.

The actual goal of Paul's argumentation becomes evident in verse 13. He would like for Onesimus to remain with him and serve him during imprisonment for the sake of the gospel. Nevertheless, he does not want to accept the service of Onesimus without the voluntary agreement of Philemon (v. 14), which, however, he in fact presupposes (v. 21). The apostle hopes, of course, soon to be able himself to visit Philemon (v. 22), and this is not made superfluous by the present and perhaps also future service of Onesimus to Paul. According to the testimony of the Letter to Philemon, Christian freedom does not result in the abolishing of social structures but is realized concretely first of all in the context of the community. It is not the removal or retention of legal relationships that changes the situation of the slave Onesimus; rather, through the death and resurrection of Jesus Christ, the slave

---

[124] Cf. J. Gnilka, *Philemon*, pp. 7–12.
[125] On the problem of slavery cf. ibid., pp. 54–81 (excursus: 'Die Sklaven in der Antike und im frühen Christentum').

becomes the beloved brother Onesimus in the community. It is the Letter to Philemon that shows that for Paul freedom is not an attribute of the human essence in the modern sense. Paul indirectly asks for the liberation of Onesimus so that the latter may be helpful to him in the proclamation of the gospel. Only on the basis of this goal is the apostle's request to be understood. Individual freedom represents no value in itself but stands in service to the gospel proclamation.

In the Corinthian letters freedom is never understood as freedom from the law, from sin, or from death; this meaning appears first in Galatians and Romans.[126] In the Letter to the Romans a derivative of the word for freedom appears for the first time in 6:18, 22, where both this location and the passive form of ἐλευθερόω ("make free") have a programmatic character. Christian freedom results from liberation from the power of sin achieved by Jesus Christ and appropriated in baptism. Thus freedom is not a possibility of the human essence; human beings can neither attain it nor realize it. The universal power of sin excludes freedom as a goal of human striving. It is true that people can have an individual feeling of freedom and deny the power of sin, but this does not alter the fact of the enslaving reign of sin in the lives of these people. Only the salvific activity of God in Jesus Christ can be understood in a comprehensive sense as a liberating event, because now the powers of sin and death that oppress people have been conquered. In baptism as a one-time historical act individuals share in the liberating activity of God in Jesus Christ, and they are now themselves people who have been liberated from sin. Paul understands this process not as the substantial transformation of a person but as something historical: as someone freed from sin, the baptized person now serves righteousness (Rom. 6:18b, 22b). The discontinuity between the old and the new being, clearly indicated with νυνί ("but now") in Rom. 6:22, is to be maintained and proven in ethical activity.

At the same time, freedom from sin for Paul includes freedom from the law. With polemical polish, he treats this fundamental connection for the first time in the Letter to the Galatians.[127]

---

[126] With S. Jones, *'Freiheit,'* pp. 67–9 and elsewhere, versus S. Vollenweider, *Freiheit,* p. 21 and elsewhere, who understands freedom in Paul entirely as freedom from the law.

[127] Cf. on the understanding of the law in Galatians esp. H. Hübner, *Gesetz bei Paulus,* pp. 16–43.

Already at the Apostolic Council he had to guard against the attempt of the 'false believers ... to spy on the freedom we have [κατασκοπῆσαι τὴν ἐλευθερίαν ἡμῶν] in Christ Jesus' (Gal. 2:4b). This represented an attack on the Pauline mission concept, in which freedom from the law for Gentile Christians was taken for granted as the basis. A new situation arose at the time of the writing of Galatians through the successful penetration of Judaizing missionaries into the Galatian church. They demanded the observation of cultic times (4:3, 9–10) and circumcision (5:3, 11–12; 6:12–13) by all church members.[128]

Paul responded to this new situation with his doctrine of justification, which is supposed to furnish, among other things, proof of the freedom of the individual Christian from the law.[129] Paul formulated the core of his doctrine of justification in Gal. 2:16a: 'A person is justified not by works of the law.' Human beings cannot obey the law in all its specifications and thus, by falling short of the demands of the law, fall under its curse (3:10–12). Christ redeemed us from the curse of the law when he took the curse of the law upon himself (3:13). In this way the law itself is nullified; it has no more power over Christ and those who have died the death of Christ with him. Those who were crucified with him in baptism have died to the law and now live only for God (2:19–20). The Galatians received the Spirit not from the law but from the preaching of faith (3:1–5). As people 'who have received the Spirit' (πνευματικοί, 6:1) and are 'a new creation' in Christ (6:15), the Galatians are no longer under the law (5:18). When they want to be under the law (4:21), they fall short of the attained salvific state of freedom.

Paul makes clear to the Galatians the senselessness of their behavior through a scriptural proof that is connected with the person of Abraham (4:21–31).[130] For Paul the law itself attests that Christians have freedom from the law. Descent from Abraham occurred in two ways: according to the flesh and through the promise (4:23). If the child of the flesh corresponds to the Sinai covenant, which leads into slavery and is manifested in the earthly

---

[128] On the religious-historical backgrounds cf. esp. D. Lührmann, 'Tage, Monate, Jahreszeiten, Jahre (Gal 4,10),' pp. 428ff.

[129] For an extensive substantiation of the thesis that it was the discussions in Galatia that first led to the development of the specifically Pauline doctrine of justification, cf. U. Schnelle, *Wandlungen*, pp. 49–76.

[130] Cf. for interpretation H. D. Betz, *Galater*, pp. 410–32.

Jerusalem, then the child of the free woman is represented by the heavenly Jerusalem, which is the mother of Christians. Therefore, 'Now you, my friends, are children of the promise, like Isaac' (4:28). At the same time, the Galatians are thus τέκνα τῆς ἐλευθέρας ("children of the free woman"; cf. 4:31), and thus everything depends on preserving the freedom founded in the Christ event, appropriated in the gift of the Spirit, and confirmed by the scripture – and not distorting it into its opposite through observance of the Torah. Christian existence by its nature is freedom, for τῇ ἐλευθερίᾳ ἡμᾶς Χριστὸς ἠλευθέρωσεν ('For freedom Christ has set us free,' 5:1). The freedom attained by Christ is realized in love (5:13); hence it is understood not as license but as responsibility for others. Circumcision and calendar observance would revoke all of this; freedom would again become slavery; living by the Spirit would again become living by the flesh. In the Letter to the Galatians, as in no other letter of Paul, freedom is seen as freedom from the law. This depends on the special situation but is at the same time objectively determined: the power of sin uses the law to enslave people (3:22).

Paul develops this argumentation extensively in Romans 7,[131] where freedom appears as the impossible possibility of humankind in the situation between sin and law. Human beings are torn between the powers of sin, the law, and death; their wanting to do good comes up empty and turns against them. They are embedded in a legalism of unfreedom from which they cannot extract themselves. Only the salvific act of God in Jesus Christ can free them from their hopeless situation (cf. Rom. 8:2). The Spirit breaks through the legalism of disaster and unfreedom and places humankind into a new legalism: that of the life appearing in Jesus Christ. In the center of Romans Paul designates precisely with ἐλευθεροῦν ("set free") the breakthrough from the level of the law to the plane of the Spirit, which took place on Golgotha and was given to the individual in baptism as freedom from sin and freedom from the law. Now it is true: οὐ γὰρ ἐστε ὑπὸ νόμον ἀλλὰ ὑπὸ χάριν ('For ... you are not under law but under grace,' Rom. 6:14b).

The universal dimensions of the Pauline concept of freedom are seen in Rom. 8:18ff.[132] Here the freedom of the believer and the freedom of the creation are brought together and embedded

---

[131] Cf. the interpretation of Romans 7 on pp. 67–73 above.
[132] Cf. here S. Jones, *'Freiheit,'* pp. 129–35; S. Vollenweider, *Freiheit*, pp. 375–96.

in a comprehensive future perspective. Through Adam's failure creation fell involuntarily under the dominion of perishability, yet in hope (8:20; cf. 4 Ezra 7:11–12): creation participates in the hope of believers 'that the creation itself will be set free from its bondage to decay and will obtain the freedom of the glory of the children of God' (Rom. 8:21). The present δουλεία ("slavery") and the future ἐλευθερία ("freedom"), perishability and glory, stand over against each other. God's eschatological creative activity includes both the whole creation (8:22: πᾶσα ἡ κτίσις) and the believers. Just as the creation groans, so also do believers under the perishability of the earthly. They long for the redemption of their bodies (8:23) and desire the transition into immediate communion with God. The certainty of this future event is conveyed by the Spirit, who as the first fruit is not only the down payment of hope but in the situation of hopeful persistence comes to the aid of the believers (8:26–27). The Spirit, in appropriate divine language, intercedes before God for the saints. The certainty of faith enables Paul to describe extensively in 8:28–30 the 'glorious freedom of the children of God': 'We know that all things work together for good for those who love God, who are called according to his purpose. For those whom he foreknew he also predestined to be conformed to the image of his Son, in order that he might be the firstborn within a large family. And those whom he predestined he also called; and those whom he called he also justified; and those whom he justified he also glorified.' God himself will bring the freedom of the children of God, which has its goal in the participation in the glory of God appearing in the Son. If for Paul discontinuity determines the relationship of past and present, then present and future stand in the continuity of the Spirit. For believers and the whole creation God himself opens up a perspective that leads to him as the origin and perfecter of all being.

As in Paul generally, here too freedom does not appear as an object accessible to human beings but as an attribute of God. Human beings can neither free themselves from the powers of the past (sin, law, and death) nor reach the future by their own power. Freedom is the gift of God alone, who in the Spirit overcomes the past and opens the future.

3.11 The Appeal to an Inner Court: Conscience in Paul

The term συνείδησις ("conscience") appears in the New Testament thirty times, fourteen times in Paul's letters. Eight occurrences of συνείδησις are concentrated in the discussion of the meat offered to idols in 1 Corinthians 8 and 10. In addition Paul uses συνείδησις three more times each in 2 Corinthians and Romans. Moreover the verb σύνοιδα is found once in 1 Cor. 4:4. Thus one can say that Paul introduced the concept συνείδησις into Christian literature. The Old Testament has no linguistic equivalent for the Greek συνείδησις.[133] Yet לֵב ("heart") can take over corresponding functions. Thus the pounding of the heart can be regarded as the expression of a bad conscience (cf. 1 Sam. 24:5 [Hebrew 24:6]; 2 Sam. 24:10); the heart can be pure or defiled (*T. Jos.* 4.6a; *T. Benj.* 8.2); and the heart can accuse (Job 27:6). Paul probably adopted συνείδησις from Hellenistic popular philosophy, in which συνείδησις mostly means the awareness that one's own deeds are morally condemned or approved. Frequently the noun συνείδησις is followed by a genitive object, which clarifies the particular understanding of συνείδησις. Also in Paul the sense of συνείδησις comes not from the word itself but from the particular narrower or broader context.

The central text complex for ascertaining the meaning of συνείδησις in Paul is the conflict over meat sacrificed to idols in 1 Corinthians 8 and 10. Paul deals intensively with the relationship of the 'strong' and 'weak' in 8:7–13. With συνείδησις in this section he means neither a 'bad conscience'[134] nor 'conscience about God';[135] rather, συνείδησις appears here as the court of self-judgment. The object of judgment by the conscience is human behavior, which is checked for agreement with pregiven norms.[136] When the strong make use of the freedom appropriate to them to continue eating meat offered to idols, they lead the weak to behave likewise. In this way they bring the weak into conflict, for the latter now eat meat offered to idols even though this does not agree with their own will and self-understanding. The weak are pressured by the strong to abandon accepted norms and thereby fall into a conflict of conscience. Yet indirectly Paul is also addressing here the conscience of the strong. When they sin against their brothers and sisters, they likewise sin against Christ (1 Cor. 8:12). Christ

---

[133] Cf. H.-J. Eckstein, *Syneidesis*, pp. 105ff.
[134] R. Bultmann, *Theologie*, p. 217.
[135] W. Gutbrod, *Anthropologie*, p. 63.
[136] Cf. H.-J. Eckstein, *Syneidesis*, pp. 242–3.

also died for the weak (8:11), and thus the strong do not have the right through their behavior to lead the weak away from Christ. The freedom of the individual clearly has a boundary in the conscience of another person, which must not be burdened.

Paul continues the discussion with the strong in Corinth in 1 Cor. 10:25–29. Of central significance is the phrase διὰ τὴν συνείδησιν ('on the ground of conscience') in verses 25, and 27, which also appears in Rom. 13:5. In 1 Cor. 10:25, 27 Paul is speaking of the συνείδησις of the strong. Here again the intended meaning is the conscience as the court of self-judgment, the court within human beings that judges their behavior according to pregiven norms and particular decisions to see how it corresponds to these presuppositions. Paul assures the strong that conscience demands no inquiries in the buying of meat, for 'the earth and its fullness are the Lord's' (10:26). Even with an invitation from pagans Christians do not have to make inquiries; they can eat whatever is set before them.

Another possible situation is discussed by Paul in verse 28. A Gentile Christian, who is one of the weak in Corinth, warns against the consumption of sacrificed meat. In order not to burden this person's conscience, the strong should forgo the consumption of meat. This is made clear in verse 29, where Paul expressly emphasizes that he does not mean the conscience of the strong but the conscience of the weak, Gentile-Christian warner. Thus συνείδησις does not designate an affect, a condition of conscience or a religio-moral capability of judgment, but a court that judges the behavior of a person according to pregiven norms. The strong do not have to make inquiries about the provenance of meat either with purchases or with invitations by pagans, because for them there is only one God, who is the source of all being. They are acting in complete agreement with their own convictions, and thus their consciences are not burdened. They should surrender their own freedom only if a weak person points out to them that meat has been offered to idols and the weak person's conscience would be burdened by the consumption of this meat. Thus the apostle's argumentation in 1 Cor. 10:25–29 seems in complete agreement with 8:7–13.[137]

In 2 Cor. 1:12 Paul has to deal with reproaches from the Corinthian church regarding his person. Some complain that he

---

[137] Cf. ibid., p. 271.

is unreliable, that he changes his travel plans, and that one cannot trust him. 'Indeed, this is our boast, the testimony of our conscience: we have behaved in the world with frankness and godly sincerity, not by earthly wisdom but by the grace of God – and all the more toward you' (1:12). Paul brings in conscience as an independent witness for his statements, and here there are echoes of the original meaning of *conscience,* "to know with."[138] The apostle is telling the truth not only subjectively but also objectively, for conscience values the life transformation and missionary activity of Paul in the Corinthian church positively. The judgment of conscience is not made by God, but Paul traces the purity of his life transformation back to the grace of God.

In a similar way συνείδησις also appears in 2 Cor. 4:2: 'We have renounced the shameful things that one hides; we refuse to practice cunning or to falsify God's word; but by the open statement of the truth we commend ourselves to the conscience of everyone in the sight of God.' Paul opens himself to the decision of the Corinthians and appeals to their conscience as a human court of judgment. Here συνείδησις cannot be understood as the voice of God or an entity directly dependent on God, since ἐνώπιον τοῦ θεοῦ ("before God") relates to the commending, not to the *syneidesis.* Paul likewise appeals to the consciences of the Corinthians in 5:11: 'Therefore, knowing the fear of the Lord, we try to persuade others; but we ourselves are well known to God, and I hope that we are also well known to your consciences.' In his missionary work Paul submits himself to testing by God and the consciences of the Corinthians in the firm hope of being recognized as pure and honest. The *syneidesis* in this passage, exactly as in 4:2, is the court that has observed the behavior of Paul and his co-workers and is now summoned to judge and to test.

In Rom. 2:14–15 συνείδησις appears as a comprehensive anthropological phenomenon: 'When Gentiles, who do not possess the law, do instinctively what the law requires, these, though not having the law, are a law to themselves. They show that what the law requires is written on their hearts, to which their own conscience also bears witness; and their conflicting thoughts will accuse or perhaps excuse them.' For Paul it is a question in Rom. 1:18–3:20 of the negative equation of Jews and Gentiles before God: all have sinned and all are without the grace of God (cf. 3:20). In

[138] Cf. F. Lang, *Korintherbriefe,* p. 255.

order to achieve this argumentative aim, in Rom. 2:12–16 Paul concedes to the Gentiles a knowledge of the law. Like the Jews the Gentiles also had the possibility of living according to God's law; like the Jews the Gentiles also failed at the law. The *syneidesis* as a phenomenon characteristic of all people confirms the existence of the law even for Gentiles. Here conscience can be understood as the moral self-judgment of people, the knowledge of people about themselves and their behavior.[139] The conscience of the Gentiles, their consciousness of moral values, proves for Paul that the law of God was not given only to the Jews.

In Rom. 9:1–2 Paul emphatically asserts the truthfulness of his feelings: 'I am speaking the truth in Christ – I am not lying; my conscience confirms it by the Holy Spirit – I have great sorrow and unceasing anguish in my heart' (cf. also 2 Cor 1:23; 2:17; 11:38; 12:19). His sincere sorrow over his people is confirmed both by the ultimate authorities, by Christ and the Holy Spirit, and by his own conscience. He brings in the *syneidesis* as independent, personified witness for the truth of his following comments. Conscience once again verifies agreement between convictions and behavior.

In Rom. 13:5 there is a substantiation for the necessity of submission to state power:[140] 'Therefore one must be subject, not only because of wrath but also because of conscience.' Christians are supposed to subject themselves to authorities out of insight into the significance of power and order, not out of fear. Governmental authorities come from the will of God in that they resist evil and promote good. Yet it is not only the fear of possible anger and punishment by authority that should cause the Christian to submit but also conscience. Here as in Rom. 2:15 Paul is thinking of the conscience of each person, not of a specifically Christian conscience. Just one's responsibility with regard to the dispositions of God and the rational insight into the necessity of the ordering function of the state are enough to bring the conscience to affirm its existence.

In substantive continuity with the foregoing usage of συνείδησις is 1 Cor. 4:4, where Paul uses the verb σύνοιδα: 'I am not aware of anything against myself, but I am not thereby acquitted. It is the Lord who judges me.' Paul knows of no shortcoming in regard to

---

[139] Cf. D. Zeller, *Römer*, p. 70.
[140] Cf. for exegesis H.-J. Eckstein, *Syneidesis*, pp. 276–300.

the Corinthian church, but this self-judgment represents only a human, internal vote. The conscience cannot speak the final judgment; rather, it is only a judging but by no means justice-dispensing court. The conscience can err; as a purely anthropological entity it is relativized by God.

Paul understands συνείδησις as the neutral court for judging completed activity (reflexively and in regard to others) on the basis of internalized value standards. The conscience for Paul does not contain the principled knowledge of good and evil, but it judges and confirms as a neutral court, in which the verdict can turn out positive as well as negative.[141] Conscience is thus a relational concept; it does not itself set norms but judges conformity to them. Nor can the conscience be regarded as a peculiarity of Christians, pagans, or Jews; it is a general human phenomenon. The function of conscience is the same for all people, but the norms that form the presupposition for judgment can be quite different. On the basis of their norms and standards Christians judge their own behavior and that of others.

Of fundamental significance here is the renewal of the mind asserted by Paul in Rom. 12:2: 'Do not be conformed to this world, but be transformed by the renewing of your minds, so that you may discern what is the will of God – what is good and acceptable and perfect.' By νοῦς ("mind") the apostle means the rational knowledge to whose insights the conscience is also open. The gift of the Spirit appropriated in baptism works itself out concretely as the renewal of a person's reason. Reason led by the Holy Spirit orients itself not toward the idea of autonomy but toward the evident will of God and the resulting responsibility.[142]

For Paul, another fundamental Christian value standard, to which the conscience feels obligated, is the commandment of love. 'Owe no one anything, except to love one another; for the one who loves another has fulfilled the law' (Rom. 13:8). It is reason renewed by the Holy Spirit that knows love as the basic norm of Christian action and feels obligated to it (Gal. 6:2: 'Bear one another's burdens, and in this way you will fulfill the law of Christ'). Beyond this basic orientation of Christian existence Paul can name

---

[141] Cf. in this sense esp. ibid., pp. 311ff. Imprecise is U. Wilckens, *Römer* 1:138, who designates *syneidesis* as 'a person's inner court, which substantiates and safeguards his or her responsibility.'

[142] Cf. on the structure of the new life in Paul esp. W. Schrage, *Ethik*, pp. 191ff.

very concrete individual instructions, to which the conscience of a Christian orients itself. Thus he lists in the catalogs of vices and virtues (Gal. 5:16–18, 19–21, 22–26) all the things that on the one hand are impossible for a Christian and on the other are to be regarded as the hallmarks of his or her new life. Fornication, impurity, licentiousness, idolatry, sorcery, strife, and jealousy belong to the past for Christians; now their lives are determined by love, joy, peace, kindness, and faith. Christians practice hospitality (Rom. 12:13b); they bless their persecutors (12:14); they do not repay evil for evil (12:17a); they do not claim to be wise (12:16c); they do not avenge themselves but leave all vengeance to God (12:19). They feed their enemies (12:20a), for their rule of life is: 'Do not be overcome by evil, but overcome evil with good' (12:21). Finally, the responsibility of a person before conscience corresponds to the responsibility before God, although the two are not to be equated. From the will of God the conscience of Christians receives value standards according to which their own behavior or the behavior of others is judged. The conscience is thus not an absolute court but rather is dependent on the will of God for right judgments and receives only from God its significance for the life of the Christian.

3.12 Human Dignity: εἰκών in Paul

Paul takes up the concept of the εἰκών ("image, likeness, archetype") in various argumentative contexts. In the tradition of Hellenistic Judaism (cf. Wis. 14:27) he describes in Rom. 1:23[143] the foolishness of alleged wisdom: 'They exchanged the glory of the immortal God for images resembling a mortal human being or birds or four-footed animals or reptiles.' With εἰκών Paul is referring to the pagan world's manifold images of idols, which often had the form of animals. Those who considered themselves wise worshiped idols but not God. They created for themselves idols and thus abandoned their destiny as creatures. Human beings cannot tolerate being creatures; they themselves want to become creators of their own divinities. By exchanging the glory of the immortal God for the perishable products of their own making, they commit themselves at the same time to the realm of hubris:

---

[143] For a comprehensive interpretation cf. J. Jervell, *Imago Dei*, pp. 312–31.

they put themselves in God's place and let nothing matter but their own abilities.

The εἰκών concept in Paul achieves fundamental theological significance in his talk of Christ as the image of God. In 2 Cor. 4:4 the apostle explains[144] how the veiling of the gospel to the perishing came about: the god of this world has blinded them 'to keep them from seeing the light of the gospel of the glory of Christ, who is the image of God [ὅς ἐστιν εἰκὼν τοῦ θεοῦ].' The preaching of the gospel does not occur within a neutral field; rather, those who follow the gospel submit themselves thereby to the power of Christ; those who shut themselves off from him, to the power of Satan. The gospel reveals the glory of Christ, who is the image of God (cf. Col. 1:15). Here εἰκών appears equally as an ontological and relational concept: like God, Christ is according to his essence δόξα ("glory"); in the Son the true essence of the Father is revealed. In Jesus Christ, God is present; as a person he is the image of God. The glory of God can be known only in Jesus Christ as the face (πρόσωπον) of God turned toward us. For Paul, Jesus Christ is like God (Phil. 2:6), which brings to expression both his mode of existence and his position. At the same time he is the Son sent by the Father (cf. Rom. 8:3; Gal. 4:4), the Son who empties himself (Phil. 2:7) and assumes the fleshly form of a slave (Rom. 8:3) in order to reconcile God and human beings (2 Cor. 5:19–21).

Jewish wisdom theology forms the religious-historical background of the εἰκών concepts.[145] Thus wisdom (Wis. 7:25) is the pure emanation of the glory of the Almighty. 'For she is a reflection of eternal light, a spotless mirror of the working of God, and an image of his goodness' (Wis. 7:26c: καὶ εἰκὼν τῆς ἀγαθότητος αὐτοῦ). In Philo the Logos as Son of God is also the *eikon* of God, cf. *Fug.* 101: 'αὐτὸς [i.e., λόγος θεῖος] εἰκὼν ὑπάρχων θεοῦ ...'; see also *All.* 1.31–32; *Op.* 25; *Conf.* 62–63, 97.

All statements about the relationship of believers to the image of Christ are based on the concept of Christ as the image of God. In 1 Cor. 15:49 Paul stresses, *vis-à-vis* the Corinthians oriented toward a present concept of salvation, that they will not bear the image of the 'man of heaven' Jesus Christ until the end event. By

---

[144] Cf. here ibid., pp. 214–18.
[145] On the religious-historical references cf. comprehensively F. W. Eltester, *Eikon*, pp. 26–129; J. Jervell, *Imago Dei*, pp. 15–170.

contrast, the present is still determined by the 'man of dust,' Adam.[146]

If up until now believers were subjected to perishability, that will no longer be true in the resurrection because they will then participate in the eternal essence of Christ in that they will be stamped with the image of the resurrected Jesus Christ. Thus as a relational concept εἰκών designates the special relationship of believers to their Lord. According to Rom. 8:29, it is the aim of God's election that believers 'be conformed to the image of his Son, in order that he might be the firstborn within a large family.'

This event is completed in the resurrection of the believers, but at the same time it also has a present dimension: in baptism believers already participate in the essence of Christ as the image of God (Rom. 6:3–5), because they share in the work of salvation effected through Christ. Here, through the Holy Spirit, is the beginning of the salvific activity of God for humankind, which will reach its goal in the end event in the transformation of the σῶμα ψυχικόν ("physical body") into the σῶμα πνευματικόν ("spiritual body"). Then the believers will be fully shaped according to the image of their Lord, who as the archetype of the new being is the firstborn among many brothers and sisters. Substantively very close to Rom. 8:29 is 2 Cor. 3:18.[147] Through the work of the Spirit the believers see the glory of the resurrected One 'as though reflected in a mirror' and are thereby transformed into the image of their Lord. Divine glory in all its fullness rests on the resurrected One; he is thus both the archetype and the aim of the Christian's transformation. As the bearer of the likeness of the invisible God, the resurrected One releases a dynamic borne by the Spirit (cf. 2 Cor. 3:17) that results in the believers acquiring the same form as their Lord. Paul interprets this process not as a transformation of substance[148] but as a historical-eschatological event, for already at work in the lives of believers is that power of God that in the end event will fully reveal itself and prevail.

If the human image of God expressed in Gen. 1:26–27 already stands in the background in Rom. 8:29 and 2 Cor. 3:18, then in 1

---

[146] Cf. Chr. Wolff, *1. Korinther*, p. 203. The human image of God in creation is translated by Paul into the eschatological dimension of the new creation of humanity already present in the Spirit and completed at the parousia; cf. J. Eckert, 'Gottebenbildlichkeit des Menschen,' pp. 350ff.

[147] On the problems of 2 Cor. 3:18 cf. H.-J. Klauck, *2. Korinther*, pp. 41–2.

[148] Versus H. Windisch, *2. Korinther*, p. 129, who suspects here the influence of mystery concepts.

Cor. 11:7–8 Paul refers explicitly to this concept: 'For a man ought not to have his head veiled, since he is the image and reflection of God; but woman is the reflection of man. Indeed, man was not made from woman, but woman from man.' Here Paul is addressing the custom – apparently widespread in Corinth – of the participation of women in the worship service without covering their heads. It is probably a question of a new practice, unknown in other churches (cf. 1 Cor. 11:16), which possibly arose from the enthusiastic striving for emancipation in parts of the Corinthian church.[149] Paul uses creation theology to argue against this elimination of previous arrangements by basing the difference between man and woman and the practical consequences following therefrom on the man's being the image of God. The man shares the glory of God; he is the 'reflection' of God. By contrast, the woman is the 'reflection' of the man because she was formed from the man (cf. Gen. 2:22). In his interpretation of Gen. 1:27 Paul follows the Jewish exegesis of his day, in which the tension between the statements related to one person in Gen. 1:27a–b ('So God created man in his own image, in the image of God he created him' [RSV]) and 1:27c ('male and female he created them') is resolved in favor of the first two parts of the verse.[150] Serving as a substantive argument here is the indication that the divine image (of the man) is the topic only in verses 27a–b and not in relation to man and woman in 27c. This interpretation does not do justice to the original intention of Gen. 1:27, for אָדָם in Gen. 1:27a must be understood as a collective term for humankind. In this way verses 27a–b and 27c explain each other and must be seen as a substantive unit.[151] The divine image of humankind is not a gender-specific one but a gender-inclusive assertion.

In the relationship between God and Jesus Christ the εἰκών concept is to be comprehended as both an ontological and a relational term. In the relationship between Christ and believers, however, εἰκών always appears as a purely relational term. As εἰκών τοῦ θεοῦ ("image of God"; 2 Cor. 4:4) Christ draws believers into the historical process at the end of which their own transformation will stand. Only in relationship to Christ as the archetype will human beings be equal to their destiny as εἰκὼν τοῦ θεοῦ. Being

---

[149] Cf. Chr. Wolff, *1. Korinther*, pp. 70–1.
[150] For evidence cf. J. Jervell, *Imago Dei*, pp. 107–12.
[151] Cf. for interpretation of Gen. 1:27 esp. G. von Rad, *Genesis*, pp. 37ff.

human is not exhausted in pure creatureliness; rather, the Creator bestows on creatures the dignity to be and to live in accordance with his image. God constitutes human existence, and only in correspondence to God do human beings realize their created destiny as the image of God, a destiny that is revealed through faith in Jesus Christ as the archetype of God.

3.13 Centers of the Human Self: καρδία, ψυχή, νοῦς, ὁ ἔσω ἄνθρωπος

The innermost parts of a human being all described by Paul in a variety of ways. For him καρδία ("heart") seems to be the center of the human self. Through the Holy Spirit the love of God was poured into human hearts (Rom. 5:5). The Holy Spirit works in the heart. God sent the Spirit of his Son 'into our hearts' (Gal. 4:6) and in baptism gave the Spirit as an ἀρραβών ("first installment") 'in our hearts' (2 Cor. 1:22). Baptism leads to an obedience from the heart (Rom. 6:17); human beings stand in a new, salvation-bringing dependency relationship: they serve God and thus righteousness. There is a circumcision of the heart that is accomplished in the Spirit and not in the letter (Rom. 2:29), an inner transformation of a person from which arises a new relationship to God. The church in Corinth is a letter of Christ, 'written not with ink but with the Spirit of the living God, not on tablets of stone but on tablets of human hearts' (2 Cor. 3:3). Faith has its place in the heart; God sent the bright light of the knowledge of Jesus Christ into the heart (2 Cor. 4:6); the heart is strengthened by God (1 Thess. 3:13), and the peace of God, which surpasses all understanding, guards the hearts of believers (Phil. 4:7).[152] The heart can open or close itself to the saving message of faith in Jesus Christ (cf. 2 Cor. 3:14–16). Conversion and confession begin in the heart, for 'if you confess with your lips that Jesus is Lord and believe in your heart ... you will be saved. For one believes with the heart and so is justified ...' Here mouth and heart correspond on the one hand, as do the acts of confession and faith on the other; the whole person is affected by the saving Christ event.

---

[152] Both in Phil. 1:7–8 (φρονεῖν, "to think"; σπλάγχνα, "innard") and in Phil. 4:7 (νόημα, 'idea'; νοῦς, 'reason') Paul connects καρδία with Greek concepts.

Hence faith 'in the heart' is by no means a purely inner event but rather expresses itself in confession; it is thus an outward-oriented event. As the 'innermost' organ the heart defines the whole person. In both the positive and negative sense, it is the center of decisions of the will (1 Cor. 4:5). The heart knows the will of God (Rom. 2:15); it stands firm against the passions (1 Cor. 7:37) and is willing to support the needy (2 Cor. 9:7). At the same time, however, the heart can also be unwise and darkened (Rom. 1:21; 2:5); it is the source of lusts (1:24; 2:5) and the place of hardness (2 Cor. 3:14–15). God tests and probes the heart (1 Rom. 8:27; Thess. 2:4) and makes the leanings of the heart apparent (2 Cor. 4:5). The heart is the seat of feelings and emotions, the place of anguish (2 Cor. 2:4), of love (7:3), of openness (6:11), and of sincere desire (Rom. 9:2; 10:1). The especially good relationship of the apostle to the Philippians is revealed in the fact that he has them in his heart (Phil. 1:7). In contrast to his opponents Paul does not work with letters of recommendation. The Corinthian church is his letter of recommendation, 'written on our hearts, to be known and read by all' (2 Cor. 3:2). The opponents in 2 Corinthians boast in outward appearance, not in the heart (5:12); Paul fights for his church and requests of them, 'Make room in your hearts for us' (7:2). He opens his heart to the church (6:11) and assures it 'that you are in our hearts, to die together and to live together' (7:3). With καρδία Paul designates the interior of a person, the seat of understanding, emotion, and will, the place where the decisions of life are really made and God's activity for humankind begins through the Spirit.

In the use of καρδία Paul stands in the tradition of Old Testament anthropology.[153] The LXX mostly translates the Hebrew לֵב (ca. 850 times in the Old Testament) with καρδία. In the Old Testament the heart designates the dynamic middle of a person, one's innermost center. Settled here are willing, thinking, and longing (1 Sam. 16:7; Ps. 44:22; Prov. 15:11; 24:12; etc.). Thinking and reflection take place in the heart (Gen. 17:17; 1 Sam. 27:2; Job 34:10; Prov. 28:16; Hos. 7:2; etc.). The heart is the place of feelings, of sensitivity (1 Sam. 2:1; Pss. 13:6; 25:17; 104:15; Prov. 15:13; 17:22; 23:77; etc.). The rational capabilities of human beings, their reason (Job 8:10; Ps. 90:12; Prov. 15:14; 16:23; 18:15; etc.) and insight

---

[153] Cf. H. W. Wolff, *Anthropologie*, pp. 68ff.

(Deut. 29:3; Prov. 10:11; 18:15; Isa. 42:25; Jer. 11:8) are located in the heart. Obedience to God's word and love of God have their place in the heart (Deut. 6:5–6; 8:2; Prov. 7:3; Jer. 17:1; etc.). In the Old Testament understanding of καρδία we see a total view of humankind; people are seen from their center in all their aspects and capabilities.

Appearing relatively seldom (eleven times) in Paul is the term ψυχή ("life, human being"); in the LXX it is mostly the translation of נֶפֶשׁ. Paul also uses ψυχή to designate life in its entirety (Rom. 2:9) or every person (Rom. 13:1). Frequently ψυχή appears in the sense of "give one's life." Paul is ready to spend his life for the church (2 Cor. 12:15). Epaphroditus risks his life for the sake of Christ's work; he came close to death (Phil. 2:30). Prisca and Aquila risked their necks for Paul's life (Rom. 16:4). In 2 Cor. 1:23 Paul offers the Corinthians his life as a pledge that his calling on God as witness to his plans is true. In the quotation from 1 Kings 19:10, 14 in Rom. 11:3 the enemies of Elijah are seeking his life. Paul grants the Thessalonians a share in his life; he lets them participate in his gifts and his work (1 Thess. 2:8). In 1 Cor. 15:45a the first human being Adam in antithesis to Christ is designated a living *psyche* (ψυχὴ ζῶσα) and thus a perishable being. The natural person (ψυχικὸς ἄνθρωπος) is incapable of perceiving the works of God through the Spirit (1 Cor. 2:14). Parallel to ἐν ἑνὶ πνεύματι ("in one spirit") in Phil. 1:27 is μιᾷ ψυχῇ in the sense of "as one person, unanimous."

A special problem in Pauline anthropology is brought up by 1 Thess. 5:23: 'May the God of peace himself sanctify you entirely; and may your spirit and soul and body be kept sound and blameless at the coming of our Lord Jesus Christ.' The trichotomous sounding phrase τὸ πνεῦμα καὶ ἡ ψυχὴ καὶ τὸ σῶμα reflects no Hellenistic anthropology according to which a person is divided into body, soul, and spirit. Paul is merely emphasizing that the sanctifying work of God concerns the whole person. This interpretation is suggested both by the adjectives ὁλοτελής ("complete") and ὁλόκληρος ("entire, intact") and by the observation that in 1 Thessalonians πνεῦμα is for Paul not a component of the human essence but the expression and sign of the new creative activity of God in humankind. With ψυχή and σῶμα Paul is only adding what constitutes each person as an individual. What is actually new and determinative is the Spirit of God.[154] With

---

[154] Cf. T. Holtz, *1. Thessalonicher*, p. 265.

his use of ψυχή Paul stands in Old Testament tradition, where נֶפֶשׁ designates the whole person.[155] Human beings are not the sum of their body parts; rather, the totality can be concentrated in one part.

The Hebrew language has no equivalent for νοῦς ("thinking, reason, being, mind"), a central concept of Hellenistic anthropology. Paul uses νοῦς in 1 Cor. 14:14–15 in his comments on glossolalia as the critical authority *vis-à-vis* uncontrolled and incomprehensible speaking in tongues. In Paul's understanding glossolalia by itself is inadequate, for in it the mind is turned off, and the church gains nothing (14:14). For Paul prayer and praise occur equally in the divine Spirit and in the human mind (14:15). In 14:19 νοῦς means the clear understanding in which the church is instructed: 'In church I would rather speak five words with my mind ... than ten thousand words in a tongue.' Also in Phil. 4:7 νοῦς designates rational understanding, the human power of comprehension, which is surpassed by the peace of God. In 1 Cor. 1:10 Paul appeals to the unity of the Corinthian church; it should be of one mind and one opinion. In 1 Cor. 2:16 and Rom. 11:34 Paul speaks of the νοῦς of Χριστός or of the κύριος, which in each case means the Holy Spirit, who is beyond human judgment.[156] In the disagreement between the 'strong' and the 'weak' in Romans Paul urges both parties to be sure of their own judgment and thus of their own concern (Rom. 14:5). According to Rom. 7:23 the law in the members and the law of the mind are in conflict. The latter, the νόμος τοῦ νοός, corresponds substantively to the νόμος τοῦ θεοῦ ("law of God") in 7:22: the person oriented toward God. With his mind he wants to serve God, but the sin dwelling in him brings this wanting to naught. In Rom. 12:2 Paul admonishes the church not to accommodate itself to the sinful and passing aeon but to allow a transformation of their entire existence itself, which occurs as a renewing of the νοῦς.[157] Paul uses νοῦς here to designate the rational knowledge and thought that through the work of the Spirit receive a new orientation. Christians receive a new power of judgment and capability of judgment that put them in a position to test what God's will is. Humankind can know God's invisible essence, because God has turned toward humankind and revealed

---

[155] Cf. H. W. Wolff, *Anthropologie*, pp. 25–48.
[156] Cf. F. Lang, *Korintherbriefe*, p. 47.
[157] Fundamental here is the interpretation of E. Käsemann, *Römer*, pp. 313–19.

himself (Rom. 1:19). Reason cannot renew itself by itself; it is dependent on the intervention of God. God takes human reason into his service and thereby leads it to its true destiny.[158]

Thus in Paul faith and reason are not opposites; the Christian is led by reason that is renewed by the Holy Spirit. Faith does not hinder reasonable knowledge but makes it possible in a comprehensive sense. According to Rom. 1:28 God gave a 'debased mind' to all those who have pushed him out of their lives and do not want to know him. Thus God puts people in the life situation that they determine for themselves. Again we see that for Paul the νοῦς does not rest in itself and is not at the disposal of the autonomous person as a means of self-realization; rather, it knows its orientation and worth only from God. Outside of faith the νοῦς loses its possibilities and its goal.

The distinction between the ἔξω ἄνθρωπος ("outer person") and ἔσω ἄνθρωπος ("inner person") is adopted by Paul from Hellenistic philosophy.[159] Here ἔσω ἄνθρωπος designates the actual, intellectual person, who can distinguish the essential from the non-essential, who lives in discipline, free from affects, and makes him- or herself independent of external events. By contrast the ἔξω ἄνθρωπος is held captive by the senses of the external world, so that he or she is ruled as a result by passions and anxiety. Thus the Jewish-Hellenistic philosopher of religion, Philo, says: 'The person who lives in the soul of each one ... convinces us from within' (*Det.* 23; cf. also *Congr.* 97; *Plant.* 42; *Agr.* 8–9; *Prob.* 111). In Seneca we read:

> When you see a person unafraid in danger, untouched by passions, fortunate in misfortune, relaxed in the middle of storms, observing people from a higher plane, on the same [plane as] the gods, will you not be overcome by awe of him? Will you not say: Is this being not greater and nobler than one could assume appropriate for this feeble body in which it is found? A divine power has placed itself therein ...
> (*Ep.* 41.4–5; cf. also *Ep.* 71.27; 102.27 and Epictetus *Diss.* 2.7.3)

In contrast to Hellenistic anthropology, in Paul the distinction between the ἔσω ἄνθρωπος and the ἔξω ἄνθρωπος is not conceived

---

[158] This fundamental aspect is too little considered by G. Bornkamm, 'Glaube und Vernunft bei Paulus,' p. 137, who holds that 'the call, to be reasonable and prudent is for Paul synonymous with the demand for the renewal of the mind, the ἀνακαίνωσις τοῦ νοός (Rom. 12:2).'

[159] The starting point of the concept is Plato *Rep.* 9.588A–589B. For the history of research cf. R. Jewett, *Anthropological Terms*, pp. 391–5.

as an anthropological dualism. Instead, the apostle considers the one existence of believers from different perspectives.[160] In Rom. 7:22 the ἔσω ἄνθρωπος joyfully agrees with the will of God; thus such people live in agreement with themselves; they are what they always should be. Yet the power of sin distorts the actual existence of believers; in their striving toward the good, they are subject to the 'law of sin' in their members. Following the catalog of hardships in 2 Cor. 4:8–9 Paul says in 4:16: 'So we do not lose heart. Even though our outer nature [ὁ ἔξω ἄνθρωπος] is wasting away, our inner nature is being renewed day by day.' Outwardly the apostle is worn down by the many sufferings in his missionary work. At the same time, however, in the ἔξω ἄνθρωπος the δόξα θεοῦ ("glory of God"; cf. 2 Cor. 4:15, 17) is at work through the Spirit. In the innermost part of their beings believers know that they are determined by the Lord who is present in the Spirit and who strengthens and renews them. Therefore they are in a position to endure the external sufferings and afflictions, because they share in the living power of the resurrected One and in this way overcome the oppressions and the deterioration of the body.[161] With ἔσω ἄνθρωπος Paul is designating the actual 'I' of the person, which is open to the will of God and the working of the Spirit.[162]

3.14 God's Action and Human Deeds: Justification as a Christological and Anthropological Phenomenon

In the Pauline doctrine of justification in Galatians and Romans there is a concentration of christological and anthropological motifs.[163] In the center of the doctrine of justification is the question

---

[160] Cf. W. Gutbrod, *Anthropologie*, pp. 85–92.

[161] On the differences between Rom. 7:22 and 2 Cor. 4:16 cf. R. Bultmann, *Theologie*, p. 204.

[162] Bultmann, ibid., and H. Conzelmann, *Grundriss*, p. 203, do not do justice to the meaning of ἔσω ἄνθρωπος in Paul when they speak of a purely formal concept.

[163] An elaborated doctrine of justification in Paul cannot be demonstrated until Galatians and Romans (and Philippians); he developed it in the last period of his missionary activity in the East; cf. U. Wilckens, *Christologie und Anthropologie*, pp. 67ff. Less convincing is J. Becker, *Paul*, p. 289, who repeats the old thesis without text analysis and without reference to the secondary literature: 'Thus the Corinthian theology of the cross is a precondition of the apostle's Galatian position.' In this argumentation the doctrine of justification of Galatians and

of the soteriological significance of the law in view of the revelation in Christ. For a long time in Paul's missionary work there was a relatively unproblematic co-existence of freedom from the law as the foundation of the Gentile mission and an understood validity of the Torah as an ethical norm, as 1 Thessalonians and the Corinthian letters show.[164]

A new situation was brought about by the demand of the Judaizers in Galatia that the Gentiles also be circumcised (Gal. 5:3, 11–12; 6:12–13). For Paul the gospel revealed to him by God was now at risk (1:6ff.; 1:11ff.), because both the requirement of circumcision and calendar observances gave the law a soteriological significance and thus in Paul's view diminished the significance of the Christ event. The apostle's theological point of departure is exclusively the recognition that God revealed his salvific will finally and solely in Jesus Christ and that only faith in the salvific work of Jesus Christ brings salvation. 'For if justification [or: righteousness] comes through the law, then Christ died for nothing' (2:21).

For Paul there is no coexistence of faith in Christ and the requirement of circumcision, because circumcision as a *pars pro toto legis* requires the keeping of the whole law (cf. Gal. 5:3) and the law would thus receive a constitutive significance for divine-human relations. Moreover, faith in Jesus Christ and the requirement of circumcision combine two totally different anthropological points of departure. The way to salvation that is oriented toward the law allots to human beings an active role in their relationship with God: they always live their lives with the judging God in mind; human deeds appear as a fundamental, positive component of the God relationship. Without doubt, in ancient Judaism there was a basic conviction that human beings as sinners are dependent on the mercy, kindness, and love of God (cf., e.g., 1QS 11.9–12; 4 Ezra 8:32, 36). The idea of the covenant as a central form of expression of Israel's relationship with God begins with a prior election by God.[165] Nevertheless, the question of salvation remained bound to human activity, in that God as the righteous Judge was expected to have mercy on the righteous and punished the lawbreakers.

Romans is simply equated with the apostle's other points of view (cf. in this sense from the older literature, for example, P. Feine, *Theologie*, pp. 234ff.).

[164] Cf. U. Wilckens, *Gesetzesverständnis*, p. 158.

[165] Based on the idea of the covenant, E. P. Sanders, *Paul and Palestinian Judaism*, pp. 33–428, interprets in a one-sided way almost the entire literature of ancient Judaism.

Faithful is the Lord to those who love him in truth, who endure his correction, who walk in the righteousness of his commandments, in the law that he imposes on us for our lives. The godly of the Lord will live by it forever; the pleasure garden of the Lord, the trees of life are his godly ones. Their planting is rooted for eternity; they will not be pulled up all the days of heaven, for God's portion and inheritance is Israel. But not so the sinners and lawbreakers, who love the day in their participation in their sin, in the baseness of the corruption of their desires, and they do not think of God. For the ways of humankind are at all times known to him, and the chambers of the heart he knows before they come into being. Therefore their inheritance is the kingdom of the dead, darkness, and destruction, and they will not be found on the day of mercy for the righteous. But the godly of the Lord will inherit life in joy.

(Ps. Sol. 14)[166]

This Pharisaic text,[167] which originated in the middle of the first century BC, can be regarded as representative of a thinking that sees the righteousness of God in his just judicial activity (cf. for the first century AD, e.g., 4 Ezra 7:70–74; 7:105). This judicial activity occurs as mercy toward the righteous and rejection of the godless, in which the keeping of the Torah forms the substantive criterion for the anticipated activity of God.[168] Thus the relationship with God is defined by the deeds of people, not in an exclusive sense, to be sure, but probably in a fundamentally positive sense. With this the contradiction between orthodoxy and orthopraxy, presupposed in texts such as Romans 2; Mt 6:1–6, 16–18, was tendentially established.

---

[166] This quotation from the *Psalms of Solomon* follows the German translation of S. Holm-Nielsen.

[167] For analysis cf. J. Schüpphaus, *Die Psalmen Salomos*, pp. 59–60. On the theology of the *Psalms of Solomon* and their origin, cf. ibid., pp. 83–158.

[168] According to E. P. Sanders, *Paul and Palestinian Judaism*, p. 393, also in the *Psalms of Solomon* 'the salvation of the righteous is due not to their own merits, but purely to the mercy of God, who chose them and who forgives them.' In view of *Pss. Sol.* 9; 13; 15; 16, this judgment corresponds not to the textual evidence in the *Psalms of Solomon* but only to Sanders' overall conception. Pertinent here is the examination of the textual evidence by H. Braun, 'Vom Erbarmen Gottes über den Gerechten,' p. 47, who ascertains that the idea 'that God accepts sinners for his own sake' is foreign to the *Psalms of Solomon*. They are marked by a 'dialectic of self-confidence and faith in God' (p. 56).

In the light of the revelation in Christ, Paul judges the human situation fundamentally differently from his Jewish contemporaries. Outside of faith, human beings find themselves still in the situation of enslavement; they are ὑπὸ νόμον ("under the law," Gal. 3:23), ὑπὸ παιδαγωγόν ("under a disciplinarian," 3:25), ὑπὸ ἐπιτρόπους... καὶ οἰκονόμους ("under guardians and trustees," 4:2), and ὑπὸ τὰ στοιχεῖα τοῦ κόσμου ("under the elemental spirits of the world," 4:3). This basic anthropological perception from the perspective of faith excludes a fundamental significance of deeds for the God relationship. On their own, human beings are not at all in a position to shape the God relationship in a positive way. The power of sin also controls and qualifies the law: 'We know that a person is justified not by the works of the law but through faith in Jesus Christ. And we have come to believe in Christ Jesus, so that we might be justified by faith in Christ, and not by doing the works of the law, because no one will be justified by the works of the law' (Gal. 2:16). Added to this is the inferior provenance of the law (3:19) and its temporal and thus also substantive distance from the promise (3:15–18).

For Paul the scripture itself attests that righteousness comes from faith alone. Thus about Abraham it says: 'Abraham believed God, and it was reckoned to him as righteousness' (Gen. 15:6 LXX in Rom. 4:3; cf. Gal. 3:6). Because of his exemplary behavior, his faithfulness, and his faith, the figure of Abraham was of great significance for all of ancient Judaism.[169] His was the election of God (cf. also 4 Ezra 3:13ff.); he was regarded not only as the father of Israel but also the father of proselytes. Abraham followed the law even before it was written (cf. Gen. 26:5; *2 Apoc. Bar.* 57). God tested him more than once and regarded him as faithful and righteous (cf. Sir. 44:20). The sacrifice of Isaac in particular was regarded as an extraordinary act of faithfulness and righteousness and was interpreted in 1 Macc. 2:52 with Gen. 15:6 LXX: 'Was not Abraham found faithful when tested, and it was reckoned to him as righteousness?' (cf. also Jas .2:23).

Here righteousness appears as the calculation of a merit (cf. here *Jub.* 30.17–23), but Paul interprets Gen. 15:6 LXX so that God's calculation is not tied to human conditions.[170] For Paul everything depends on the sovereign act of God. There are no requirements

---

[169] On this cf. K. Berger, 'Abraham,' pp. 372–82.
[170] On the adoption of Gen. 15:6 LXX by Paul cf. esp. D.-A. Koch, *Die Schrift als Zeuge*, pp. 221–6.

vis-à-vis God but only taking hold of the promise in faith. That is exactly what Abraham does, for against all experience he trusts the promise of God that his descendants will be as numerous as the stars. Thus Abraham stands for a human attitude regarding God that renounces one's own claims and hopes for everything from God alone. For Paul the prophets also witness to the righteousness that comes from faith. In contrast to the Jewish tradition of his time (cf. 1QpHab 7:17; 8:1) and in tension with the original wording ('the righteous, because of his faithfulness, will live') and sense of the text, Paul does not relate Hab. 2:4 in Gal. 3:11b and Rom. 1:17 ('the one who is righteous through faith will live' [NRSV alternate reading]) to the conscious obedience of the laws from which righteousness follows.[171] Rather, for Paul righteousness comes only as a consequence of the righteousness of God given in faith. The foundation of salvation is the same for all people, Jews and Gentiles: the revelation of God in Jesus Christ. Before God there is no partiality (Rom. 2:11); Jews and Gentiles alike run afoul of the law (Rom. 1:18–2:29), because all are under sin (Rom. 3:9b, 23).

With the revelation in Christ the situation of humankind before God changed fundamentally, because now both God's will to salvation and humankind's need for and possibility of salvation are finally evident. For the Christian Paul, the situation of humankind before God shows itself to be completely new: the question of salvation was answered once and for all by the death and resurrection of Jesus Christ; human beings are righteous out of faith in Jesus Christ and have peace with God (Rom. 5:1).

In this way all past, present, and future efforts of humankind to achieve salvation from other sources or to realize it themselves become insignificant (Phil. 3:7: 'Yet whatever gains I had, these I have come to regard as loss because of Christ'). The transformation of time and the new existence of humankind are likewise based on the Christ event. By interpreting the righteousness of God as a gift (cf. Rom. 1:17; 3:21–22; 10:3),[172] and not as a demand, Paul separates the question of salvation from human activity. The truth has the character not of deed but event.[173] People no longer live

---

[171] Cf. here ibid., pp. 275ff., 289ff.

[172] Cf. H. Lietzmann, *Römer*, p. 95.

[173] To the point here is H. Weder, 'Gesetz und Sünde,' p. 370: 'The question is whether my truth is something to perceive, to observe, to hear, and to believe or something that only becomes apparent in what I make of myself.'

out of themselves (2 Cor. 5:15b: 'that those who live might live no longer for themselves'); they owe their new lives to the dying of Christ – a process that is of great significance for relationships to God and to the world as well as for human self-understanding. God alone, through his salvific activity in Jesus Christ, changed the situation of human beings, who now in faith find access to God.

Thus human beings now stand before God as recipients of an unearned gift; they no longer have to realize their salvation in the world to approach God. Rather, as people justified in faith who come from God, they can do God's will in the world. In Paul justification always designates God's prior activity. God has already acted in Jesus Christ, before human beings begin to act. This prior activity of God is strictly separated and distinguished by Paul from the always subsequent deeds of people. Only this foregoing deed of God creates salvation and meaning for human beings. They are thereby relieved of the impossible task of having to create meaning and salvation themselves. Human life receives a new destiny; people become free for tasks they can accomplish. And before God they are not the sum of their deeds; they are distinguishable from their works. Human essence is not defined by doing but only by relationship with God.

The solo activity of God does not, however, exclude human activity. Rather, in Christian existence God lays claim to the activity of people in the power of the Holy Spirit. But the activity of God and the deeds of humankind are not reversible or exchangeable, 'for it is God who is at work in you, enabling you both to will and to work for his good pleasure' (Phil. 2:13). In Pauline theology Christology is the constant; anthropology is the variable.[174] The self-understanding of the believer is not identical with faith as a gift of God; there is a fundamental difference between the reality of the salvific activity of God in Jesus Christ and the human experience or interpretation of this event.[175] God's deed alone

---

[174] Versus H. Braun, 'Der Sinn der neutestamentlichen Christologie,' p. 272, who asserts that for Paul 'the anthropology is the constant; the Christology, by contrast, is the variable.' R. Bultmann, 'Das Verhältnis der urchristlichen Christusbotschaft,' p. 463, expressly agrees with this thesis: 'The constant is the self-understanding of the believer; Christology is the variable.' For a justified criticism of this conception cf. U. Wilckens, 'Christologie und Anthropologie,' pp. 67ff.

[175] Versus H. Braun, 'Die Problematik einer Theologie des Neuen Testaments,' p. 341, whose total anthropologization of theology logically leads to the

establishes salvation, not human understanding or doing. God's reality and human self-realization are not identical. When people confuse the two, they miss God and their own existence.

assertion that 'the human being as human being, the human being in his fellow humanity, implies God. Based on the New Testament, that would be discoverable ever anew. God would then be a certain kind of fellow humanity.' Here human beings are again left to their own devices.

4

Johannine Anthropology

4.1 The Human Realization of God and the Self-realization of Human Beings: Incarnation in John

The starting point and center of Johannine thought is the incarnation of God in Jesus Christ. We find it already in the middle of the Johannine prologue, which, as the programmatic opening text, prejudices the understanding of the entire Gospel.[1] Jn 1:1–4 speaks of the Logos being initially with God, his identity with God, his mediation in creation, and the presence of life in the Logos as light for humankind.

Found here are two central assertions of Johannine anthropology: human beings are creatures of the Logos (1:3) and thus in their origin are shaped by the Logos.[2] For John there is an original determination of humankind by the Word of God, for life as a specific sign of the human essence is an attribute of the Logos (1:4). The Logos appears as the light that 'was the light of all people' (1:4b, 9b). Human beings are not themselves the light; rather, they encounter the light and find themselves already illuminated by this light. Their whole existence is essentially shaped by the Logos, who calls them into life and as the epitome of life and true light grants them their existence. In the Logos life is present; he is the place of life, and only the light of the Logos illuminates the lives of human beings. Human vitality is understood by John as the reflection of the light that belonged to the Logos from the beginning. The Logos wants to illuminate the lives of human beings; he moves toward humankind. This movement of the Logos shapes the whole prologue.[3] The Logos appears in the

---

[1] Cf. on Jn 1:1–18 U. Schnelle, *Antidoketische Christologie*, pp. 231–47.
[2] Cf. J. Blank, 'Der Mensch,' p. 151.
[3] Cf. H. Weder, 'Der Mythos vom Logos,' p. 53.

darkness (1:5); he comes into the world (1:9c), to what is his own (1:11), and gives people the power to be children of God (1:12–13).

In Jn 1:14a the movement of the turning of the Logos toward the world reaches its goal: καὶ ὁ λόγος σὰρξ ἐγένετο ('and the Word became flesh'). The Logos wants to be close to humankind so much that he himself becomes human. The Creator himself becomes a creature; the light for human beings becomes a human being. In the Gospel of John σάρξ designates the creaturely human being made of flesh (cf. 1:13; 3:6; 6:51–56; 6:63; 8:15; 17:2) and blood, the 'pure humanity.' The Logos is now what he was not before: a true and real human being.[4] The event of the incarnation of the pre-existent Logos likewise contains an assertion of identity and essence: the Logos who was with God in the beginning became really and truly human. Although time and history owe their existence to God and the Logos, the Logos really entered time and history without being absorbed by them. He submitted himself to the historicalness of all earthly being without becoming subject to it. Verse 14b ('and lived among us') stresses the bodily presence of the pre-existent Logos among human beings. The Logos not only became human but also lived as a human being 'among us,' which is confirmed by the circle of the first witnesses from Andrew to Thomas.

At the same time, however, even in the incarnation the Logos remained what he was from the beginning: the Son of God. The Johannine community looks at the human being Jesus of Nazareth and sees in him the glory of God (1:14c–d: 'and we have seen his glory, the glory as of a father's only son'). This seeing comprises the true essence of Jesus: he was with the Father before all time, he reveals himself precisely in his humanity as Son of God, and after glorification in death and resurrection he will again be with the Father. The experience of the presence of the glory of God in the incarnate Word gives life that is not accessible to humankind and can be received only as grace.

If the prologue of John describes the event of the incarnation of the life-giving Logos, then the rest of the Gospel unfolds the way of the Logos among human beings and considers the salvific significance of the Logos Jesus Christ.[5] From the beginning in

---

[4] Versus E. Käsemann, *Jesu letzter Wille* , p. 28, who claims to see in Jn 1:14a only the 'contact with the earthly.'

[5] Concerning the relationship prologue-Gospel see Y. Ibuki, *Wahrheit*, pp. 177–8: 'The beginning determines the whole. This corresponds to the Johannine idea that origin forms the determination of essence.'

John, Jesus' activity is also seen from the perspective of the cross.[6]

Already in Jn 1:29 and 36 John the Baptist says of Jesus: 'Here is the Lamb of God.' John places the cleansing of the temple at the beginning of Jesus' public activity (2:14–22) in order thus to underscore the salvific significance of cross and resurrection. He who has life and is life gives his life for those who are his: 'I am the good shepherd. The good shepherd lays down his life for the sheep' (10:11; cf. 10:15, 17). Love does not hold fast to life: 'No one has greater love than this, to lay down one's life for one's friends' (15:13). The incarnate One is none other than the crucified One, who through his self-sacrifice on the cross makes life possible for those who are his. Therefore John can say precisely to the suffering Jesus Christ: ἰδοὺ ὁ ἄνθρωπος ('Here is the man!'; 19:5). Here the paradox of the incarnation of the pre-existent One is intensified in the extreme. On the surface Jesus appears to be the king of fools, yet he is the true king. He is pure humanity. He creates room for life through his self-sacrifice as the living Word. Also in John's Gospel the revelation reaches its goal at the cross. Here the incarnate Logos speaks: τετέλεσται ('It is finished'; 19:30).

For John everything depends on the identification of the pre-existent and incarnate One with the crucified and exalted One, as the Thomas pericope (20:24–29) documents in an almost tangible way. The one who died so shamefully on the cross was exalted by God and is the living Word of God. If believers remain in the Word Jesus Christ, they will participate in his abundant life. When they receive the love of the Son of God, they become true human beings themselves and thus become human to each other. The human realization of God in Jesus Christ, as the revelation of the glory of life, of truth and grace in the Word, makes possible for John the self-realization of human beings in the way of love.

If the cross is the concrete form of Jesus' love for his people, then foot washing is the act that corresponds to Jesus' deed.[7] In Jn 13:1 ('Now before the festival of the Passover, Jesus knew that his hour had come to depart from this world and go to the Father. Having loved his own who were in the world, he loved them to the

---

[6]   On the significance of the cross in Johannine theology cf. H. Kohler, *Kreuz und Menschwerdung;* M. Hengel, 'Schriftauslegung,' pp. 271ff.; P. Bühler, 'Ist Johannes ein Kreuzestheologe.'

[7]   Cf. here the interpretation of H. Kohler, *Kreuz und Menschwerdung,* pp. 192–229.

end') Jesus himself defines his 'hour' as an act of love, and with it he connects cross and foot washing.

In both cases the everlasting love of the incarnate One is revealed; ἀγάπη ("love") determines Jesus' relationship with his own. The paradoxical form of this love is recounted in Jn 13:4–5: the washing of the servants' feet by the master. Love characterizes not only the being and essence of Jesus; in the foot washing love assumes concrete form and becomes the defining event. In the recipients the surprising role reversal evokes misunderstanding and even consternation (13:6–10a). Peter energetically rejects Jesus' action; he cannot comprehend that Jesus' lordship is accomplished and perfected precisely in serving. In the foot washing Jesus comes to human beings and effects their purity (13:10). A reversal occurs: both in ancient Judaism and in the pagan cults it is human beings who through their own behavior produce purity and thus the prerequisite for meeting God, but here God himself comes to people and makes them pure. Human beings do not have to and cannot contribute anything. In this way human existence is converted by God into a new quality that is achieved in abiding in Jesus and thus in abiding in the Word (15:4, 7).

This new existence is realized in correspondence to Jesus' deed in the foot washing. 'So if I, your Lord and Teacher, have washed your feet, you also ought to wash one another's feet' (13:14). Jesus' deed contains within it the disciples' obligation to do likewise. 'For I have set you an example, that you also should do as I have done to you' (13:15).

Jesus' deed here is both archetype and example for human action. If Jesus were exclusively the example, human beings would again be left to their own abilities in that they would have to emulate his example as best as they could. This would run counter to the movement of God's prevenient love. Human beings cannot imitate Jesus, because Jesus' deed alone is the basis of human existence and human action. This special quality of Jesus' deed is revealed in 13:15 in the double substantiation with γάρ ("for") and καθώς ("as"). The disciples cannot imitate Jesus, for he is going to a place where they cannot go (13:36b).

They can, however, join the love movement initiated by God and in it be in accord with Jesus. 'I give you a new commandment, that you love one another. Just as I have loved you, you also should love one another' (13:34). The commandment of brotherly love as the central ethical instruction of the Johannine school (cf. Jn 15:9–10; 1 Jn 2:7–11; 4:10, 19; 2 Jn 4–7) clearly reveals the relationship of indicative (= divine activity toward human beings) and imperative (= resulting activity of human beings): as Jesus loved his own in his archetypal and exemplary activity, even in the self-sacrifice of death (15:13), so also his own are to love one another.[8] Thus the love of Jesus that becomes evident in the foot washing appears as a foreshadowing of the crucifixion event. It is the presupposition and enabling of the disciples' service of love. At the same time Jesus' deed becomes the substantial norm of the disciples' deeds. Foot washing was a humble service counted among the duties of slaves, a concrete and also dirty activity[9] that was in no way only a liturgical or symbolic act. Jesus gives his disciples a paradigm of Christian existence and conduct of life; he inducts them into the loving activity of God, which opens up for them a new existence in brotherly love. Incarnation, foot washing, and cross are equally movements of love downward into the depths of human existence. Thus Johannine theology is shaped by the idea of the divine assuming form:[10] in Jesus Christ, God really became human and made true human existence possible.[11]

4.2 The Enabling of the New Life: Faith in John

No other New Testament author reflected as intensively on the nature of faith as the evangelist John. Even the linguistic evidence is significant. In John the verb πιστεύειν ("believe") occurs eighty-eight times, compared to eleven times in Matthew, fourteen in Mark, and eight in Luke. In the majority of cases πιστεύειν occurs with εἰς ("in"), which reveals a fundamental trait of the Johannine understanding of faith: the linking of faith with the person Jesus Christ.[12]

For John faith in Jesus Christ means at the same time believing 'his word' (4:41, 50; 5:24), believing Moses and the scripture, who

---

[8] On the love commandment in the Johannine writings cf. G. Strecker, *Johannesbriefe*, pp. 328–33.

[9] Cf. the texts in Str-B 2:557; also *Jos. As.* 7.1; 20.2–5.

[10] H. Weder, 'Die Menschwerdung Gottes,' p. 352, rightly emphasizes 'that the decisive conceptual initiative of John's Gospel is the incarnation.'

[11] Here there is no equating of redeemer and redeemed, which fundamentally distinguishes John from gnostic systems; cf. K. W. Tröger, *Ja oder Nein zur Welt*, p. 74: 'Human beings do not have the light in themselves; they themselves are not the light (1:8!) but can only "grasp" (1:5) it.'

[12] Cf. F. Hahn, 'Glaubensverständnis,' pp. 56–7.

witness to Jesus (5:46–47), and above all believing the one who sent him (cf. 5:24; 6:29; 11:42; 12:44; 17:8). The unity of Father and Son forms the basis of the Johannine understanding of faith: 'The Father and I are one' (10:30). Jesus appears as *the* representative of God; 'Whoever sees me sees him who sent me' (12:45), and 'Whoever has seen me has seen the Father' (14:9). Therefore Jesus can also say: 'Believe in God, believe also in me' (14:1b). Faith in God and faith in Jesus Christ are identical because Jesus Christ is the Son of God. The whole Gospel of John was written 'so that you may come to believe that Jesus is the Messiah, the Son of God, and that through believing you may have life in his name' (20:31).[13] In the Gospel of John faith in Jesus is faith in the God who reveals himself in the sending of Jesus.

In John *seeing* (ὁρᾶν) and *knowing* (γινώσκειν) appear as structural elements of faith. Even the prologue shows that for the evangelist the incarnation of the pre-existent Logos and 'seeing' the δόξα ("glory") belong inseparably together. The incarnation is thus not the surrender of the glory; rather, it is precisely in the incarnation of the Logos and in the earthly activity of Jesus that God's glory becomes evident.

Within the earthly activity of Jesus it is above all in the miracles that he reveals his *doxa*, his glory. For John the miracles of Jesus have revelatory character. The *doxa* of the Son,[14] bestowed by the Father before the foundation of the cosmos (17:5b–c, 24c–d; 12:41) and visible in the incarnation of the pre-existent One (1:14a–b), is manifested in the miracles (2:11; 11:4, 40) and perfected on the cross, in order to return to the one *doxa* with the Father (17:1b, 5, 10b, 22, 24c). Already in the miracle of the wine at Cana the *doxa* of Jesus becomes evident (2:11), and the last and greatest miracle serves exclusively the glorification of the Son (11:4) and the revelation of the *doxa* of the Father (11:40). It is hardly coincidental that the evangelist interprets the first and last miracle of Jesus with the *doxa* concept, for in this way Jesus' entire working of miracles appears as a repeated revelation of the *doxa*.[15] The miracles are manifestations of the *doxa* of Jesus, but here John uses *doxa* in the

---

[13] Jn 1:1–18 and 20:31 are both instructions for reading that are supposed to lead the reader or hearer of the Gospel to the correct understanding; on the interpretation of Jn 20:31 cf. F. Neugebauer, *Entstehung*, pp. 10–20.

[14] Still basic for understanding δόξα in John is W. Thüsing, *Die Erhöhung und Verherrlichung Jesu im Johannesevangelium*.

[15] Cf. here U. Schnelle, *Antidoketische Christologie*, pp. 182–5.

revelation-theological sense in connection with Jesus' public activity. If Jesus' entire revelatory activity serves the glorification of the Father through the Son and of the Son through the Father (cf. 8:54; 12:28; 13:31–32; 14:13), then the miracle is the special locus of this event. It is not only an indication of the *doxa* but an expression of the *doxa* itself. This revelation of Jesus' *doxa* in miracles evokes faith.

At the wedding in Cana the evangelist develops his understanding of miracle and faith, using the disciples as an example ('Jesus did this, the first of his signs, in Cana of Galilee, and revealed his glory; and his disciples believed in him'; 2:11). Faith does not see the miracle; rather, faith arises through the revelation of the *doxa* in the miracle. Because the miracle has revelatory character and witnesses powerfully to the unity of the Son with the Father, it can awaken faith.

After the disciples it is the crowd that believes in Jesus because of the miracles ('When he was in Jerusalem during the Passover festival, many believed in his name because they saw the signs that he was doing'; 2:23). Anyone who accomplishes such deeds can only be the true prophet who has come into the world or the Christ (6:14; 7:31; cf. also 6:2; 9:13; 12:18). Through a miracle the man born blind acquires faith in the one who opened his eyes (9:35–38). How closely miracle and faith belong together for the evangelist is shown by Jn 10:40–42: 'He went away again across the Jordan to the place where John had been baptizing earlier, and he remained there. Many came to him, and they were saying, "John performed no sign, but everything that John said about this man was true." And many believed in him there.' Because Jesus and the Baptist were essentially different in that only Jesus performed miracles, the 'many' could only believe in Jesus. Likewise Jn 11:15 makes clear that faith arises through miracles. For the disciples Jesus is glad that he was not present at the death of Lazarus. Now he can raise his friend from the dead, so that the disciples can come to faith. Here the miracle is not the accidental cause of faith; rather, it is consciously performed in order to evoke faith.

The Johannine connection between seeing and believing also plays an important role in the resurrection and appearance reports. The redactional verse 20:8 says of the beloved disciple that he entered the tomb καὶ εἶδεν καὶ ἐπίστευσεν ('and he saw and believed'). Thomas[16] makes the seeing of his Lord's wounds the

---

[16] On John 20:24–29 cf. the analyses in ibid., pp. 156–61; H. Kohler, *Kreuz und Menschwerdung*, pp. 173–91.

condition for faith (20:25: 'Unless I see the mark of the nails in his hands, and put my finger in the mark of the nails and my hand in his side, I will not believe'). Jesus does not reject these demands but fulfills them (20:28), and thus verse 25 cannot be claimed as a Johannine criticism of miracles. In a miraculous way Thomas is permitted to verify the identity of the resurrected One and thereby comes to faith. With the admonition in verse 27c, 'Do not doubt but believe' (καὶ μὴ γίνου ἄπιστος ἀλλὰ πιστός), Jesus expressly accepts the connection between the miraculous seeing and the believing that arises from it. The real seeing of the resurrected One brings Thomas to faith and evokes the confession in verse 28: 'My Lord and my God.' The question from the lips of Jesus, 'Have you believed because you have seen me?' (v. 29a), stresses again the connection between the miraculous seeing and the resulting faith.

The shift in accent produces the following beatitude: 'Blessed are those who have not seen and yet have come to believe' (v. 29b). It is for the generations who can no longer come to faith through the direct seeing of the resurrected One. Exemplified in Thomas is what at the time of the Gospel of John is already the case: faith without the miraculous direct vision of the resurrected One that was granted to Thomas, and dependence on the tradition of eyewitnesses. The different temporal perspectives are crucial for the interpretation of the Thomas pericope. While Jn 20:24–29a reports an event that was possible only at the time of the epiphanies of the resurrected One and the first generation of disciples, verse 29b looks toward the future, and this alone makes clear the form of the beatitude. Thus verse 29b does not criticize or relativize the foregoing vision of Thomas but merely formulates what is already true for the following generations in distinction to that of the eyewitnesses. Direct seeing is limited to the generation of the eyewitnesses. But because this seeing is the foundation of the Johannine tradition, it has present meaning in the kerygma for the Johannine community. In this sense the connection between seeing and believing is in no way limited to the life of Jesus but has present meaning in the proclamation of the community.

Also in Jn 2:24–25; 4:48; 6:30 there is no fundamental criticism of miracles,[17] for Jesus is only rejecting the naked demand for

---

[17] Versus L. Schottroff, *Der Glaubende*, pp. 236ff., who sees in Jn 4:48 the proof of a fundamental criticism of miracles; for a critique of this type of interpretation cf. esp. W. J. Bittner, *Jesu Zeichen*, pp. 122–34.

miracles (4:48; 6:30) or a doubtful faith on the part of the crowd (2:24–25). Jn 4:48 in particular ('Unless you see signs and wonders, you will not believe') cannot be taken as proof of a fundamental Johannine criticism of miracles; rather, the Johannine Jesus – as already in 2:4 – first rejects the naked demand for a miracle, in order then, however, to perform the miracle.

For the evangelist John the miracle effects faith; the seeing of the σημεῖον ("sign", "miracle") is followed by a πιστεύειν εἰς Ἰησοῦν Χριστόν. This totally undualistic connection between seeing and believing is explicitly expressed in 2:11, 23; 4:53; 6:14; 7:31; 9:35–38; 10:40–42; 11:15, 40, 45; 12:11; 20:8, 25, 27, 29a, and thus in the fourth evangelist's understanding of faith, it receives a central significance. Faith is the result of a previously occurring miracle and not what makes it possible. Thus miracle faith for John is in no way only a 'preliminary faith'; the miracle gives rise not just to an inferior or incomplete faith[18] but to faith in the full sense of the word: knowing and acknowledging the divine sonship of Jesus Christ. If faith arises in the encounter with Jesus, who reveals his *doxa* in the miracle, then it includes equally Jesus' fleshly and heavenly existence. Hence its content includes not just the *fact* of the revelation; rather, the miracles also describe with virtually unsurpassable vividness and reality the activity of the Revealer in history.[19] Thus the seeing of the miracle is not a spiritual seeing but a manifest seeing.[20] Since the revelation of the *doxa* of the incarnate One makes possible a θεᾶσθαι, a corporeal and vivid seeing (1:14), and the miracles of the fleshly Jesus are the places of the repeated manifestation of the *doxa*, the seeing of the miracle can be the foundation of faith.

Believing in Jesus is for John synonymous with 'knowing' Jesus.[21] This is what Jn 14:7 says: 'If you know me, you will know my Father

---

[18] Versus R. Bultmann, *Theologie*, p. 425, who asserts: 'Genuine faith may not be confused with an apparent kind that is awakened, for example, through the σημεῖα of Jesus...' This judgment is followed by, among others, D. Lührmann, 'Glaube,' p. 74 ('preliminary faith'); F. Hahn, 'Glaubensverständnis,' p. 54 (defense against a false faith oriented 'toward visibility and provability'); J. Gnilka, *Theologie*, p. 132 ('superficial miracle faith').

[19] Versus R. Bultmann, *Theologie*, p. 419: 'Thus in his Gospel John presents only the fact of revelation without making its content apparent.'

[20] Versus R. Bultmann, *Johannes*, p. 43, who calls the vividness of the revealer 'pietistic misunderstanding' and says: 'Thus the Johannine representation of the incarnate Revealer also lacks any vividness; the encounter with him is only question and not persuasion.'

[21] On γινώσκειν cf. G. Strecker, *Johannesbriefe*, pp. 319–25.

also. From now on you do know him and have seen him.' Jesus says of himself: 'I am the good shepherd. I know my own and my own know me' (10:14). The believers have known Jesus (Jn 6:69; 1 Jn 4:16); they know him and know who he is: the one sent by God, the Son of Man, the truth (cf. Jn 7:17; 8:28; 14:6, 17, 20; 17:7–8, 25; 1 Jn 2:13–14; 5:20).

Those who abide in Jesus' word receive the promise: 'You will know the truth, and the truth will make your free' (John 8:32). Johannine knowing is not oriented toward external things; it penetrates to the essence of the known. In Jesus of Nazareth the glory of God is revealed; he is the Savior of the world sent by God (4:42). Therefore in John 'knowing' includes acknowledging Jesus as Lord and thereby entering into a personal relationship with him. To know Jesus means to follow him (10:27: 'My sheep hear my voice. I know them, and they follow me'). Therefore the knowing of Jesus and the acceptance of the message of Christ lead to observing the will of God.

> Now by this we may be sure that we know him, if we obey his commandments. Whoever says, "I have come to know him," but does not obey his commandments, is a liar, and in such a person the truth does not exist; but whoever obeys his word, truly in this person the love of God has reached perfection. By this we may be sure that we are in him.
>
> (1 Jn 2:3–5; cf. also 3:19, 24; 4:13)

Brotherly love is the mark of those who know God or the love of God (cf. 3:16; 4:7–8). By contrast, the one who sins does not know God (3:6). The τηρεῖν τὸν λόγον ("keeping the word"; Jn 8:51; 14:23; 15:20; 17:6) and the μένειν ἐν τῷ λόγῳ ("abiding in the word"; 8:31) belong to the essence of faith, because the knowledge of the Revealer includes confessing his word and will.[22] Knowledge does not separate itself from faith; rather, faith is a knowing faith. In the relationship of Father and Son, on the other hand, direct knowledge replaces faith: '… just as the Father knows me, and I know the Father' (10:15a; cf. 17:25).

Faith for John is a saving event. It is not without consequence, for the will of the Father is 'that all who see the Son and believe in him may have eternal life; and I will raise them up on the last day' (Jn 6:40). Faith opens up the salvific abundance of eternal life because it is directed toward the One who is life (cf. 3:15–16; 5:24; 6:47; 11:25–26; 20:31). For believers judgment already belongs to

---

[22] Cf. here J. Heise, *Bleiben*, pp. 44ff.

the past, for faith saves one from the coming wrath of the Judge (3:18: 'Those who believe in him are not condemned; but those who do not believer are condemned already'). Hence faith appears not as an arbitrary process; rather, it decides life and death. Therefore the message of saving faith in Jesus Christ must be passed on to humankind.

For John the natural result of faith is mission.[23] The sending of the Son into the world provides the rationale and the requirement for sending the disciples into the world (20:21). Because Jesus' death and exaltation are the presupposition and substantiation for mission in the Johannine school, there are appropriately also mission statements in the farewell discourses.[24] In Jn 17:15 Jesus expressly asks the Father not to take the disciples, and thus the church, out of the world; rather: 'As you have sent me into the world, so I have sent them into the world' (17:18). Thus as Jesus came into the world in order to awaken faith and bring salvation, so also the disciples are sent 'so that the world may believe that you have sent me' (17:21c). In 17:20 Jesus even petitions for those who come to faith through the proclamation of the disciples: 'I ask not only on behalf of these, but also on behalf of those who will believe in me through their word.'

Jesus appears programmatically as a missionary in Jn 4:5–42.[25] Every initiative comes from him; he addresses the woman of Samaria at the Jacob's well (4:7b) and reveals himself to her as the water of life (4:14b) and as the Messiah (4:26). There is a mutual recognition between Jesus and the woman. Jesus perceives the woman in her essence and reveals her past; she perceives the messianic significance of the person of Jesus. This leads the Samaritans to Jesus: 'Many Samaritans from that city believed in him because of the woman's testimony, "He told me everything I have ever done"' (4:39). The Samaritans come to the crucial recognition: 'This is truly the savior of the world' (4:42). Also in dialogue with the disciples the idea of mission predominates. Jesus uses the image of the harvest to describe the missionary activity of the disciples: 'I sent you to reap that for which you did not labor.

---

[23] On the relationship of faith to mission in John cf. M. R. Ruiz, *Missionsgedanke*, pp. 347–8.

[24] The farewell discourses (Jn 13:31–17:26) are an original component of the Gospel of John; cf. U. Schnelle, 'Abschiedsreden,' pp. 65ff.

[25] On the Samaritan mission in the Gospel of John cf. M. R. Ruiz, *Missionsgedanke*, pp. 41–72.

Others have labored, and you have entered into their labor' (4:38). From the post-Easter perspective, John 4:38 formulates the pre-Easter transference of harvest activity to the disciples. All missionary activity, all harvesting, stands in a continuous relationship with the mission and activity of Jesus. In regard to the Samaritan woman just as with the royal official (cf. 4:53), it becomes clear that people are called by Jesus, gathered, and led to faith in order then to be actively in mission themselves. Faith, as the sole access to salvation,[26] cannot remain with oneself; rather, it must necessarily spread, cross boundaries, and lead people into God's kingdom of life.

The sending of Jesus into the world evokes faith but also unfaith. This state of affairs is formulated almost programmatically by the evangelist in 12:37: 'Although he had performed so many signs in their presence, they did not believe in him.' Even Jesus' brothers did not believe in him (7:5), although they saw his works (7:3). The result of the healing of the man born blind was faith and unfaith on the part of the Jews (cf. 9:16). The raising of Lazarus also led many Jews to faith (11:45); at the same time this great miracle of Jesus becomes the cause of Jesus' betrayal (11:46). Especially with regard to the miracles John demonstrates the essence of unfaith, for in the face of the σημεῖα unfaith denies an obvious fact: Jesus Christ is the Son of God. The marks of unfaith are not ignorance or inability but the conscious rejection of an unavoidable fact. 'You have seen me and yet do not believe' (6:36). Precisely because Jesus is the truth and tells the truth, many do not believe in him (8:45: 'But because I tell the truth, you do not believe me'). John knows about human imprisonment by the powers of the world; he knows how people close themselves off from the truth (cf. 5:47; 6:64; 8:46; 10:26; 16:9). Jesus' discourses and miracles do not work automatically or magically; despite their character of revelation they require a decision from the human side.

4.3 The Elect of God: Predestination in John

Because faith for John is always an act of decision in response to the truth that has become evident in Jesus Christ, the question arises: Must faith therefore be understood as a human achievement? How are human activity and divine action, human

---

[26] Pertinent here is R. Bultmann, *Theologie*, p. 427: 'For John … faith is the way to salvation, and that means faith alone.'

responsibility and divine determination related to each other in John?

A number of statements seem to suggest that we speak of a Johannine determinism or predestination in John. For example, Jn 6:44a says: 'No one can come to me unless drawn by the Father who sent me.' Not only the sending of the Son but also faith appears here as a work effected by God (6:65: 'For this reason I have told you that no one can come to me unless it is granted by the Father'). 'No one can receive anything except what has been given from heaven' (3:27). The Father has 'given' to the Son his own, so that they now share in eternal life (cf. 17:2, 6, 9). No one can snatch the believers from the Son's hand, for 'what my Father has given me is greater than all else, and no one can snatch it out of the Father's hand' (10:29). Not one of them will be lost, except the betrayer, who was destined for that from the beginning (cf. 6:64; 17:12). All of them will see the *doxa* of the Son (cf. 17:24). John formulates his position fundamentally in 8:47: ὁ ὢν ἐκ τοῦ θεοῦ τὰ ῥήματα τοῦ θεοῦ ἀκούει ('Whoever is from God hears the words of God'). Only his own hear the voice of the shepherd (10:3–4), while the unbelievers do not belong to his sheep (10:26). Those to whom God does not give faith cannot believe. Natural human beings judge by outward appearances (cf. 7:24; 8:15); they perceive in Jesus only Joseph's son (cf. 6:42). Just as unfaith as imprisonment to the world is much more than an individual decision (cf. the adoption in 12:40 of the concept of the hardening of hearts from Isa. 6:9–10), so also faith ultimately goes back to God's initiative.[27] Only those who come from the truth hear the voice of the Son (cf. Jn 18:37c). Only what the Father gives to the Son comes to the Son (cf. 6:37, 39; 10:29; 17:2, 9, 24). Jesus chooses his disciples from the world, not they him (cf. 15:16, 19). In the Johannine understanding faith is a work of God: 'This is the work of God, that you believe in him whom he has sent' (6:29). The believer must be born anew or from above (ἄνωθεν; 3:3, 5). Because natural human beings belong to the sphere of the flesh (3:6) and cannot reach God on their own, they receive a new origin from God.

---

[27] R. Bultmann, *Theologie*, pp. 377–8, does not do justice to this text passage when he says: 'The essence of a human being is constituted definitively in the decision of faith or unfaith, and only then does the origin of a human being receive clarity.' According to numerous Johannine texts, it is not the decision of faith but God's action that determines the origin of a human being.

If these statements point in the direction of predestination and determinism, then there are on the other hand numerous assertions in the Gospel of John that have the character of demand and decision. Jn 6:27a is formulated imperatively: 'Do not work for the food that perishes, but for the food that endures for eternal life.' The Johannine Christ can call for faith: 'Believe me that I am in the Father and the Father is in me; but if you do not, then believe me because of the works themselves' (14:11; cf. 10:38; 12:38; 14:1). Jn 8:12 is a call to decision: 'I am the light of the world. Whoever follows me will never walk in darkness but will have the light of life' (cf. also 5:24; 6:35; etc.). The Johannine Revealer directly invites faith in himself: 'I have come as light into the world, so that everyone who believes in me should not remain in the darkness' (12:46; cf. also 3:36). The invitation, as well as the promise or threat, belongs to the basic form of the ἐγώ-εἰμι ("I am") sayings (cf. 6:35, 51a; 8:12; 11:25–26; 14:6; 15:5).[28] The entire Gospel can be understood as a call to faith, for it was written 'so that you may come to believe that Jesus is the Messiah, the Son of God' (20:31a).

How are the two series of statements related to each other? For the fourth evangelist neither faith nor unfaith is simply an individual decision; rather, their source lies outside the individual.[29] As God effects faith, so unfaith as imprisonment to the world arises through the work of the devil (cf. 8:41–46; 13:2) or as God's act of hardening hearts (cf. 12:37–41). According to John, God alone decides salvation and disaster, and this preserves the inaccessibility of God's action. At the same time the procedural action of God touches human existence, so that decision for faith and persistence in disobedience as possible subsequent reactions to God's offer of salvation are also real for the evangelist. Human beings are supposed to let themselves be moved to faith, for God's salvific will does not abolish human freedom of decision. The tension thus asserted is appropriate, because the two series of statements cannot be related without contradiction.[30]

The concept of the inaccessibility of salvation, which is also constitutive for John, has God appear as the sole universal subject

---

[28] Cf. here S. Schulz, *Komposition und Herkunft*, pp. 84ff.

[29] In this way John also emphasizes 'the priority of grace' (J. Gnilka, *Theologie*, p.136).

[30] To the point is R. Bergmeier, *Glaube*, p. 231: 'The evangelist thinks in a predestinarian way but does not develop a doctrine of predestination that satisfies the laws of logic'; cf. also F. Hahn, 'Glaubensverständnis,' pp. 62–3.

of the salvation event in all its dimensions. At the same time the idea of human freedom and responsibility subsequent to God's action requires the emphasis on decision with regard to the salvation event. What is seen as predestination on the level of theological reflection in John is, on the historical level, the subsequent attempt to explain the experience that there is faith and unfaith. Such an attempt at explanation must necessarily run up against boundaries, because in it human beings are to a certain extent putting themselves in God's place and wanting to achieve insights into God's mysteries. Predestination statements are always theological boundary statements.

4.4 Humankind between Good and Evil: Johannine Dualism

The anthropological dimensions of Johannine dualism have already become visible: faith and unfaith as possible orientations of human existence stand antithetically opposed and totally determine the life of the individual. With ἐκ ("from") John names precisely the particular source and thus also the essence of human existence. The believers are ἐκ τοῦ θεοῦ ("from God"); they hear God's word (cf. Jn 8:47) and do the will of God (cf. 1 Jn 3:10; 4:6; 5:19). They are children of the light (Jn 12:36a), born from God (1:13) and from the truth (Jn 18:37; 1 Jn 2:21; 3:19). By contrast unfaith is trapped in the world. Non-believers (Jn 8:23) and false teachers are ἐκ τοῦ κόσμου ("from the world"; 1 Jn 4:5). They have the devil for a father (Jn 8:44; cf. 1 Jn 3:8, 10) and are 'from below' (Jn 8:23: εἶναι ἐκ τῶν κάτω). These distinctions in John come from the idea of revelation itself, for the Revealer is 'from above' (8:23: ἐγὼ ἐκ τῶν ἄνω εἰμί; 3:31: 'The one who comes from above is above all; the one who is of the earth belongs to the earth and speaks about earthly things. The one who comes from heaven is above all'). Because the Revealer himself is not ἐκ τοῦ κόσμου, his own are also not from the world (cf. 17:16). Hence Johannine dualism appears as a necessary consequence of the idea of revelation; it is christologically and not protologically conceived.[31] The Gospel of John grew out of the post-Easter, Spirit-effected anamnesis of the Christ event (cf. 2:17, 22; 10:6; 12:16; 13:7; 14:26; 18:32; 20:9) and considers the decision of human

---

[31] Cf. T. Onuki, *Gemeinde und Welt*, pp. 41ff.

beings *vis-à-vis* the incarnate Logos in the categories of rejection and acceptance.[32]

Only the Revealer came 'from above,' not the believers. In gnostic systems, by contrast, the believers belong from the beginning to the higher sphere, and dualism has a protological function.[33] Thus the revealer Eleleth in the writing *Hypostasis of the Archons* can say to Norea about the immortal children of light: 'You and all your sons belong to the Father, who has existed from the beginning. Their souls came from above from the eternal light. Therefore the powers can no longer approach them – because of the spirit of truth that dwells in them. But all who have known this way are immortal in the midst of mortal human beings' (NHC 2.4, p. 96.19–27).[34] Here predestination, a protological dualism, and substantial identification between Redeemer and redeemed come together.

John is a long way from these ideas, because for him the transition from being trapped in the world to being in the realm of God occurs through faith and thus historically. The universe is in no way considered completely negatively. The world of God and the human world originally belong together. Already in the creation the temporal priority of the good is seen. It is a work of the Logos that was with God in the beginning; only after the creation statements in Jn 1:1–4 does the dualistic light-darkness antithesis appear in 1:5. Out of love God sent his Son into the world (3:16; cf. 10:36; 1 Jn 4:9, 14; 2:2; 4:14). Jesus Christ is the prophet or Son of God who has come into the world (Jn 6:14; 11:27). As the bread that came down from heaven he gives life to the world (6:33; cf. 6:51); he is the light of the world (9:5). Jesus came in order to save the world (cf. 3:17; 12:47); he is the σωτὴρ τοῦ κόσμου ('Savior of

---

[32] F. Mussner, 'Die "semantische Achse" des Johannesevangeliums,' p. 252, who says concisely of the author of the Gospel of John: 'He reflects on the Jesus history as the history of faith and decision and reduces the antithetical behavior of opponents and supporters regarding the Logos–Christ to the basic linguistic opposition *accept/not accept ...*'

[33] Cf. on this K. W. Tröger, 'Gnostische Anthropologie,' p. 34ff. Versus L. Schottroff, *Der Glaubende*, p. 275, who interprets Johannine dualism in the framework of Gnosticism and asserts: 'It has been shown that even the statement complexes in John represented by 1:14 and 3:16 do not go beyond the framework of gnostic dualism, which is the foundation of the Johannine conception throughout.'

[34] Following the translation of P. Nagel, cited according to K. W. Tröger, 'Gnostische Anthropologie,' p. 31.

the world'; 4:42; cf. 1 Jn 2:2). Quite consciously, the departing Christ asks the Father not to take the church out of the world (Jn 17:15) but to protect it from the evil one. The church lives in the world, but it is not ἐκ τοῦ κόσμου ("from the world"; cf. 15:19; 17:14). Jesus sends his disciples into the world (17:18), and the world is even given the abilities of perception and faith in Jesus' mission (cf. 17:21, 23). The world itself is not appraised negatively; rather, unfaith turns the world against God (cf. 1:10; 7:7; 8:23; 9:39; 14:17; 16:9).[35]

Because a new situation for humankind has begun through the coming of the light and the question of salvation is decided solely in faith in Jesus Christ (cf. only Jn 3:16–17; 12:46; and the ἐγώ-εἰμι sayings in 6:35; 8:12; 10:7, 11; 11:25; 14:6; 15:1), all those who reject the message of Christ consequently remain in darkness. Thus Johannine dualism can appropriately be called a dualism of decision, since the decisions of human beings with regard to the revelation in Christ determine their origin and their destiny.[36] If in faith they allow God's salvific devotion in Jesus Christ also to be valid for them, their existence thereby receives, as a rebirth 'from above' in the power of the Spirit (cf. 3:5–6), a new foundation and orientation. By contrast, unfaith remains in the realm of darkness and death.

4.5 Decision Today: Johannine Eschatology

The strong emphasis on the present in Johannine eschatology results from the elementary experience and conviction that the salvation event in Jesus Christ does not belong to the past but in its soteriological dimensions is immediately present: in the sacraments and in the activity of the Paraclete. Therefore in John the levels of time and space are intertwined.[37] The spheres of the divine 'above' and the earthly 'below,' which were separated in the ancient world, are united in Jesus Christ. The Revealer who comes 'from above' really enters the realm of the earthly. The believing community is drawn into this intertwining of spheres. In baptism as rebirth 'from above' (ἄνωθεν, Jn 3:3, 7) the existence

---

[35] Cf. R. Bultmann, *Johannes*, p. 34.
[36] On the tensions between human freedom and supra-individual determination in John, cf. section 4.3 above.
[37] Cf. J.–A. Bühner, 'Denkstrukturen,' pp. 224ff.

of the believer experiences a new orientation. In the Eucharist the Johannine church receives the bread of life that came down from heaven. 'I am the living bread that came down from heaven. Whoever eats of this bread will live forever' (6:51a–b; cf. 6:33, 50, 58).[38] In the Paraclete the heavenly Revealer is also present in his church after the exaltation; the basic difference between heaven and earth is abolished precisely in the Paraclete.[39] The church does not come 'from above,' but here the heavenly world extends into the earthly realm.

The intertwining of spheres corresponds in John to an intertwining of the levels of time. Traditionally future events already reach into the present in John. 'Very truly, I tell you, the hour is coming, and is now here [ἔρχεται ὥρα καὶ νῦν ἐστιν], when the dead will hear the voice of the Son of God, and those who hear will live' (5:25). The eschatological events already have a present reality; the future reaches into the present (cf. 3:18). Also the present reaches into the past: 'Before Abraham was, I am' (8:58). Moses already wrote about Jesus (5:46), and before the Baptist, Jesus already was (1:15, 30). In the present encounter with Jesus Christ or with the word of the Revealer, judgment already takes place; in the present the decision is made about the future (12:48: 'The one who rejects me and does not receive my word has a judge; on the last day the word that I have spoken will serve as judge'). Faith now offers full participation in life; whoever does not obey the Son will not see life but will remain under the wrath of God (cf. 5:14, 26). The salvific content of eternal life is present in faith; consequently the step from death to life is not accomplished in the future; rather, for the believer it lies already in the past (5:24: 'Very truly, I tell you, anyone who hears my word and believes him who sent me has eternal life, and does not come under judgment, but has passed from death to life').

The fundamental significance of the incarnation of the Son of God Jesus Christ and the resulting Christology of the present lead in the fourth evangelist to an overlapping of time levels and to the strong emphasis on the comprehensive presence of salvation. Present and future in John no longer appear primarily as formal categories of time but rather are determined exclusively on the basis of Christ.[40] Faith does not abolish time; it gives it a new quality.

38 On the sacraments cf. sections 4.6; 4.8 below.
39 On the Paraclete cf. section 4.6.
40 Cf. J. Gnilka, 'Christologie des Johannesevangeliums,' p. 97.

The anthropological dimensions of this conception are evident: believers know themselves removed from the realm of death already in the present; their existence as a new creation from water and Spirit is no longer imprisoned in the world; it is rather ἐκ τοῦ θεοῦ ("from God"). Judgment as God's decision about the life of a person already lies in the past. The full transition into the realm of salvation is also conceived by John not substantially but historically. Faith is an inaccessible event, believers continue to live under the conditions of the world, and the Johannine community knows itself called to realize the commandment of love where it is (cf. Jn 13:34–35; 15:9–10; 1 Jn 4:19; etc.). The appearance of false teachers from the middle of the Johannine school (cf. 1 Jn 2:19; 2:22–23; 4:1–3) and the reality of sin (cf. Jn 8:34; 1 Jn 1:8–10; 3:4ff.; 5:16) make clear finally that for John there is also backsliding from the attained state of salvation.

Finally, the statements about the present do not cover the whole spectrum of Johannine eschatology.[41] Not only in the Johannine letters (cf. 1 Jn 2:18, 25, 28; 3:2–3; 4:17; 2 Jn 7) but also in the Gospel there are future eschatological statements. The very presence of salvation opens for the Johannine community a future that is shaped by the work of the Spirit and by the expectation of the parousia. The evangelist develops these themes accordingly above all in the farewell discourses, whose real addressee is the community of hearers and readers outside the text.[42] They are to live according to the will of the Father and the Son consciously in the world (cf. Jn 17:15a: 'I am not asking you to take them out of the world'), where they are subject to the tribulations of the age (cf., e.g., 15:18: 'If the world hates you, be aware that it hated me before it hated you').

The prospects of the return of Christ serve to interpret and overcome the community situation marked by grief (λύπη in Jn 16:6, 20–22). Thus 14:2–3 undoubtedly refers to the parousia of Christ: 'In my Father's house there are many dwelling places. If it were not so, would I have told you that I go to prepare a place for you? And if I go and prepare a place for you, I will come again and will take you to myself, so that where I am, there you may be also.' Only the return of the Son enables believers to be forever with the

---

41 Versus R. Bultmann and others who regard only the statements about the present as 'genuinely' Johannine. On Bultmann's argumentation cf., for example, the interpretation of John 5:24–30 (idem, *Johannes*, pp. 183–97).

42 Cf. on this U. Schnelle, 'Abschiedsreden,' pp. 66ff.

Father and be removed from the troubles of the present and future. This does not relativize the present assertions of salvation but rather makes them more precise from the perspective of community reality: the life of the believer is encompassed in the present and future by the Father's salvific will and salvific action. The prospects of the parousia of Christ in Jn 14:18–21, 28; 16:13e, 16 must also be seen from this perspective, for the promise of seeing the Son again is directed toward the transformation of the community-oppressing λύπη ("grief, sorrow") into the eschatological χαρά ("joy"; cf. 16:20–22).

Also the announcement of an eschatological waking of the dead[43] in Jn 5:28–29; 6:39–40, 44, 54 is directed toward the community of readers outside the text. In faith the Johannine Christians have already moved from death into life; in the present the decision is made about the future. Yet faith does not effect the resurrection of the dead; no passage in the Johannine writings says that the believer has already risen. The Johannine conception of life does not exclude physical death. Rather, the resurrection takes place as a reawakening or new creation of the body in meeting Jesus, to whom the Father has given the power to awaken people from death (cf. 5:21). On the text-internal level of the Gospel story this is illustrated by the Lazarus pericope (11:1–44), in which Jesus appears as Lord over life and death. In contrast to the Jewish hope for the future (cf. 11:24) Jesus stresses: 'I am the resurrection and the life. Those who believe in me, even though they die, will live, and everyone who lives and believes in me will never die' (11:25–26). Because Jesus himself meets Lazarus in space and time and brings him back into life, in this case there is no need for a future resurrection from the dead. By contrast, the Johannine community is in a fundamentally different situation. Jesus is with the Father; not until his parousia will the believers meet him. On his return Jesus will perform what is decided for believers in the present but not yet reality: the resurrection from the dead.

In John present and future eschatology are not antitheses but rather complement each other: what is established in the present will also stand in the future.[44]

---

43 For analysis of the texts cf. J. Blank, *Krisis*, pp. 172ff. (but cf. the slight self-correction in idem, *Johannes*, pp. 38–9).

44 Voting for the objective necessity of future statements within Johannine theology are, among others, W. G. Kümmel, *Theologie*, pp. 261–2; L. Goppelt, *Theologie*, pp. 640–3; C. K. Barrett, *St John*; J. Gnilka, *Theologie*, pp. 140–1. The

4.6 The Powerful Presence of the Divine: Spirit in John

In the Gospel of John, Jesus appears as the quintessential bearer of the Spirit. Thus Jesus' baptism in 1:29–34 is presented exclusively as baptism of the Spirit, and the remaining of the Spirit on Jesus receives emphatic stress:

> And John [the Baptist] testified, 'I saw the Spirit descending from heaven like a dove, and it remained on him [καὶ ἔμεινεν ἐπ' αὐτόν]. I myself did not know him, but the one who sent me to baptize with water said to me, "He on whom you see the Spirit descend and remain [καὶ μένον ἐπ' αὐτόν] is the one who baptizes with the Holy Spirit."'

Because the Spirit remains on Jesus and becomes an attribute of his person, the whole appearance of Jesus, his deeds and discourses, can be understood as a happening in the power of the Spirit.[45]

Since Jesus baptizes in the Holy Spirit, in John's Gospel baptism also appears as a Spirit-effected event (3:5: 'No one can enter the kingdom of God without being born of water and Spirit'). This is a logical parallelism, for only the Johannine school anchors its own baptismal practice in the life of Jesus (cf. 4:1).[46] For the evangelist John, reproduction/birth out of water and Spirit, and thus baptism, is the condition for participation in eschatological salvation. The generalizing τις ("anyone") and the formulation ἐὰν μή ... οὐ ("if not ... then not"), which suggests a claim to exclusivity, show the fundamental meaning of the statement. Without baptism there is no access to the kingdom of God. Baptism alone conveys the eschatological, salvific gift of the Spirit. In the Johannine school, as in Paul, the bestowal of the Spirit is a primary datum of Christian existence. The Johannine community sees baptism as an entrance requirement into the kingdom of God and thus as the rite of initiation necessary for salvation. There can be no natural passage into the kingdom of God, for 'what is born of the flesh is flesh, and what is born of the Spirit is spirit' (3:6).

various perspectives (temporal: Jesus before all time, past, present, future, pre- and post-Easter; spatial: realms 'above' and 'below'; literary: way of the eternal Logos within the text – community of readers outside the text) are characteristic of the Johannine Gospel writing precisely in their overlapping. John thinks synthetically – not in 'pure forms' like many of his interpreters.

45 Cf. here G. M. Burge, *Anointed Community*, pp. 50ff.
46 On the analysis of the Johannine baptismal texts cf. U. Schnelle, *Antidoketische Christologie*, pp. 196–213.

For John origin determines essence, so that the designation of origin with ἐκ ("from, out of") represents at the same time a statement of essence. Because the essence of a being is determined by its provenance, like can produce only like. If something reproduced from flesh belongs in its essence to the sphere of the σάρξ ("flesh"), then it is thereby fundamentally separated from the sphere of the πνεῦμα, the Spirit. For the fleshly person there is no access to the kingdom of God; only through a new origin granted by God can one gain entrance into God's sovereign realm[47] (Jn 6:63a: 'it is the Spirit that gives life; the flesh is useless'). Thus *pneuma* does not designate simply a gift; it must be understood in a more comprehensive sense as the divine working principle or creative power. Rebirth ἐξ ὕδατος καὶ πνεύματος ('of water and Spirit') in John designates a comprehensive new creation that takes place in baptism with water and leads into a life determined by the Spirit. If the Spirit effects the qualitative ontological difference from the fleshly human being, then baptism has a salvific reality in that it is the place where the transition from the sphere of the *sarx* and death to the sphere of God occurs. This reproduction out of the Spirit is not within human power; rather, 'The wind blows where it chooses, and you hear the sound of it, but you do not know where it comes from or where it goes. So it is with everyone who is born of the Spirit' (3:8). This emphasizes the inaccessibility of the rebirth; it is exclusively a divine and not a human possibility. John preserves the *extra nos*, the 'outside of us' aspect of the salvation event and at the same time gives the place where human beings can participate in salvation: in the baptism of the Johannine community.

The First Letter of John makes clear that in the Johannine school baptism and Lord's Supper were understood as Spirit-effected events. 'This is the one who came by water and blood, Jesus Christ, not with the water only but with the water and the blood. And the Spirit is the one that testifies, for the Spirit is the truth. There are three that testify: the Spirit and the water and the blood, and these three agree' (1 Jn 5:6–8). The Spirit recalls and witnesses to the salvific event that takes place in the sacraments of baptism and Lord's Supper. The life of the baptized now takes place within the field of influence of the Spirit. The Spirit given by God abides (μένειν) in the believers and determines their lives: 'By this we

---

[47] Cf. F. Porsch, *Pneuma und Wort*, pp. 124–5.

know that we abide in him and he in us, because he has given us
of his Spirit' (1 Jn 4:13; cf. 3:24). Thus the words of Jesus present
in the Gospel are spirit and life (cf. Jn 6:63b). Because the
enlivening Spirit is present and active in the words of Jesus, they
are life and they give life. The whole worship of God in the
Johannine community occurs as adoration of the Father in the
Spirit, for 'God is spirit, and those who worship him must worship
in spirit and truth' (Jn 4:24).

The mission of the Johannine school also occurs in the power
of the Spirit, whom the resurrected One gave to his disciples:
'"Peace be with you. As the Father has sent me, so I send you."
When he had said this, he breathed on them and said to them,
"Receive the Holy Spirit"' (Jn 20:21b–22).[48] In John 7:39 the
exaltation of Jesus is expressly named as precondition for the gift
of the Spirit: 'Now he said this about the Spirit, which believers in
him were to receive; for as yet there was no Spirit, because Jesus
was not yet glorified.' The Johannine community lives in the time
after the exaltation of Jesus, and thus all the statements in the
Gospel about the Spirit are already reality for them.

The special consciousness of Johannine Christians as bearers of
the Holy Spirit is seen in the concept of the Paraclete.[49] The
Paraclete appears in the post-Easter situation of the community as
the present Christ, as the representation of the glorified Jesus Christ
in his church.[50] The Paraclete, expressly identified with the $\pi\nu\epsilon\hat{\upsilon}\mu\alpha$
$\dot{\alpha}\gamma\iota o\nu$ ("Holy Spirit") or the $\pi\nu\epsilon\hat{\upsilon}\mu\alpha$ $\tau\hat{\eta}\varsigma$ $\dot{\alpha}\lambda\eta\theta\epsilon\dot{\iota}\alpha\varsigma$ ("Spirit of truth";
cf. Jn 14:17, 26; 15:26; 16:30), abides and works in the church
forever (cf. 14:16–17). He teaches and reminds the church of what
Jesus said (cf. 14:26). The Paraclete testifies about Jesus (cf. 16:13–
14). He takes from the revelatory abundance of Jesus and passes it
on the church: 'All that the Father has is mine. For this reason I

---

[48] On interpretation cf. M. R. Ruiz, *Missionsgedanke*, pp. 257–6.

[49] On the possible religious-historical background of the Paraclete concept cf.
R. Schnackenburg, *Johannes* 3:156–73.

[50] Yet the exalted Christ and the Paraclete are not simply identical, as shown by
the differentiations in John 14:16 ($\check{\alpha}\lambda\lambda o\nu$ $\pi\alpha\rho\dot{\alpha}\kappa\lambda\eta\tau o\nu$ ["another Paraclete"]);
14:26 ($\dot{\epsilon}\nu$ $\tau\hat{\omega}$ $\dot{o}\nu\dot{o}\mu\alpha\tau\dot{\iota}$ $\mu o\upsilon$ ["in my name"]); 15:26c ('he will testify on my
behalf'); and the sending of the Paraclete by Jesus in 15:26a; 16:7e. The exalted
One works in the Paraclete and through the Paraclete, but he is not the
Paraclete. Versus R. Bultmann, *Johannes*, p. 477: 'As the prophecy of the
Paraclete adopts the early Christian idea of Pentecost, so also that of the return
of Jesus adopts the early Christian expectation of the Parousia; it is precisely
in the coming of the Spirit that he himself comes...'

said that he [i.e., the Paraclete] will take what is mine and declare it to you' (16:15).

The Paraclete is thus the basis that makes possible the Spirit-effected interpretation of the Christ event developed in the Gospel of John as the comprehensive representation of this salvation event. Ultimately the Paraclete makes impossible a separation between the proclaiming Jesus and the proclaimed Christ. Through the Paraclete the glorified Christ himself speaks, so that in the Paraclete the distance between past and present if overcome. There is a joining of perspectives made possible by the emphasis on the unity of the pre-existent, present, glorified, and returning Christ.[51] The whole Gospel of John is nothing but an interpretation of the Christ event through the Paraclete, in which the glorified Christ speaks and legitimizes the Johannine tradition. The presence of the Spirit in the Christian community cannot be imagined more broadly than in John.[52] The Spirit effects the transition into the realm of God; worship and life in the Johannine community take place in the Spirit, and in the Spirit Jesus is present with his own; he teaches them, reminds them of what he has told them, reveals to them what is to come, and protects them from the hate of the world.

4.7 Human Beings: Sinful or Righteous?

The First Letter of John, like the Gospel of Matthew (cf. Mt 18:15ff.) and the Letter to the Hebrews (cf. Heb. 6:4–6; 10:26–31; 12:13–17), bears witness to a vigorous disagreement within early Christianity over the question whether a baptized Christian can still sin and how the community should treat sinners in their midst (cf. also 2 Thess. 3:6–15; 1 Tim. 1:20; 5:19–20; Tit. 3:10–11; Jas. 5:14–16, 19–20).

The First Letter of John offers at first a contradictory picture.[53] The beginning of the letter stresses emphatically that the assertion of the sinlessness of Christians is contrary to the truth. 'If we say

---

[51] Fundamental here is F. Mussner, *Die johanneische Sehweise*, pp. 56ff.

[52] J.-A. Bühner, 'Denkstrukturen,' p. 228, correctly designates pneumatology as the deepest level of Johannine thought: 'The cultic intensification of the overlapping of spaces and times in the gathered community is borne by pneumatic access to the heavenly world, as it is granted to Jesus and as he passes it on …' (p. 229).

[53] A detailed exegesis of all relevant texts is found in I. Goldhahn-Müller, *Die Grenze der Gemeinde*, pp. 27–72.

that we have no sin, we deceive ourselves, and the truth is not in us. If we confess our sins, he who is faithful and just will forgive us our sins and cleanse us from all unrighteousness. If we say that we have not sinned, we make him a liar, and his word is not in us' (1:8–10). Thus the writer of 1 John not only affirms the fact of sin in his community but also polemicizes against community members who apparently deny this (cf. 1:8).

A completely different statement is found in 1 Jn 3:9: 'Those who have been born of God do not sin, because God's seed abides in them; they cannot sin, because they have been born of God.' Here the writer of 1 John asserts the impossibility of sin for Christians. Because God is the origin and basis of Christian existence, sin seems to be an impossible possibility. 'No one who abides in him sins; no one who sins has either seen him or known him' (3:6). Being born of God and being bound to Christ exclude sin. There is a clear separation between the children of God and the children of the devil (3:10).

Another direction is indicated by 1 Jn 5:16–17: 'If you see your brother or sister committing what is not a mortal sin, you will ask, and God will give life to such a one – to those whose sin is not mortal. There is sin that is mortal; I do not say that you should pray about that. All wrongdoing is sin, but there is sin that is not mortal.' The distinction between sin that is mortal and sin that is not makes it possible for 1 John not to deny the fact of sinning in its community but at the same time to hold fast to the idea that sinning and being a Christian are mutually exclusive (5:18a: 'We know that those who are born of God do not sin').

The obvious tensions between individual series of statements document a fundamental anthropological problem: Is the Christian fundamentally separated from sin by passage into the new being effected by God? The description of the new life in 1 John seems to suggest this. God bestows on believers the χρῖσμα ("anointing"; cf. 2:20, 27),[54] which remains in them and teaches them everything. They were created anew by the divine seed (cf. 3:9; also 2:29; 4:7; 4:18; 5:1); they are now ἐκ θεοῦ ("of God"; cf. 3:10; 4:1ff.; 5:19) and thus τέκνα θεοῦ ('children of God'; cf. 3:1–2). The church knows that it is led by the Spirit and thus by God himself (cf. 3:24; 4:13); God protects them from the attacks of the evil one; evil is already conquered (cf. 2:13–14; 3:8, 10; 5:18b–19). Believers belong to the realm of life (cf. 5:11–13, 16, 20), for 'we know that we have

---

[54] On χρῖσμα cf. R. Schnackenburg, *Johannesbriefe*, pp. 210ff.

passed from death to life' (3:14a). Sins were already forgiven (2:12); the believers have already known God (2:13). God not only enables the new existence but also protects Christians in their new being (cf. 5:18b). The emphasis on the presence of salvation and the comprehensive reality of salvation, which is characteristic of the whole Johannine theology, led to the consequence that Christians are fundamentally separated from sin and can no longer sin (cf. 3:6, 9; 5:18a). Their being in the living reality of God excludes communion with sin.

Yet this judgment is opposed by the reality of sin and sinning in the church: brotherly love is not universally practiced; there is hatred between members of the community (cf. 3:11–12, 15); rich Christians look on as their brothers and sisters live in want (cf. 3:17). Readers are emphatically exhorted to love not only with words but with deeds (3:18). The experience of sin is reflected in the community in a fundamental way in 1:8–10 and also articulated in 2:1–2, where Jesus appears as the advocate of sinful Christians with the Father. Thus in the First Letter of John we have side by side the claim of the sinlessness of Christians and the reality of sin and forgiveness of sins in the church – not an antithesis for 1 John but a co-existence in tension. This corresponds to the salvation-historical situation of the church. On the one hand, through the gift of the Spirit believers share in the abundant life and holiness of God; on the other, their existence is also still under the eschatological reservation (3:2a: '... what we will be has not yet been revealed').

The assertions of sinlessness in 1 John must also be understood in the context of eschatology.[55] Only with the parousia of Christ (cf. 2:28) can one say: 'What we do know is this: when he is revealed, we will be like him [ὅμοιοι αὐτῷ ἐσόμεθα], for we will see him as he is' (3:2b). The statements of sinlessness of 1 John express not a new ontological quality but only being and abiding in the living reality of God.[56] The aim of the letter's paraenesis is the separation between God's and the devil's children, which appears in 3:10 as the consequence of the *non posse peccare* in 3:9 and prepares the solution of the problem with the distinction between mortal and non-mortal sin in 5:16–17.[57]

---

[55] Cf. I. Goldhahn-Müller, *Die Grenze der Gemeinde*, p. 70.

[56] Cf. G. Strecker, *Johannesbriefe*, p. 303.

[57] Cf. I. Goldhahn-Müller, *Die Grenze der Gemeinde*, p. 71.

With mortal sin the First Letter of John holds fast to the incompatibility of being a Christian and sinning. Those who sin are not in the realm of the Spirit and life; they belong in the realm of death. On the other hand, the author of 1 John takes community reality into account when he speaks of sins that are not mortal. For these sins the brother or sister may ask God for forgiveness. It is hardly accidental that a definition of the two kinds of sin is missing.[58] The community retains the freedom to decide itself in each case in its midst which failing is to be regarded as forgivable sin and which is a matter of mortal sin. With this conception the essential antithesis between sin and being Christian is basically maintained while the imperative is intensified: there are sins that destroy one's relationship with God, and thus even the baptized can fall away from God's realm of life.

In the Gospel of John human beings outside of faith always appear as sinners. The marks of sin are the failure to belong to God and to know the truth. Thus for John sin is identical with unfaith, which shows itself already in the rejection of the pre-existent Logos (1:10–11) and reaches its high point in the decision to kill him (11:53). The Paraclete reveals the sin of the world: 'They do not believe in me' (16:9b). Therefore only faith in Jesus Christ overcomes the human lapse into sin (8:24: 'For you will die in your sins unless you believe that I am he'; cf. 8:21). If the Redeemer had not come, human beings would have no sin (15:22). If he had not done works among them, they would be guiltless (15:24a). But now they have no excuse, and sin is revealed as conscious hatred of Jesus and the Father (15:24b). Human beings cannot free themselves from sin; rather, 'Everyone who commits sin is a slave to sin' (8:34b); 'So if the Son makes you free, you will be free indeed' (8:36).

The Son has conquered the world (16:33c), and the ruler of this world has been deposed (12:31b). Right at the beginning of the Gospel Jesus is called 'the Lamb of God who takes away the sins of the world' (1:29). God appears in the weakness of a lamb in order to take away human sins.[59] The cross is the extreme sign of the reconciling God; on the cross Jesus sanctifies himself for

---

[58] This is not the case in *Did.* 5.1, for example, where among the sins of 'the way of death' we find, among others, murder, adultery, desires, fornication, theft, idolatry, sorcery, deception, greed, jealousy, and pride.

[59] For a comprehensive analysis of Jn 1:29 cf. M. Hasitschka, *Befreiung von der Sünde*, pp. 15–175.

the disciples (17:19). Jesus alone, who is without sin (7:18; 8:46), like God and in place of God abolishes the power of sin and in the Paraclete opens for believers a life in brotherly love. With this presupposition the word of the resurrected One to the disciples in 20:23 is consistent: 'If you forgive the sins of any, they are forgiven; if you retain the sins of any, they are retained' (cf. Mt. 18:18).[60] With this the resurrected One transfers his power to bind and loose to the church, which now under full authority continues the work of Jesus in its midst. Jesus' unique act of atonement (cf. Jn 1:29, 36; 3:16; 6:51c; 10:11, 15, 17–18; 11:47ff.; 12:24; 13:1; 18:14; etc.) makes possible the forgiveness of sins, but at the same time people exclude themselves from salvation through serious, unforgivable shortcomings. The text does not say in what manner the binding and loosing take place, but this event can in no way be limited to baptism and preaching. Rather, it is a question of an obligatory stance with regard to church members who through their behavior have called their being Christian into question.

The subject has an unmistakable similarity to the problems of the First Letter of John: in both cases there are forgivable and unforgivable sins. An exact definition of these sins is also lacking in the Gospel of John, and thus the power of decision within the community is preserved. Jn 20:23 is possibly an indication of the solution of the internal community conflict, recognizable in 1 John, regarding the essence of sin and the consequences of sinning:[61] the church created a practice of penance, legitimated by the resurrected One, within the framework of which the church itself decides who belongs to it and who has separated from it. Thus the Gospel of John also attests to the earnest will of Johannine Christians to keep its community free from sin. Sinning and being a Christian are actually mutually exclusive.

4.8 Everlasting Communion with God: Life and Eternal Life in John

The new being of Christians is fully qualified by John as ζωή ("life") or ζωὴ αἰώνιος ("eternal life"). Thus only in faith is the essence of

---

[60] Apt here is H. von Campenhausen, *Kirchliches Amt*, p. 152: 'John sees in the power of forgiveness something that the church must value above all, because she herself lives on the strength of forgiveness.'

[61] On the ordering of the letters of John before the Gospel of John, cf. U. Schnelle, *Antidoketische Christologie*, pp. 65–75.

being human revealed as the life made possible through God. In John life is first of all an attribute of the Father,[62] who gives life to the Son: 'For just as the Father has life in himself, so he has granted the Son also to have life in himself' (5:26; cf. 6:57).

The Son in turn receives from the Father authority over all people 'to give eternal life to all whom you have given him' (17:2b). The pre-existent Logos already had within him the life that became the light of humankind (1:4; 1 Jn 1:2). Here we see the mixing of the time and subject areas that is characteristic of John: it is not just the resurrection that enables one to say that Jesus is life and gives life. Rather, Jesus comes from God as the epitome of life; as the pre-existent One he is at the same time the incarnate, crucified, and resurrected One. In a concrete historical person, divine life is present in the cosmos.[63] Precisely as the presupposition of the deliverance of humankind from subjection to death, the whole incarnation is directed toward the gift of eternal life for believers. 'For God so loved the world that he gave his only Son, so that everyone who believes in him may not perish but may have eternal life' (Jn 3:16; cf. 3:36a). Jesus came so that his own may have abundant life (cf. 10:10b). Faith alone, as participation in the living reality of Jesus Christ, overcomes human subjection to death.

Knowledge of God and the One he sent opens up eternal life (17:3), for in Jesus Christ the divine power of life broke into the world of death. Neither the way of knowledge of the true self that is traveled in philosophy nor faith in a substantial identity with a heavenly redeemer in Gnosticism frees a person from the realm of death.[64] For John, Jesus alone gives the water that becomes a spring gushing up to eternal life (4:14). Out of Jesus' body will flow rivers of living water (7:38),[65] namely, the Spirit (cf. 7:39), which as the divine principle of life gives the salvific gift of eternal life. As the light of the world, Jesus is at the same time the light of life (8:12). He can say of himself: 'I am the resurrection and the life' (11:25) and 'I am the way, and the truth, and the life' (14:6).

---

[62] Cf. on this F. Mussner, *ZΩH*, pp. 70ff.

[63] Cf. ibid., pp. 82ff.

[64] K. W. Tröger, *Ja oder Nein zur Welt*, p. 75, names this fundamental difference between the Gospel of John and Gnosticism: 'The idea of identity is left behind, and the redeemed person does not become the redeemer.'

[65] The αὐτοῦ in verse 38 must refer to Jesus and not to the believer. This is supported by the parallel in 4:14, the indirect reference to 19:34, and the following verse 39, for God or Jesus is, in the Johannine view, the Giver of the Spirit; for analysis cf. R. Schnackenburg, *Johannes* 2:215ff.

The healing by the Son of a royal official in Jn 4:46–54 and above all the raising of Lazarus, already dead four days (11:1–44), show Jesus as Lord over death and life. Jesus makes life possible when he brings people back to life or overcomes limited possibilities for life (healing of the lame and blind in 5:1–9a; 9:1–41). Jesus turns away hunger (6:1–15) and distress at sea (6:16–25) as threats to life. Jesus Christ, the mediator of creation, gives life and makes clear the ongoing dependence of the creature upon the Creator. The Creator's gift of life reaches beyond what is temporal and thus transitory and limited; those who have eternal life are not lost and do not come into judgment (cf. 3:36; 5:24; 10:28). Jesus' promise has only one content: eternal life (cf. 1 Jn 2:25). Jesus is the bread of life (Jn 6:35a). Whoever eats from it never dies (6:50) but lives forever (6:58).

Whereas the ancestors died in the wilderness (6:49), the bread that has come down from heaven gives eternal life. The allusions to the Lord's Supper in the bread-of-life discourse (6:30–51b) and the eucharistic section in 6:51c–58 make clear the sacramental dimension of the Johannine concept of life:[66] in the community meal the resurrected One is revealed to believers as the epitome of life, and he grants them participation in his own abundant life. At no place in the Gospel is the identification of gift and Giver – so fundamental in Johannine thought – as visible as in the eucharistic section. All dimensions of the Son's work of salvation come together in one union: Jesus' death and exaltation are the prerequisite for the gift of life, in the Lord's Supper the living connection between believer and exalted One takes place, and the gift of life in the Lord's Supper opens the way to eternal life for the believer (6:53–54). Past, present, and future, as well as life and death, lie in the hands of the Son.

Just like the Lord's Supper, baptism appears in John as the epitome of a life-giving event. In baptism, as the place of transition from the sphere of the *sarx* into the realm of the Spirit, true life is given to the believer in rebirth. The new birth in the power of the Spirit occurs as a vertical invasion into the person's present life. As the living power of God, the Spirit places the believer in a new reality. The continued reality of physical death no longer limits life; one can say to the church: 'We know that we have passed from

---

[66] The eucharistic section 6:51c–58 was composed by the evangelist John and added by him to the traditional bread-of-life discourse in 6:30–35, 41–51b; for detailed substantiation cf. U. Schnelle, *Antidoketische Christologie*, pp. 214–30.

death to life' (1 Jn 3:14; cf. Jn 5:24). Whoever accepts Jesus' word 'will never see death' (Jn 8:51; cf. 11:26). In the Son the Father gives a life that is not destroyed by biological death. As a communion of the believer with God beginning in the present, eternal life opens up a never-ending future. John promises believers not immortality but ongoing true life with God.

5

God's Reality and Human Life:
New Testament Anthropology and the People of Today

Christian faith perceives reality in a specific way. It sees the world not simply in the light of cosmic theories of origin or models of evolution; rather, for faith the world is first of all God's good work of creation. Christians experience their place in reality as acceptance of their own creatureliness, which is fundamentally related to the Creator and is defined by this relationship. As creatures human beings are part of creation, not something over against it. The anthropological dimensions of this view represented by Jesus, Paul and John are evident. Human beings are defined by their being embedded in creation as creatures, but not thinking or acting on their own. Activity and passivity as basic categories of human existence experience different assignments in these two possibilities of human self-understanding. If human beings are understood as creatures of God, then activity is accorded first of all to the Creator. He gives humankind life and bestows meaning. Human beings are thereby relieved of the task of actively having to create meaning themselves. Rather, out of the experience of being given something and thus out of passivity, they can actively shape their lives.

Where God the Creator no longer appears as Giver of life and Giver of meaning, human beings must reorient themselves. Intentionally or unintentionally they take God's place and realize themselves in the process of actively shaping the world and thereby subjugating it. They do not receive the meaning of their lives but must create it themselves. Thus activity defines all areas of life; human beings are not oriented toward God but toward themselves and their needs. Karl Marx, in his eleventh thesis on Feuerbach, gave classical formulation to the human grasp toward creation: 'Philosophers have only *interpreted* the world in various ways; what is important is changing it.'[1] Beyond all ideological boundaries, in

1 K. Marx, *Thesen über Feuerbach*, p. 141.

modern times it is human beings making themselves through work, planning, and formation who want to turn the wheel of history under their own power. Science and technology provide them with the means. In this process human beings have understood themselves even in the present day as the subjects of this event, while at the same time beginning to sense that they are already its objects. The possible destruction of the world through atomic weapons, the ecological threat, the obvious failure of old and new teachings of salvation, as well as individual and societal crises of orientation, are much more than warning signs. They stand at the end of the path that people who trust in themselves have taken. The creatures wanted to escape their limitation and determine themselves. They claimed for themselves the creativity that befits God alone. In so doing human beings did not fulfill the hope placed in them by human beings. Modern subjectivism and its concomitant anthropocentrism of thought and action led precisely not to the discovery and practice of humaneness. Faith knows that natural human beings are also by no means in a position to do this, for 'if God is absent, Satan is present.'[2]

The Christian faith and the perception of human beings outside of faith are fundamentally different in their understandings of sin. Everywhere, of course, human fallibility is beyond question, but at the same time every epoch has the repeated expectation of being able to overcome this fallibility through insight or force. Reason in particular is still accorded this capability. This is not a new hope, for the gift of reason has repeatedly been considered characteristic of humankind.[3] Both in regard to the individual shaping of life and in the overcoming of global problems, reason, as a good gift of God, has undoubtedly been given a central role. But according to the New Testament understanding, it is capable neither of recognizing the real situation of humankind nor of freeing people from it. Outside of faith human beings stand under the power of sin; they are ruled by sin and are not free.

Increasingly these statements are felt as provocation, for they call human freedom and self-determination into question. Thus the theology of this century has also not been lacking in attempts to relativize or overcome the offensiveness of New Testament statements. Paul Tillich claims to give a new hearing to the objective

---

[2] M. Luther, 'De servo arbitrio,' p. 159: 'Si Deus abest Satan adest.'
[3] Cf. e.g., Seneca, *Ep.* 41.8: 'Rationale enim animal est homo' ("the human being is namely a rational animal").

content of the New Testament understanding of sin through the concept of 'estrangement.' By the word *sin* he means 'the personal act of turning away from that to which one belongs. Sin expresses most sharply the personal character of estrangement over against its tragic side. It expresses personal freedom and guilt in contrast to tragic guilt and the universal destiny of estrangement.'[4] The concept of estrangement is foreign to Pauline theology; it comes from a philosophical-political tradition that still shapes its understanding. Also, the many-leveled nature of the Pauline understanding of sin cannot be expressed through a new overall concept. The New Testament understanding of reality cannot be developed apart from the concepts that bear it; rather, the interpretation must take place not as a paraphrase but as an opening up of what is meant.

The New Testament concept of sin was given a completely new evaluation in political theology. 'Sin cannot be understood in a specialized religious sense as the lack of God's love or as rebellion against a master; rather, it must be considered in a secular, political way. It is not the profaned temple or the now empty churches that accuse us, but the state of the world.'[5] Here humankind is credited with the possibility of freeing itself by its own strength from the shackles of sin. Righteousness and peace appear as comprehensive counterconcepts, and human beings as acting subjects in a process of liberation. A promising message! Suddenly it is human beings who can turn away evil and bring about good. With the pathos of decisiveness the radicality of the Pauline understanding of sin is abolished. At the same time sin appears again as a moral category that can be variously filled according to the standpoint of the observer. What one person holds to be the war of liberation against sin *is* sin for another. This supposed domestication of sin encounters the human endeavor to be master/mistress of all things – an illusion, for according to Paul it is part of the very essence of sin to deceive people about their true situation, to leave them under the illusion that they can master life under their own power.

The obvious objection is that such argumentation serves only the reimposition of the will of the Christian faith on people and the legitimization and stabilization of the dominance of people over people. The concept of sin was often used in this spirit in the

---

[4]   P. Tillich, *Systematic Theology* 2:46.
[5]   D. Sölle, *Politische Theologie*, p. 115.

history of the church, but this misuse does not determine the truth of the New Testament statements. Rather, at this point the question of the truth and necessity of the New Testament understanding of reality is raised in all clarity on the level of the modern perception of the world. A relativization especially of the Pauline understanding of sin with reference to a modified understanding of reality would amount to doing away with the Pauline perception. Reality would be limited to the dimensions imaginable and acceptable to people of the modern age.

Here a decision is unavoidable: either the present interpretation of the world acquires a normalizing and thus also content-determining function, or the New Testament writings are given the advantage that they assert for themselves as the word of God (1 Thess. 2:13: 'We also constantly give thanks to God for this, that when you received the word of God that you heard from us, you accepted it not as a human word but as what it really is, God's word'). Naturally, the interpretation of the word of God occurs on the level of a particular reality of life, which, however, may not govern the word of God but claims to be opened up on the basis of this word.

For New Testament anthropology and the debatable question of the understanding of sin, this means that New Testament talk of the power of sin is not a mythical concept to be overcome; it names precisely the reality of humankind and the world outside of faith. Unavoidably colliding here are two interpretations of reality that can be neither united nor harmonized, but rather confront human beings with a decision.

Directly connected with the concept of sin is the question of human freedom. In the modern age freedom appears primarily as freedom of the will and of action. Freedom 'is the possession of space in which to be able to make a choice, space within which human beings themselves can on their own make decisions about themselves.'[6] Choice, decision, and self-determination as attributes of a philosophical concept of freedom designate unsurrenderable values of human existence. For the New Testament, however, not all dimensions of human freedom are included. Rather, human freedom is defined there paradoxically as being bound to God. How do people free themselves from their permanent self-centeredness and self-overestimation? Who can tear them away from the enslaving yoke of sin? What enables them to do good?

---

[6] W. Weischedel, *Skeptische Ethik*, p. 137.

Only attachment to God puts human beings into the area of freedom where they can find themselves, become fellow human beings with others, and learn to respect creation as a gift. This is a concept that runs counter to the familiar one, hurts our self-evaluation, and is hard to take: freedom is an attribute of God alone, who bestows it on those who attach themselves to him and orient themselves toward his will. Only God tears people away from the power of sin and enables them thereby to do good.

The presupposition for the appearance of humaneness in history is not the good will of people but liberation from the power of sin in Jesus Christ. When human beings submit themselves to God and escape from sin, they gain freedom from themselves and thus the possibility of devoting themselves to humankind and to the creation. The human inclination toward the self, self-love, and self-sufficiency can be broken up neither through the subjectively honest willing of the individual nor through moral appeal, legal precepts, or optimistic doctrines of salvation. Required here is the intervention of God, who in contrast to human beings knows the true human situation. In the one true human being Jesus Christ, God freed human beings for themselves and opened for them the kingdom of freedom.

The basis, center, and aim of all anthropological statements in the New Testament are found in the one human being Jesus Christ, in whom God himself became human. In him the humanity willed by God took form, and God's reality moved into the life of humankind. 'The human being that I am, Jesus was also. Of him alone it is really true that nothing human remained foreign to him.'[7] Those who seek the human essence must look to Jesus. They will know that the one human being Jesus Christ is entirely God. Jesus' humanity is only to be understood on the basis of his divinity, for Jesus lived not from himself but in a unique relationship with the Father. At the same time Jesus' divinity is revealed precisely in his humanity, for God is just what Jesus of Nazareth proclaimed him to be. Anyone who ignores Jesus' humanity or takes offense at his divinity will miss him completely.

---

[7] D. Bonhoeffer, *Jesus Christus*, p. 108.

Bibliography

The abbreviations correspond to lists of abbreviations in the *JBL* (where applicable) or the *EWNT* (*Exegetisches Wörterbuch zum Neuen Testament*). In the notes, works are cited in abbreviated form by the author's name and a key word or phrase from the title.

The bibliography also offers an overview of important publications on theological anthropology.

A. Systematic Anthropology

Althaus, P. *Paulus und Luther über den Menschen.* 2nd edn. Gütersloh, 1951.

Barth, K. *Kirchliche Dogmatik* 3/2. Zurich, 1948. ET: *Church Dogmatics.* Edinburgh: T&T Clark, 1936.

Ben-Chorin, S. *Was ist der Mensch?* Tübingen, 1986.

Brunner, E. *Der Mensch im Widerspruch.* 4th edn. Zurich, 1965.

Ebeling, G. *Dogmatik des christlichen Glaubens* 1:334–414. Tübingen, 1979.

——. *Lutherstudien II. Disputatio de homine III.* Tübingen, 1979.

Fischer, H., ed. *Anthropologie als Thema der Theologie.* Göttingen, 1978.

——. 'Tendenzen zur Verselbständigung der theologischen Anthropologie.' In ibid., pp. 9–19.

Frey, Chr. *Arbeitsbuch Anthropologie.* Stuttgart, 1979.

Gollwitzer, H. *Krummes Holz – aufrechter Gang. Zur Frage nach dem Sinn des Lebens.* 10th edn. Munich, 1985.

Härle, W., and E. Herms. *Rechtfertigung. Das Wirklichkeitsverständnis des christlichen Glaubens.* Göttingen, 1980.

Joest, W. *Dogmatik II. Der Weg Gottes mit dem Menschen.* Göttingen, 1986.

Jüngel, E. 'Der Gott entsprechende Mensch.' In idem, *Entsprechungen*, pp. 290–317. BEvT 88. Munich, 1980.

Moltmann, J. *Mensch.* 2nd edn. Stuttgart, 1983.

Pannenberg, W. *Was ist der Mensch?* 4th edn. Göttingen, 1972. ET: *What Is Man? Contemporary Anthropology in Theological Perspective.* Philadelphia: Fortress, 1970.

——. *Anthropologie in theologischer Perspektive.* Göttingen, 1983. ET: *Anthropology in Theological Perspective.* Philadelphia: Westminster, 1985.

Pesch, O. H. *Frei sein aus Gnade. Theologische Anthropologie.* Freiburg, 1983.

Peters, A. *Der Mensch*. Gütersloh, 1979.

Sauter, G. 'Mensch sein – Mensch bleiben. Anthropologie als theologische Aufgabe.' In H. Fischer, ed., *Anthropologie*, pp. 71–118.

——. 'Die Wahrnehmung des Menschen bei Martin Luther.' *EvT* 43 (1983): 489–503.

Scheffczyk, L., ed. *Der Mensch als Bild Gottes*. Darmstadt, 1969.

Schütz, P. *Das Wagnis des Menschen*. Hamburg, 1966.

Thielicke, H. *Mensch sein – Menschen werden*. Munich, 1976.

B. Old Testament Anthropology

Schmidt, W. H. '"Was ist der Mensch?" Anthropological Einsichten des Alten Testaments.' *GuL* 4 (1989): 111–29.

Wolff, H. W. *Anthropologie des Alten Testaments*. 4th edn. Munich, 1984. ET: *Anthropology of the Old Testament*. Philadelphia: Fortress, 1974.

Zimmerli, W. *Das Menschenbild des Alten Testaments*. TEH 14. Zurich, 1949.

——. *Der Mensch und seine Hoffnung im Alten Testament*. Göttingen, 1968.

C. Themes of Old and New Testament Anthropology

Gerstenberger, E., and W. Schrage. *Leiden*. Stuttgart, 1977.

——. *Frau und Mann*. Stuttgart, 1980.

Hermisson, H. J., and E. Lohse. *Glauben*. Stuttgart, 1978.

Kaiser, O., and E. Lohse. *Tod und Leben*. Stuttgart, 1977.

Krieg, M., and H. Weder. *Leiblichkeit*. ThStud 128. Zurich 1983.

Seybold, K., and U. B. Müller. *Krankheit und Heilung*. Stuttgart, 1978.

D. New Testament Anthropology

1. Overviews

Fascher, E. *Das Menschenbild in biblischer Sicht*. Berlin, 1962.

Kümmel, W. G. *Römer 7 und das Bild des Menschen im Neuen Testament*. TB 53. Munich, 1974 (= 1929/1948).

Schelkle, K. H. *Theologie des Neuen Testaments* 1:91–169. Düsseldorf, 1968.

Schnackenburg, R. 'Der Mensch vor Gott – Zum Menschenbild der Bibel.' In idem, *Christliche Existenz* 1:11–34. Munich, 1967.

2. The Image of Humanity in Jesus' Proclamation

Bornkamm, G. *Jesus von Nazareth.* 9th edn. Stuttgart, 1971.

Braun, H. *Jesus.* 2nd edn. Stuttgart, 1969 (repr. 1988).

Bultmann, R. *Jesus.* 4th edn. Hamburg, 1970.

Conzelmann, H. S.v. 'Jesus Christus.' *RGG* (3rd edn.) 3:619–53.

Dautzenberg, G. *Sein Leben bewahren. Ψυχή in den Herrenworten der Evangelien.* SANT 14. Munich, 1966.

Eckert, J. 'Wesen und Funktion der Radikalismen in der Botschaft Jesu.' *MTZ* 24 (1973): 301–25.

Flusser, D. *Jesus.* Hamburg, 1968.

Goppelt, L. *Theologie des Neuen Testaments.* Edited by J. Roloff. 3rd edn. Göttingen, 1978.

Jeremias, J. *Neutestamentliche Theologie.* 3rd edn. Gütersloh, 1979. ET: *New Testament Theology.* New York: Scribners, 1971–.

Merklein, H. *Jesu Botschaft von der Gottesherrschaft.* SBS 111. Stuttgart, 1983.

——. *Die Gottesherrschaft als Handlungsprinzip.* 3rd. edn. FzB 34. Würzburg, 1984.

Petzoldt, M. *Gleichnisse Jesu und christliche Dogmatik.* Berlin, 1983.

Schweizer, E. S.v. 'Jesus Christus.' *TRE* 16:670–726.

Strecker, G. *The Sermon on the Mount.* Nashville: Abingdon, 1988.

Weder, H. *Die Rede der Reden.* 2nd edn. Zurich, 1987.

——. 'Einblick ins Menschliche. Anthropologische Entdeckungen in der Bergpredigt.' In *Vom Urchristentum zu Jesus,* FS J. Gnilke, edited by H. Frankemölle and K. Kertelge, pp. 172–93. Freiburg, 1989.

3. Pauline Anthropology

Barth, G. 'Pistis in hellenistischer Religiosität.' *ZNW* 73 (1982): 110–26.

Bauer, K.-A. *Leiblichkeit – das Ende aller Werke Gottes. Die Bedeutung der Leiblichkeit des Menschen bei Paulus.* Gütersloh, 1971.

Baumbach, G. 'Die Schöpfung in der Theologie des Paulus.' *Kairos* 21 (1979): 196–205.

Becker, J. *Paul: Apostle to the Gentiles.* Louisville: Westminster John Knox, 1993.

Binder, H. *Der Glaube bei Paulus.* Berlin, 1968.

Brandenburger, E. *Fleisch und Geist. Paulus und die dualistische Weisheit.* WMANT 29. Neukirchen-Vluyn, 1968.

Braun, H. 'Römer 7,7–25 und das Selbstverständnis der Qumran-Frommen.' In idem, *Gesammelte Studien zum Neuen Testament und seiner Umwelt*, pp. 100–19. 3rd edn. Tübingen, 1971.

Bultmann, R. 'Römer 7 und die Anthropologie des Paulus.' In idem, *Exegetica*, pp. 198–209. Tübingen, 1967.

——. *Theologie des Neuen Testaments*, edited by O. Merk, pp. 193–353. 9th edn. Tübingen, 1984. ET: *Theology of the New Testament.* New York: Scribners, 1951–55.

Conzelmann, H. *Grundriss der Theologie des Neuen Testaments*, pp. 192ff. 4th edn. Tübingen, 1987. ET: *An Outline of the Theology of the New Testament.* New York: Harper and Row, rpt. 1969

Dobbeler, A. von. *Glaube als Teilhabe.* WUNT 2/22. Tübingen, 1987.

Eckert, J. 'Christus als "Bild Gottes" und die Gottebenbildlichkeit des Menschen in der paulinischen Theologie.' In *Vom Urchristentum zu Jesus*, FS J. Gnilka, edited by H. Frankemölle and K. Kertelge, pp. 337–57. Freiburg, 1989.

Eckstein, H.-J. *Der Begriff Syneidesis bei Paulus.* WUNT 2/10. Tübingen, 1983.

Eichholz, G. *Die Theologie des Paulus im Umriss.* 2nd edn. Neukirchen-Vluyn, 1977.

Eltester, F. W. *Eikon im Neuen Testament.* BZNW 23. Berlin, 1958.

Friedrich, G. 'Glaube und Verkündigung bei Paulus.' In *Glaube im Neuen Testament*, FS H. Binder, BThSt 7, edited by F. Hahn and H. Klein, pp. 93–113. Neukirchen-Vluyn, 1982.

Gundry, J. *Soma in Biblical Theology, with Emphasis on Pauline Anthropology.* SNTSMS 29. Cambridge, 1976.

Gutbrod, W. *Die paulinische Anthropologie.* BWANT 4/15. Stuttgart, 1934.

Güttgemanns, E. *Der leidende Apostel und sein Herr.* FRLANT 90. Göttingen, 1966.

Jervell, J. *Imago Dei. Gen 1,26f im Spätjudentum, in der Gnosis und in den paulinischen Briefen.* FRLANT 76. Göttingen, 1960.

Jewett, R. *Paul's Anthropological Terms. A Study of Their Use in Conflict Settings.* Leiden, 1971.

Jones, S. *'Freiheit' in den Briefen des Apostels Paulus.* GTA 34. Göttingen, 1987.

Käsemann, E. 'Zur paulinischen Anthropologie.' In idem, *Paulinische Perspektiven*, pp. 9–60. 2nd edn. Tübingen, 1969.

Kertelge, K. 'Exegetische Überlegungen zum Verständnis der paulinischen Anthropologie nach Römer 7.' *ZNW* 62 (1971): 105–14.

Lührmann, D. *Glaube im frühen Christentum.* Gütersloh, 1976.

Maier, G. *Mensch und freier Wille.* WUNT 12. Tübingen, 1971.

Mell, U. *Neue Schöpfung.* BZNW 56. Berlin, 1989.

Ridderbos, H. *Paulus,* pp. 71ff. Wuppertal, 1970.

Röhser, G. *Metaphorik und Personifikation der Sünde.* WUNT 2/25. Tübingen, 1987.

Sand, A. *Der Begriff Fleisch in den paulinischen Hauptschriften.* Regensburg, 1966.

——. S.v. 'σάρξ.' *EWNT* 3:549–57.

——. S.v. 'ψυχή.' *EWNT* 3:1197–203.

Schlatter, A. *Der Glaube im Neuen Testament.* 4th edn. Stuttgart, 1927.

Schmithals, W. *Die theologische Anthropologie des Paulus.* Stuttgart, 1980.

Schnackenburg, R. 'Römer 7 im Zusammenhang des Römerbriefs.' In *Jesus und Paulus,* FS W. G. Kümmel, edited by E. E. Ellis and E. Grässer, pp. 283–300. Göttingen, 1975.

Schnelle, U. 'Der erste Thessalonicherbrief und die Entstehung der paulinischen Anthropologie.' *NTS* 32 (1980): 207–24.

——. *Gerechtigkeit und Christusgegenwart. Vorpaulinische und paulinische Tauftheologie.* 2nd edn. Göttingen, 1986.

Schrage, W. 'Die Stellung zur Welt bei Paulus, Epictet und in der Apokalyptik. Ein Beitrag zu 1 Kor 7,29–31.' *ZTK* 61 (1964): 125–54.

Schweizer, E. S.v. 'πνεῦμα.' *TDNT* 6:332–451.

——. S.v. 'σῶμα.' *EWNT* 2:770–9.

——. S.v. 'σῶμα.' *TDNT* 7:1024–94.

——. 'Die Leiblichkeit des Menschen.' In idem, *Beiträge zur Theologie des Neuen Testaments,* pp. 165–82. Zurich, 1979.

Schweizer, E., F. Baumgärtel, and R. Meyer. S.v. 'σάρξ.' *TDNT* 7:98–151.

Scroggs, R. *The Last Adam: A Study in Pauline Anthropology.* Oxford, 1966.

Stuhlmacher, P. 'Erwägungen zum ontologischen Charakter der καινὴ κτίσις bei Paul.' *EvT* 27 (1967): 1–35.

Taeger, J. W. 'Paulus und Lukas über den Menschen.' *ZNW* 71 (1980): 96–108.

Vollenweider, S. *Freiheit als neue Schöpfung.* FRLANT 147. Göttingen, 1989.

Weber, R. 'Die Geschichte des Gesetzes und des Ich in Römer 7,7–8,4. *NZSTh* 29 (1987): 147–79.

Weder, H. 'Der Mensch im Widerspruch.' *GuL* 4 (1985): 130–42.

——.'Gesetz und Sünde. Gedanken zu einem qualitiven Sprung im Denken des Paulus.' *NTS* 31 (1985): 357–76.

Wendland, H. D. *Vom Leben und Handeln der Christen.* Stuttgart, 1972.

Wilckens, U. 'Christologie und Anthropologie im Zusammenhang der paulinischen Rechtfertigungslehre.' *ZNW* 67 (1976): 65–82.

4. Johannine Anthropology

Barrett, C. K. *The Gospel According to St. John.* 2nd edn. Philadelphia: Westminster, 1978.

Bergmeier, R. *Glaube als Gabe nach Johannes.* BWANT 112. Stuttgart, 1980.

Blank, J. *Krisis. Untersuchungen zur johanneischen Christologie und Eschatologie.* Freiburg, 1964.

———. 'Der Mensch vor der radikalen Alternative.' *Kairos* 22 (1980): 146–56.

Bühner, J.-A. 'Denkstrukturen im Johannesevangelium.' *TBei* 13 (1982): 224–31.

Bultmann, R. *Das Evangelium des Johannes.* 19th edn. MeyerK 2. Göttingen, 1968. ET: *The Gospel of John: A Commentary.* Philadelphia: Westminster, 1971.

———. *Theologie des Neuen Testaments.* pp. 367–445.

Fischer, K. M. 'Der johanneische Christus und der gnostischer Erlöser.' In *Gnosis und Neues Testament*, edited by K. W. Tröger, pp. 245–66. Berlin, 1973.

Gnilka, J. 'Zur Christologie des Johannesevangeliums.' In *Christologische Schwerpunkte*, edited by W. Kasper, pp. 92–107. Düsseldorf, 1980.

Hahn, F. 'Das Glaubensverständnis im Johannesevangelium.' In *Glaube und Eschatologie*, FS W. G. Kümmel, edited by E. Grässer and O. Merk, pp. 51–69. Tübingen, 1985.

Hasitschka, M. *Befreiung von Sünde nach dem Johannesevangelium.* ITS 27. Innsbruck, 1989.

Kohler, H. *Kreuz und Menschwerdung im Johannesevangelium.* ATANT 72. Zurich, 1987.

Lips, H. von. 'Anthropologie und Wunder im Johannesevangelium.' *EvT* 50 (1990): 296–311.

Mussner, F. *ZΩH. Die Anschauung vom Leben im vierten Evangelium.* MThS 1/5. Munich, 1952.

———. *Die johanneische Sehweise.* QD 28. Freiburg, 1965.

———. '"Kultische" Aspekte im johanneischen Christusbild.' In idem, *Praesentia salutis*, pp. 133–45. Düsseldorf, 1967.

Onuki, T. *Gemeinde und Welt im Johannesevangelium.* WMANT 56. Neukirchen-Vluyn, 1984.

Schnackenburg, R. 'Christ und Sünde nach Johannes.' In idem, *Christliche Existenz nach dem Neuen Testament* 2:97–122. Munich, 1968.

———. 'Leben und Tod nach Johannes.' In ibid., pp. 123–48.

———. *Das Johannesevangelium* 1–3. HTKNT 4/1–3. Freiburg, vol. 1, 5th edn., 1981; vol. 2, 3rd edn., 1980; vol. 3, 3rd edn., 1979.

Schnelle, U. *Antidoketische Christologie im Johannesevangelium.* FRLANT 144. Göttingen, 1987. ET: *Antidocetic Christology in the Gospel of John.* Minneapolis: Fortress, 1992.

Tröger, K. W. *Ja oder Nein zur Welt. War der Evangelist Johannes Christ oder Gnostiker?* Theol. Vers. 7, pp. 61–80. Berlin, 1976.

———. 'Die gnostische Anthropologie.' *Kairos* 23 (1981): 31–42.

Weder, H. 'Die Menschwerdung Gottes.' *ZTK* 82 (1985): 325–60.

———. 'Der Mythos vom Logos (Johannes 1).' In *Mythos und Rationalität*, edited by H. H. Schmid, pp. 44–75. Gütersloh, 1988.

E. Additional Cited Literature

Baumgarten, J. *Paulus und die Apokalyptik.* WMANT 44. Neuchirchen-Vluyn, 1975.

Berger, K. S.v. 'Abraham II.' *TRE* 1:372–82.

Betz, H. D. *Der Galaterbrief.* Munich, 1988.

Billerbeck, P. *Kommentar zum Neuen Testament aus Talmud und Midrasch* 1–4 (Str-B). Reprint. Munich, 1926–61.

Bittner, W. J. *Jesu Zeichen im Johannesevangelium.* WUNT 2/26. Tübingen, 1987.

Blank, J. *Das Evangelium nach Johannes.* Geistliche Schriftlesung 4/1b. Düsseldorf, 1981.

Bonhoeffer, D. *Wer ist und wer war Jesus Christus?* Hamburg, 1962. ET: *Christ the Center.* New York: Harper and Row, 1966.

Bornkamm, G. 'Glaube und Vernunft bei Paulus.' In idem, *Studien zu Antike und Christentum, Ges. Aufsätze* 2:119–37. 3rd edn. BEvT 28. Munich, 1970.

Braun, H. 'Vom Erbarmen Gottes über den Gerechten.' In idem, *Gesammelte Studien zum Neuen Testament und seiner Umwelt*, pp. 8–69. 3rd edn. Tübingen, 1971.

———. 'Der Sinn der neutestamentlichen Christologie.' Ibid., pp. 243– 82.

——. 'Die Problematik einer Theologie des Neuen Testaments.' Ibid., pp. 325–41.

Breytenbach, C. *Versöhnung.* WMANT 60. Neukirchen-Vluyn, 1989.

Brockhaus, U. *Charisma und Amt.* Wuppertal, 1987 (= 1972).

Bühler, P. 'Ist Johannes ein Kreuzestheologe?' In *Johannes- Studien*, FS J. Zumstein, edited by M. Rose, pp. 191–207. Zurich, 1991.

Bultmann, R. 'Die Geschichtlichkeit des Daseins und der Glaube.' *ZTK* 11 (1930): 339–64.

——. 'Das Verhältnis der urchristlichen Christusbotschaft zum historischen Jesus.' In idem, *Exegetica*, pp. 445–69. Tübingen, 1967.

——. *Die Geschichte der synoptischen Tradition.* 8th edn. FRLANT 29. Göttingen, 1970. ET: *The History of the Synoptic Tradition*, rev. edn. New York: Harper and Row, 1968.

——. *Der zweite Brief an die Korinther.* MeyerK Sonderband. Göttingen, 1976.

——. 'Welchen Sinn hat es, von Gott zu reden?' In idem, *Glauben und Verstehen* 1:26–37. 8th edn. Tübingen, 1980.

——. 'Die liberale Theologie und die jüngste theologische Bewegung.' Ibid., pp. 1–25.

Burchard, Chr. 'Jesus von Nazareth.' In *Die Anfänge des Christentums*. Edited by J. Becker, pp. 12–58. Stuttgart, 1987. ET: *Christian Beginnings*, pp. 15–72. Louisville: Westminster John Knox, 1993.

Burge, G. M. *The Anointed Community.* Grand Rapids, 1987.

Campenhausen, H. von. *Kirchliches Amt und geistliche Vollmacht in den ersten drei Jahrhunderten.* 2nd edn. BHT 14. Tübingen, 1963.

Conzelmann, H. *Der erste Brief an die Korinther.* MeyerK 5. Göttingen, 1969.

Dihle, A. *Die Vorstellung vom freien Willen in der Antike.* Göttingen, 1985.

Epictetus. In two volumes with an English translation by W. A. Oldfather. London, 1925/1928.

Ernst, J. *Johannes der Täufer.* BZNW 53. Berlin, 1989.

Fascher, E. *Der erste Brief des Paulus an die Korinther.* THKNT 7/1. Berlin, 1975.

Feine, P. *Theologie des Neuen Testaments.* 4th edn. Leipzig, 1922.

Foerster, W., ed. *Die Gnosis* 1. 2nd edn. Zurich, 1979.

Gadamer, H. G., and P. Vogler, eds *Neue Anthropologie* 1–7. Stuttgart, 1972–75.

Gnilka, J. *Der Philemonbrief.* HTKNT 10/4. Freiburg, 1982.

——. *Das Evangelium nach Markus.* 2nd edn. EKKNT 2/1. Neukirchen-Vluyn, 1986.

——. *Das Matthäusevangelium.* HTKNT 1/1. Freiburg, 1986.

——. *Neutestamentliche Theologie im Überblick.* NEB.EB 1 zum Neuen Testament. Würzburg, 1989.

Goldhahn-Müller, I. *Die Grenze der Gemeinde.* GTA 39. Göttingen, 1989.

Grässer, E. 'Kolosser 3,1–4 als Beispiel einer Interpretation secundum homines recipientes.' In idem, *Text und Situation,* pp. 123–51. Gütersloh, 1973.

——. '"Ein einziger ist Gott" (Röm 3,30).' In idem, *Der Alte Bund im Neuen,* pp. 231–58. WUNT 35. Tübingen, 1985.

Haenchen, E. *Der Weg Jesu.* 2nd edn. Berlin, 1968.

Hahn, F. 'Die Nachfolge Jesu in vorösterlicher Zeit.' In *Die Anfänge der Kirche im Neuen Testament,* edited by F. Hahn et al., pp. 7–36. Göttingen, 1967.

Hampel, V. *Menschensohn und historischer Jesus. Ein Rätselwort als Schlüssel zum messianischen Selbstverständnis Jesu.* Neukirchen-Vluyn, 1990.

Harnisch, W. *Die Gleichniserzählungen Jesu.* Göttingen, 1985.

Hegermann, H. 'Das hellenistische Judentum.' In *Umwelt des Urchristentums* 1, edited by J. Leipoldt and W. Grundmann, pp. 292–345. 4th edn. Berlin, 1975.

Heidegger, M. *Phänomenologie und Theologie.* Frankfurt, 1970.

——. *Sein und Zeit.* 14th edn. Tübingen, 1977. ET: *Being and Time.* London: SCM Press, 1962.

Heise, J. *Bleiben. Menein in den johanneischen Schriften.* HUT 8. Tübingen, 1967.

Hengel, M. *Nachfolge und Charisma.* BZNW 34. Berlin, 1968.

——. 'Die Schriftauslegung des 4. Evangeliums auf dem Hintergrund der urchristlichen Exegese.' *JBTh* 4 (1989), Neukirchen-Vluyn, 1989, pp. 249–88.

Hermann, I. *Kurios und Pneuma.* SANT 2. Munich, 1961.

Holm-Nielsen, S. *Die Psalmen Salomos.* JSHRZ 4/2. Gütersloh, 1977.

Holtz, T. *Der erste Brief an die Thessalonicher.* EKKNT 13. Neukirchen-Vluyn, 1986.

Horn, F. W. *Glaube und Handeln in der Theologie des Lukas.* 2nd edn. GTA 26. Göttingen, 1986.

Hübner, H. 'Mark. VII. 1–23 und das jüdisch-hellenistische Gesetzesverständnis.' *NTS* 22 (1976): 319–45.

——. *Das Gesetz bei Paulus.* 3rd edn. FRLANT 119. Göttingen, 1982. ET: *Law in Paul's Thought.* Edinburgh: T&T Clark, 1984.

——. *Gottes Ich und Israel.* FRLANT 136. Göttingen, 1984.

———. *Das Gesetz in der synoptischen Tradition.* 2nd edn. Göttingen, 1986.

Ibuki, Y. *Die Wahrheit im Johannesevangelium.* BBB 39. Bonn, 1972.

Jeremias, J. 'Abba.' In idem, *Abba. Studien zur neutestamentlichen Theologie und Zeitgeschichte*, pp. 15–67. Göttingen, 1966.

———. *Die Gleichnisse Jesu.* 8th edn. Göttingen, 1970. ET: *The Parables of Jesus.* New York: Scribners, 1955.

Josephus. *De Bello Judaico.*

Jülicher, A. *Der Brief an die Römer*, pp. 223–335. 3rd edn. SNT 2. Göttingen, 1917.

Kamlah, E. 'Anthropologie als Thema der Theologie bei Rudolf Bultmann.' In H. Fischer, ed., *Anthropologie*, pp. 21–38.

Käsemann, E. 'Das Problem des historischen Jesus.' In idem, *Exegetische Versuche und Besinnungen* 1:187–214. 6th edn. Göttingen, 1970.

———. *An die Römer.* 4th edn. HNT 8a. Tübingen, 1980. ET: *Commentary on Romans.* Grand Rapids: Eerdmans, 1980.

———. *Jesu letzter Wille nach Johannes 17.* 4th edn. Tübingen, 1980.

Kautzsch, E., ed. *Die Apokryphen und Pseudepigraphen des Alten Testaments* 1–2. Darmstadt, 1975 (= 1921).

Kertelge, K., ed. *Rückfrage nach Jesus.* 2nd edn. QD 63. Freiburg, 1977.

Klauck, H.-J. *2. Korintherbrief.* NEB. Würzburg, 1986.

Koch, D.-A. *Die Schrift als Zeuge des Evangeliums.* BHT 69. Tübingen, 1986.

Kuhn, H.-W. *Ältere Sammlungen im Markusevangelium.* SUNT 8. Göttingen, 1971.

Kuhn, K. G. 'Πειρασμός–ἁμαρτία–σάρξ im Neuen Testament und die damit zusammenhängenden Vorstellungen.' *ZTK* 49 (1952): 200–22.

Kümmel, W. G. *Die Theologie des Neuen Testaments.* 3rd edn. GNT 3. Göttingen, 1976.

———. 'Äussere und innere Reinheit des Menschen bei Jesus.' In idem, *Heilsgeschehen und Geschichte* 2:117–29, edited by E. Grässer and O. Merk. Marburg, 1978.

———. *Dreissig Jahre Jesusforschung (1950–1980).* BBB 60. Königstein/ Bonn, 1985.

Lang, F. *Die Briefe an die Korinther.* NTD 7. Göttingen, 1986.

Lichtenberger, H. *Studien zum Menschenbild in Texten der Qumrangemeinde.* SUNT 15. Göttingen, 1980.

Lietzmann, H. *An die Römer.* 5th edn. HNT 8. Tübingen, 1971.

Linnemann, E. *Gleichnisse Jesu.* 7th edn. Göttingen, 1978.

Lohse, E. S.v. 'σάββατον.' *TDNT* 7:1–35.

——, ed. *Die Texte aus Qumran*. 2nd edn. Darmstadt, 1971.

——. 'Jesu Worte über den Sabbat.' In idem, *Die Einheit des Neuen Testaments*, pp. 62–72. 2nd edn. Göttingen, 1973.

——. 'ὁ νόμος τοῦ πνεύματος τῆς ζωῆς. Exegetische Anmerkungen zu Röm 8,2.' In *Neues Testament und christliche Existenz*, FS H. Braun, edited by H. D. Betz and L. Schottroff, pp. 279–87. Tübingen, 1973.

Lüdemann, G. *Paulus, der Heidenapostel* 1. FRLANT 123. Göttingen, 1980.

Lührmann, D. S.v. 'Glaube.' *RAC* 11:48–122.

——. 'Tage, Monate, Jahreszeiten, Jahre (Gal 4,10).' In *Werden und Wirken des Alten Testaments*, FS C. Westermann, edited by R. Albertz et al., pp. 428–45. Göttingen, 1980.

——. *Das Markusevangelium*. HNT 3. Tübingen, 1987.

Luther, M. 'De servo arbitrio.' In *Luthers Werke* 3:94–293, edited by O. Clemen. 6th edn. Berlin, 1966. ET: *The Bondage of the Will*. In *Luther's Works*, vol. 33. St. Louis: Concordia, 1955–76.

Luz, U. 'Zum Aufbau von Röm 1–8.' *TZ* 25 (1969): 161–81.

——. 'Jesus und die Pharisäer.' *Judaica* 38 (1982): 229–46.

——. 'Jesus und die Tora.' *EvErz* 34 (1982): 111–24.

——. *Das Evangelium nach Matthäus*. EKKNT 1/1. Neukirchen-Vluyn, 1985. ET: *Matthew 1–7: A Commentary*. Minneapolis: Fortress, 1989.

Luz, U., and R. Smend. *Gesetz*. Stuttgart, 1981.

Marcus Aurelius. *Wege zu sich selbst*. Edited by W. Theiler. Zurich, 1951.

Marx, K. *Thesen über Feuerbach*. Marx-Engels Studienausgabe 1, edited by I. Fetscher, pp. 139–41. Frankfurt, 1966.

Marxsen, W. *Der erste Brief an die Thessalonicher*. ZBK 11.1. Zurich, 1979.

Michel, O. *Der Brief an die Römer*. 5th edn. MeyerK 4. Göttingen, 1978.

Müller, K. 'Jesus und die Sadduzäer.' In *Biblische Randbemerkungen*, FS R. Schnackenburg, edited by H. Merklein and J. Lange, pp. 3–24. Würzburg, 1974.

Mussner, F. 'Die "semantische Achse" des Johannesevangeliums. Ein Versuch.' In *Vom Urchristentum zu Jesus*, FS J. Gnilka, edited by H. Frankemölle and K. Kertelge, pp. 246–55. Freiburg, 1989.

Neugebauer, F. *Die Entstehung des Johannesevangeliums*. AzTh 1/36. Stuttgart, 1968.

Neusner, J. 'Die pharisäischen rechtlichen Überlieferungen.' In idem, *Das pharisäische und talmudische Judentum*, pp. 43–51. Tübingen, 1984.

Paschen, W. *Rein und Unrein.* SANT 24. Munich, 1970.

Paulsen, H. *Überlieferung und Auslegung in Römer 8.* WMANT 43. Neukirchen-Vluyn, 1974.

Pesch, R. *Das Markusevangelium.* 4th edn. HTKNT 2/1. Freiburg, 1984.

Philo. In ten volumes with an English translation by F. H. Colson, G. H. Whitaker, and J. W. Earp. Cambridge, Mass., and London, 1929–62.

Philo. Supplement 1–2. Translated by R. Marcus. Cambridge, Mass., and London, 1953.

Pöhlmann, W. 'Die Abschichtung des Verlorenen Sohnes (Lk 15,12f) und die erzählte Welt der Parabel.' *ZNW* 70 (1979): 194–213.

Porsch, F. *Pneuma und Wort.* FST 16. Frankfurt, 1974.

Rad, G. von. *Genesis.* 9th edn. ATD 2/4. Göttingen, 1972. ET: *Genesis: A Commentary.* Philadelphia: Westminster, 1961.

Rahlfs, A., ed. *Septuaginta* 1–2. 8th edn. Stuttgart, 1965.

Räisänen, H. 'Jesus and the Food Laws.' *JNST* 16 (1982): 79–100.

Roloff, J. *Das Kerygma und der irdische Jesus.* 2nd edn. Göttingen, 1973.

Ruiz, M. R. *Der Missionsgedanke des Johannesevangeliums.* FzB 55. Würzburg, 1987.

Sanders, E. P. *Paul and Palestinian Judaism: A Comparison of Patterns of Religion.* Philadelphia: Fortress, 1977.

——. *Jesus and Judaism.* Philadelphia: Fortress, 1985.

Sauer, G. *Jesus Sirach.* JSHRZ 3/5. Gütersloh, 1981.

Schade, H. H. *Apokalyptische Christologie bei Paulus.* 2nd edn. GTA 18. Göttingen, 1984.

Schaller, B. 'Die Sprüche über Ehescheidung und Wiederheirat in der synoptischen Überlieferung.' In *Der Ruf Jesu und die Antwort der Gemeinde,* FS J. Jeremias, edited by E. Lohse et al., pp. 226–46. Göttingen, 1970.

Schnackenburg, R. *Die Johannesbriefe.* 6th edn. HTKNT 13/3. Freiburg, 1979.

Schneider, G. *Das Evangelium nach Lukas.* ÖTK 3/1. Gütersloh, 1977.

Schnelle, U. 'Sachgemässe Schriftauslegung.' *NovT* 30 (1988): 115–31.

——. 'Die Abschiedsreden im Johannesevangelium.' *ZNW* 80 (1989): 64–79.

——. *Wandlungen im paulinischen Denken.* SBS 137. Stuttgart, 1989.

Schoeps, H. J. *Paulus.* Tübingen, 1959. ET: *Paul: The Theology of the Apostle in the Light of Jewish Religious History.* Philadelphia: Westminster, 1961.

Schottroff, L. *Der Glaubende und die feindliche Welt*. WMANT 37. Neukirchen-Vluyn, 1970.

———. 'Das Gleichnis vom verlorenen Sohn.' *ZTK* 68 (1971): 27–52.

Schrage, W. 'Theologie und Christologie bei Paulus und Jesus auf dem Hintergrund der modernen Gottesfrage.' *EvT* 36 (1976): 121–54.

———. *Ethik des Neuen Testaments*. 2nd edn. GNT 4. Göttingen, 1989. ET: *The Ethics of the New Testament*. Philadelphia: Fortress, 1988.

Schulz, S. *Komposition und Herkunft der johanneischen Reden*. BWANT 5/1. Stuttgart, 1960.

———. *Q: Die Spruchquelle der Evangelisten*. 1972.

Schüpphaus, J. *Die Psalmen Salomos*. ALGHJ 7. Leiden, 1977.

Schürer, E. *Geschichte des jüdischen Volkes* 2. 4th edn. Leipzig, 1907.

Sellin, G. *Der Streit um die Auferstehung der Toten*. FRLANT 138. Göttingen, 1986.

Seneca. *Opera* 1. Edited by F. Haase. Leipzig, 1862.

———. *Epistulae morales* 1–5. Edited by F. Loretto. Stuttgart, 1977–88.

Sölle, D. *Politische Theologie*. Stuttgart, 1971. ET: *Political Theology*. Philadelphia: Fortress, 1974.

Stegemann, H. 'Der lehrende Jesus.' *NZSTh* 24 (1982): 3–20.

Strecker, G. *Der Weg der Gerechtigkeit*. 3rd edn. FRLANT 82. Göttingen, 1971.

———. *Die Johannesbriefe*. MeyerK 14. Göttingen, 1989.

Stuhlmacher, P. *Der Brief an die Römer*. NTD 6. Göttingen, 1989.

Synofzik, E. *Die Gerichts- und Vergeltungsaussagen bei Paulus*. GTA 8. Göttingen, 1977.

Theissen, G. *Urchristliche Wundergeschichten*. SNT 8. Gütersloh, 1974. ET: *The Miracle Stories of the Early Christian Tradition*. Philadelphia: Fortress, 1983.

———. 'Die Starken und die Schwachen in Korinth.' In idem, *Studien zur Soziologie des Urchristentums*, pp. 272–89. 2nd edn. WUNT 19. Tübingen, 1983.

———. *Psychologische Aspekte paulinischer Theologie*. FRLANT 131. Göttingen, 1983. ET: *Psychological Aspects of Pauline Theology*. Philadelphia: Fortress, 1986.

Thüsing, W. *Die Erhöhung und Verherrlichung Jesu im Johannesevangelium*. 3rd edn. NTA 21/1–2. Münster, 1979.

Tillich, P. *Systematic Theology* 2. Chicago: Univ. of Chicago Press, 1957.

Wedderburn, A. J. M. *Baptism and Resurrection*. WUNT 44. Tübingen, 1987.

Weder, H. *Die Gleichnisse Jesu als Metaphern*. 3rd edn. FRLANT 120. Göttingen, 1984.

Weischedel, W. *Skeptische Ethik*. Frankfurt, 1980.

Weiser, A. *Die Knechtsgleichnisse der synoptischen Tradition*. SANT 24. Munich, 1971.

Wendland, H. D. 'Das Wirken des Heiligen Geistes in den Gläubigen nach Paulus.' *TLZ* 77 (1952): 457–70.

Wiefel, W. 'Die Hauptrichtung des Wandels im eschatologischen Denken des Paulus.' *TZ* 30 (1974): 65–81.

——. *Das Evangelium nach Lukas*. THKNT 3. Berlin, 1988.

Wilckens, U. *Der Brief an die Römer*. EKKNT 6/1–3. Neukirchen-Vluyn, 1978–82.

——. 'Zur Entwicklung des paulinischen Gesetzesverständnisses.' *NTS* 28 (1982): 154–90.

Windisch, H. *Der zweite Korintherbrief*. 9th edn. MeyerK 6. Göttingen, 1924.

Wolff, Chr. *Der erste Brief an die Korinther*. THKNT 7/2. Berlin, 1982.

Zeller, D. *Kommentar zur Logienquelle*. SKK.NT 21. Stuttgart, 1984.

——. *Der Brief an die Römer*. RNT. Regensburg, 1985.

Index of Modern Authors

Althaus, P., 69–70

Barth, G., 52
Barth, K., 4
Bauer, K.-A., 55–6, 58
Baumgarten, J., 37
Becker, J., 37, 51, 107
Berger, K., 110
Bergmeier, R., 127
Betz, H. D., 90
Billerbeck, P., 118
Bittner, W. J., 121
Blank, J., 133
Bonhoeffer, D., 149
Bornkamm, G., 106
Brandenburger, E., 46
Braun, H., 14–5, 112
Breytenbach, C., 40
Brockhaus, U., 48
Brunner, E., 2
Bühler, P., 116
Bühner, J.-A., 130, 137
Bultmann, R., 2–9, 14–5, 47, 50–1, 56–8, 60, 69, 74–5, 82, 93, 107, 112, 122, 125–6, 130, 132, 136
Burchard, Chr., 15
Burge, G. M., 134
Campenhausen, H. von, 141
Conzelmann, H., 45, 107

Dautzenberg, G., 12
Dihle, A., 80
Dobbeler, A. von, 51–2, 55

Eckert, J., 23, 100
Eckstein, H.-J., 93–4, 96

Eichholz, G., 4
Eltester, F. W., 99
Ernst, J., 23

Fascher, E., 86
Foerster, W., 1
Frey, Chr., 2
Friedrich, G., 50–1, 54

Gadamer, H. G., 2
Gehlen, A., 2
Gnilka, J., 12, 15–7, 21, 88, 122, 127, 131, 133
Goldhahn-Müller, I., 76, 137, 139
Goppelt, L., 35, 133
Grässer, E., 75, 83
Gutbrod, W., 93, 107

Haenchen, E., 14–5
Hahn, F., 11, 35, 118, 122, 127
Hampel, V., 16, 31, 35
Harnisch, W., 25, 28–30
Hasitschka, M., 140
Hegermann, H., 40
Heidegger, M., 2, 4, 7–8
Heise, J., 123
Hengel, M., 35, 116
Hermann, I., 45
Holm-Nielsen, S., 81, 109
Holtz, T., 104
Horn, F. W., 25
Hübner, H., 14–7, 67–8, 72, 78–9, 83, 89

Ibuki, Y., 115

Jeremias, J., 12–3, 18, 27, 30

Jervell, J., 98–9, 101
Jewett, R., 55, 106
Jones, S., 84–7, 89, 91
Jülicher, A., 51

Kamlah, E., 3
Käsemann, E., 15, 38, 44, 51, 53, 56, 58, 64, 72–3, 105, 115
Kertelge, K., 11, 69
Klauck, H.-J., 60, 100
Koch, D.-A., 65, 79, 110–1
Kohler, H., 116, 120
Krieg, M., 60
Kuhn, K. G., 16, 63
Kümmel, W. G., 2, 10, 13–15, 35, 69, 133

Lang, F., 95, 105
Lichtenberger, H., 66
Lietzmann, H., 48, 64, 111
Linnemann, E., 27
Lohse, E., 16–7, 72
Lüdemann, G., 43
Lührmann, D., 16, 52, 90
Luther, M., 9, 146
Luz, U., 11–2, 15, 19, 21–2, 25, 72, 77

Maier, G., 79, 82
Marx, K., 145
Marxsen, W., 41, 53
Mell, U., 49
Merklein, H., 12, 15, 18–9, 27–8, 31–2, 35
Michel, O., 78
Mussner, F., 11, 129, 137, 142

Nagel, P., 129
Neugebauer, F., 119
Neusner, J., 14, 31

Onuki, T., 128

Pannenberg, W., 2–3
Paschen, W., 13, 15
Paulsen, H., 61–2, 73
Pesch, O. H., 2
Pesch, R., 32
Petzoldt, M., 25–6, 28
Plessner, H., 2
Pöhlmann, W., 26
Porsch, F., 135

Rad, G. von, 101
Räisänen, H., 14–5, 72
Röhser, G., 63, 65–6, 70
Roloff, J., 16–7
Ruiz, M. R., 124, 136

Sand, A., 61
Sanders, E. P., 5, 15, 108–9
Sauter, G., 6
Schade, H. H., 41
Schaller, B., 13
Schlatter, A., 53
Schmithals, W., 61, 71
Schnackenburg, R., 136, 138, 142
Schneider, G., 24
Schnelle, U., 9, 39, 41–2, 46, 58, 74, 90, 114, 119–20, 132, 134, 141, 143
Schoeps, H. J., 51
Schottroff, L., 25, 121, 129
Schrage, W., 15, 34, 38–9, 97
Schulz, S., 31, 127
Schüpphaus, J., 109
Schürer, E., 14
Schweizer, E., 57–8
Sellin, G., 43
Sölle, D., 147
Stegemann, H., 13, 17
Strecker, G., 11–13, 19, 21–2, 25, 33, 118, 122, 139
Stuhlmacher, P., 54, 72–3

Synofzik, E., 40, 77

Theissen, G., 17, 69, 84
Thielicke, H., 2
Thüsing, W., 119
Tillich, P., 147
Tröger, K. W., 118, 129, 142

Vogler, P., 2
Vollenweider, S., 37, 86, 89, 91

Weber, R., 67–9, 71–2
Wedderburn, A. J. M., 74

Weder, H., 20, 22, 28–9, 33, 65, 111, 114, 118
Weischedel, W., 148
Weiser, A., 29
Wendland, H. D., 51
Wiefel, W., 24, 57
Wilckens, U., 67, 69, 71–2, 97, 107–8, 112
Windisch, H., 100
Wolff, Chr., 38, 42, 60, 100–1
Wolff, H. W., 60, 103, 105

Zeller, D., 12, 71, 96

Index of Ancient References

Old Testament

Genesis
1:26–27   100
1:27   101
2:2–3   16
7:2   13
15:6   110

Habakkuk
2:4   111

Psalms
78:39a   60
119:120   60

Proverbs
25:21–22a   21

New Testament

Matthew
3:9–10   23
5:3, 4, 6   32
5:21–22a   19
5:27–28   19–20
5:33–34a   19–20
5:39b–40   19, 21
5:44a   19, 21
5:45   12
6:9b   18
6:11   18
6:12   24
6:13b   17
6:25–33   12
6:32   18
6:33   12, 18
6:45   18
7:1   22
7:11   25
8:21–22   35
9:34   17
10:29–31   12
11:5–6   18, 34
11:18–19   15, 31
11:25   12, 18
13:31–32   35
18:12–14   27
18:23–35   29–30
18:23b–30   25
20:1–16   28
23:25   15

Mark
1:4   23
2:1–12   32
2:16   32
2:17c   32
2:18b–19a   15
2:21–22   34
2:27   16
3:4   17
3:27   34
7:15   13–5
7:18b, 29   14
10:2–9   13
14:36   18
14:36a   12

Luke
3:8–9   23
6:20b   32
6:21a–b   32

6:27a	19, 21, 32	3:2–3	132
6:29	19, 21	3:3	126, 130
7:33–34	15, 31	3:5	126, 134
7:36–50	32	3:6	134
10:7	15	3:7	130
10:13–14	24	3:8	160
10:18	17, 34	3:16	129, 142
10:21	12, 18	3:18	124
10:23–24	34	3:27	126
11:2b	18	3:31	128
11:3	18	4:1	134
11:4	24	4:5–42	124
11:14–19	17	4:24	136
11:20	17, 41	4:38	125
11:21–22	17	4:39	124
11:31–32	35	4:42	124, 130
11:32	24	4:46–54	143
11:39–41	15	4:48	121–2
12:30	18	4:53	125
13:1, 3–5	24	5:1–9a–b	143
13:16	17	5:24	131
13:18–19	35	5:25	131
15:1–7	27	5:26	142
15:8–10	27	5:46	131
15:11–32	25	6:1–15	143
17:21	34	6:16–25	143
18:10–14a	25	6:27a	127
		6:29	126
John		6:30	121–2
1:1–4	114	6:36	125
1:4	129, 142	6:40	123
1:14	114, 122	6:44a	126
1:15	131	5:51a–b	131
1:29	116, 140	6:53–54	143
1:29–34	134	6:63a	135
1:30	131	6:65	126
1:36	116	7:38	142
2:4	122	7:39	136
2:11	119–20	8:12	127
2:14–22	116	8:23	128
2:23	120	8:24	140
2:24–25	121–2	8:32	123

8:34b	140	17:15	124, 130
8:36	140	17:18	124
8:45	125	17:20	124
8:47	125	17:21c	124
8:51	144	19:5	116
8:58	131	19:30	116
9:1–41	143	20:8	120
9:35–38	120	20:21	124
10:14	123	20:21b–22	136
10:15a	123	20:23	141
10:27	123	20:24–29	116, 121
10:29	126	20:31	119
10:30	119	20:31a	127
10:40–42	120		
11:1–44	143	**Romans**	
11:4	119	1:3b–4a	44
11:15	120	1:5	54
11:25–26	133	1:17	111
11:40	119	1:21	37
12:37	125	1:23	98
12:45	119	2:12	65
12:46	127	2:14–15	95
12:48	131	3:9	65
13:1	116	3:21	66
13:10	117	3:23	65–6
13:14	117	3:24	52
13:15	117	3:25	39
13:34	117	4:3	110
14:2–3	132	4:16	50
14:6	142	5:8	40
14:7	122	5:12	64
14:9	119	5:12ff.	38
14:11	127	5:20	65
14:16–17	136	6	74
14:26	136	6:1–11	76
15:4, 7	117	6:3	74
15:13	116	6:3–5	100
15:18	132	6:4	74–5
15:24a	140	6:6	56, 75
16:9b	140	6:8–9	52
16:13–14	136	6:12	56
16:15	137	6:12–23	76

6:14b	91	9:10–13	78
7	66	9:14	79
7:1–4	66	9:15	79
7:4	59	9:16	79
7:5–6	61	9:17	79
7:7	61	9:19–21	79
7:7–25a	61, 77	9:22–23	80
7:7–8:4	73	10:8	50
7:8–11	68	10:9–10	52
7:12	68	10:13–14	51
7:14	69	10:17	50
7:14b	61	11:36a	38
7:14–25a	69	12:2	97
7:15–16	69–70	12:3	53
7:18–20	70	12:3–8	48
7:21	70	12:6	48
7:22–23	71	12:21	98
7:24	56, 72	13:5	96
7:25a	72	13:8	73, 97
8	72	14:14	14–5
8:1ff.	61	14:23	65
8:2	91		
8:2–3	72	**1 Corinthians**	
8:3	61	1:18ff.	37
8:3a	72	1:25ff.	37
8:4	73	1:30	40
8:5–8	61	2:4–5	50
8:9	56	3:1	60
8:9–10	70	4:4	96
8:11	49	5:1–13	76
8:14	47	6:11	46
8:15	18	6:12	85
8:18ff.	37, 91	6:13	57
8:21	92	6:15	58
8:28–30	92	6:17	45
8:38–39	38	6:19	57
9:1–2	77, 96	6:20b	57
9:3	77	7:4	55
9:6a	77	7:17–24	86
9:6–29	77	7:21b	86
9:6ff.	77	8:1–13	84
9:7–9	78	8:6	37, 38

8:7–13	93	5:10	77
8:9	85	5:11	95
8:11	94	5:16	60
8:12	85, 93	5:17	49
9	85	5:19	40
10:14–33	84	5:21	39
10:16	59	6:2b	38
10:17	59	7:3	103
10:23	85	10:3	61
10:25–29	94		
10:26	37	**Galatians**	
11:7–8	101	2:4b	90
11:27	59	2:16	110
12:3b	50	2:16a	90
12:4–11	48	2:19–20	90
12:11	45	2:21	108
12:13	46, 87	3:10–12	90
12:27	59	3:11b	111
14:1	49	3:13	90
14:14–15	105	3:15–18	110
14:19	105	3:19	110
14:26	48	3:26–28	87
15:11b	50	4:4a	38
15:17	40	4:6	18, 45
15:20	42	4:28	91
15:35–56	42–3	5:1	91
15:49	99	5:3	108
		5:5	51
		5:6	53
2 Corinthians		5:18	48
1:12	94	5:22	48
1:21–22	46	5:25	47
1:23	104	6:1	90
3:2	103	6:2	97
3:3	102		
3:17	45		
3:18	100	**Philippians**	
4:2	95	1:27	104
4:4	99, 101	1:29	50
4:14	39	2:9–11	38
4:16	107	2:13	51, 112
5:1–10	57	3:7	111
5:7	55	3:21	58

1 Thessalonians

2:13	148
4:8	47
4:13–18	41–2
5:23	104

Philemon	88–9

1 John

1:8–10	138
2:3–5	123
2:18	132
3:2a	139
3:2b	139
3:6	138
3:9	138–9
3:10	139
3:14	143–4
4:13	136
5:6–8	135
5:16–17	138–9
5:18a	138

2 John

7	132

1 Maccabees

2:52	110

Psalms of Solomon

5.4	81
9.4–7	81
14	109

Sirach

15:11–15, 20	80
33:11–15	80

Wisdom of Solomon

7:1–6	62
7:22, 24	46
7:26c	99

Dead Sea Scrolls

CD 11:16–17	16

1QS 4:15–17	82
10:18	21
11:9–12	108

1QH 15:12–17	82

Apocrypha and Pseudepigrapha

Assumption of Moses

10.1	17

1 Enoch

99.10	33

4 Ezra

8:32, 36	108

Jubilees

22.16	31

Other Writers

Epictetus

Diss. 2.26.1	69
Diss. 2.26.4–5	70
Diss. 3.22.54	21
Diss. 4.4.33	87

Josephus

Bell. 2.143–44	32

Marcus Aurelius

Semet. 7.22	21

Philo
  Det. 23   106
  Fug. 101   99

Seneca
  Ben. 4.26.1   21
  Ep. 41.4–5   106
  Ep. 47   87